Portfolio of

TIRITILLI

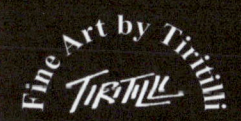
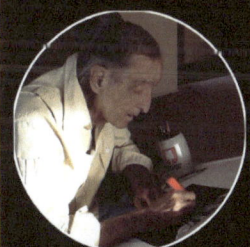
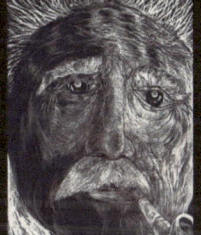
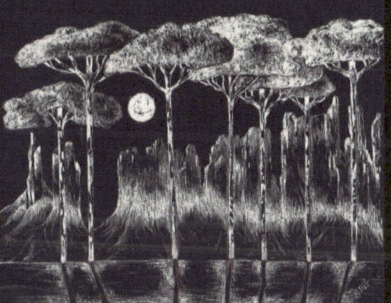
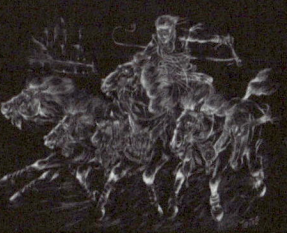

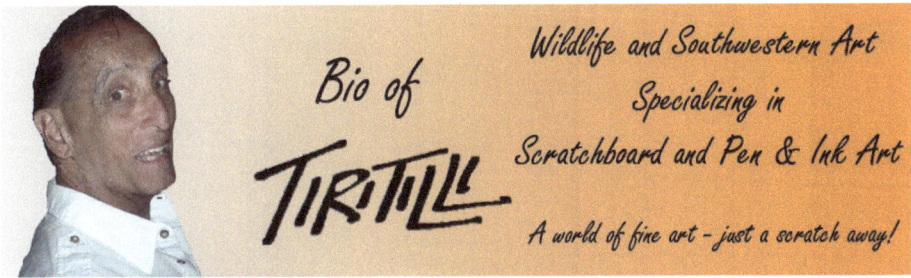

Bio of **TIRITILLI**

Wildlife and Southwestern Art
Specializing in
Scratchboard and Pen & Ink Art

A world of fine art - just a scratch away!

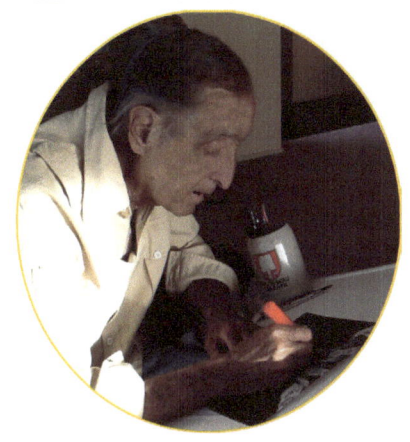

Tiritilli's passion for drawing and painting began when he was a young child in Chicago and still remains with him. Self taught, he has painted with oils, work with pen and ink, but now he is concentrating his attention to scratchboard art.

Utilizing the scratchboard process is ideal for his "perfectionist" nature. There is no forgiveness in this tedious medium – one wrong scratch or errant stroke - the drawing may be ruined.

Scratchboard art is as much of a game as a skill. The skill is to manipulate and/or stimulate the observer. The game is to not let the observer feel they are being manipulated, tricked or coerced. To the artist the creative process is both relaxing and genuinely original in a way beyond description. Without color, this has induced both a challenge and satisfaction for that tests your innate skills.

Robert learned years ago that scratchboard art is both a simple and a complex process. It's "Simple" because you can concentrate and focus on the subject while leaving much of the background open. It's "Complex" because there is always the question of what to eliminate; what to accentuate; and what to observe and focus on.

The images he draws stimulate the observer's eye and brain in a way that fills in the missing pieces without allowing them to make bold or presumptuous statements. Since the scratchboard technique leaves out parts or substantial parts of all images, it demands the observer to compare the visual to the images' total result.

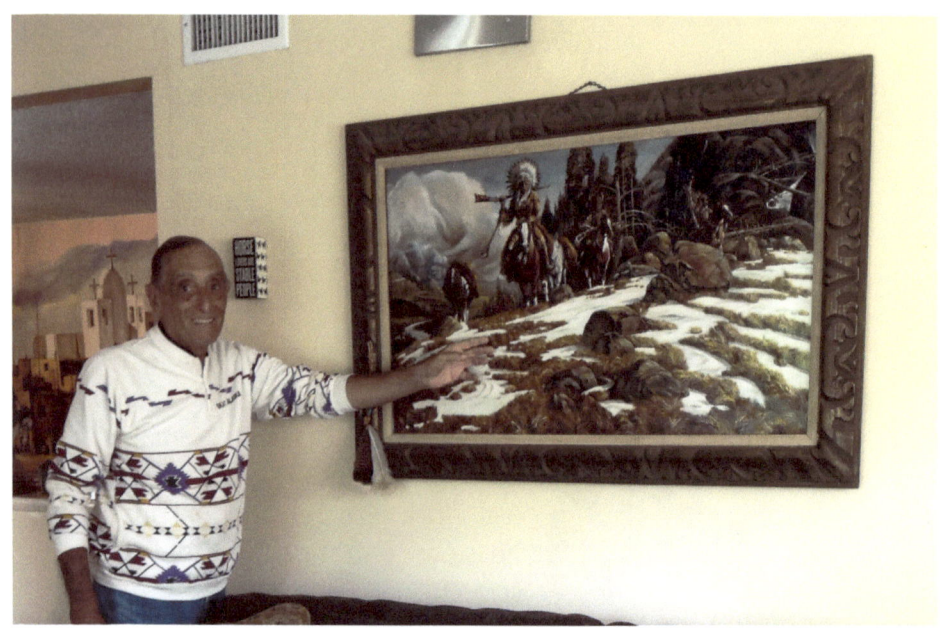

One of the most rewarding ways to collect art is to discover an emerging artist whose artwork you love. Robert A. Tiritilli is one of those artists, whose favorite medium is working with the non-traditional scratchboard because of its sensitivity to touch and its archival qualities.

Tiritilli is quickly becoming known as one of the premier wildlife and old American SouthWest scratchboard artists of today. His mastery of the difficult scratchboard medium is evident in the outstanding quality of each of his works. Highly detailed and realistic, his scratchboard art is often mistaken for photographs at a distance. Tiritilli's work is instantly recognizable due to its anatomical accuracy, strong compositions, and sense of light which help bring the viewer into the world of his artwork creations.

Scratchboarding is regarded by many artists as one of the most difficult mediums to master as it requires excellent drawing skills and attention to fine details. The medium does not allow for many mistakes and Tiritilli is able to convey many different textures all with just lines or dots. This scratcher's work is filled with intricate and meticulous designs underscored by mesmerizing contrasts and textures. Seeing him slicing his knife across the paper is like pitching a perfect game in baseball—it seems he never makes a mistake while creating something creative and inspiring.

To truly appreciate the intricacy of his work, allow yourself to see close-up all the details in his elaborate scratchboard art.

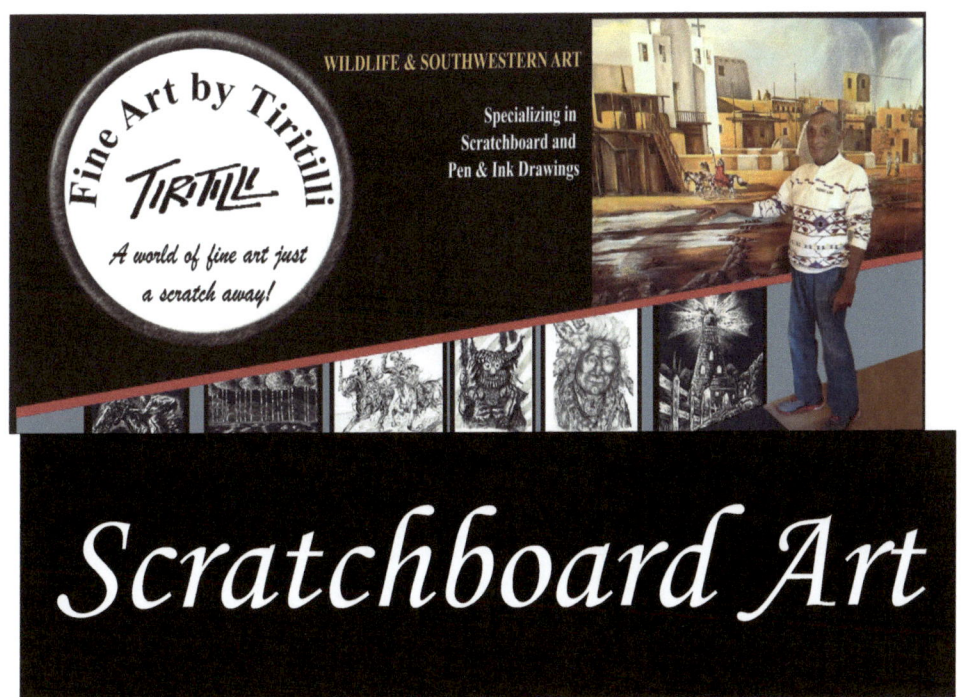

Scratchboard Art

Scratchboard is a medium that is over 100 years old but has usually been used as a commercial art and illustrating medium. With the addition of color 30+ years ago and the development of a "new" scratchboard that has a rigid subsurface, it has made its way into the Fine Art category. It is now accepted in Museum shows all over the world and the 1950s, the origin of the artistic practice dates to the early 20th century avant garde movements that sought to challenge traditional artistic media. Here are some famous artists who worked with Scratchboard Art: Virgil Finlay, Ruth Lozner, Paul Sheldon, Sally Maxwell, Kent Barton and Rudy Draguett.

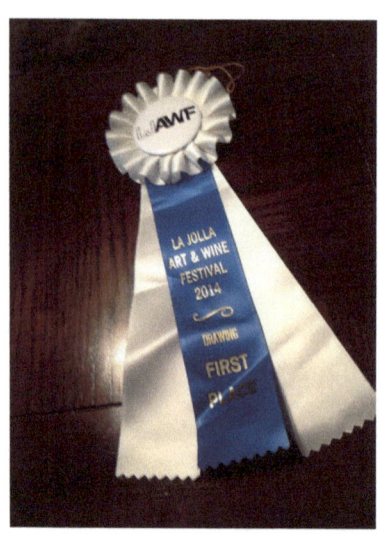
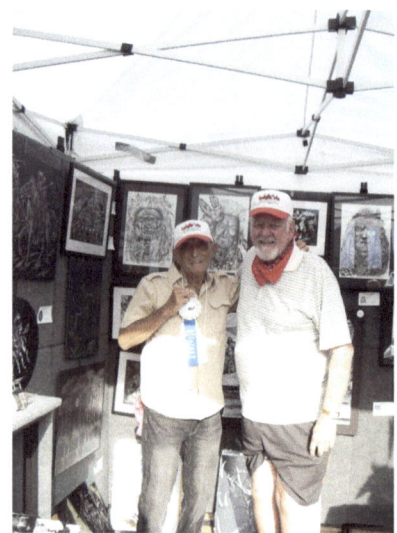

Award-winning artist, Robert Tiritilli won 1st PLACE in the drawing category at the SIXTH ANNUAL LA JOLLA ART & WINE FESTIVAL (LJAWF). The judges awarded Tiritilli 1st place due to his outstanding scratchboard and pen and ink artwork. Robert is showing off his blue-ribbon award with his business partner, Charles Hellman.

This two-day juried art show (Oct 11 -12 2014) has quickly garnered a reputation as one of the most prestigious art & wine festivals in South California.

A crowd of almost 40,000 attended this highly regarded prestigious West Coast event, located in the heart of La Jolla's iconic coastal village along Girard Ave. The bustling area of Girard Avenue transformed itself into an art lovers paradise highlighting 150 established artists from the West Coast, Baja and beyond. All of the artists at the LJAWF were judged by a highly qualified jury of artists, authors, critics and collectors.

Enjoy Robert's *"made from scratch artwork"* on the next pages.
For more information contact:
Charles Hellman
(760) 861-2174

THE OL WEST SERIES

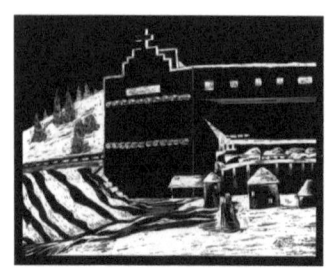

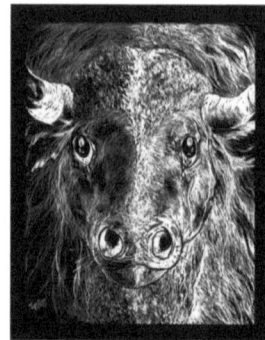

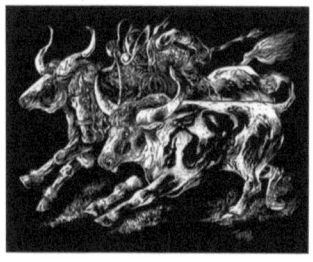

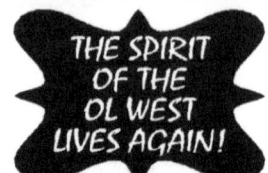

THE SPIRIT
OF THE
OL WEST
LIVES AGAIN!

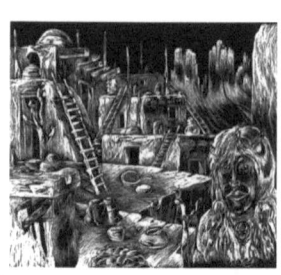

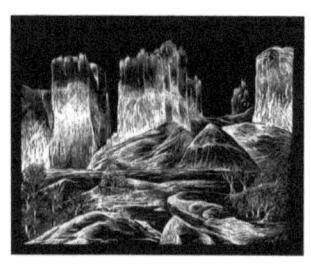

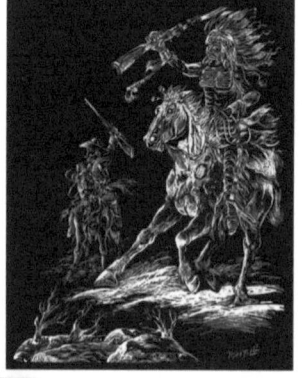

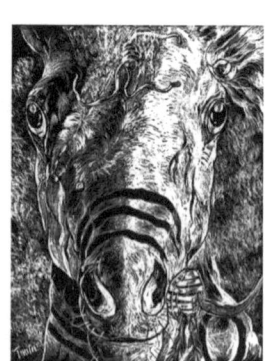

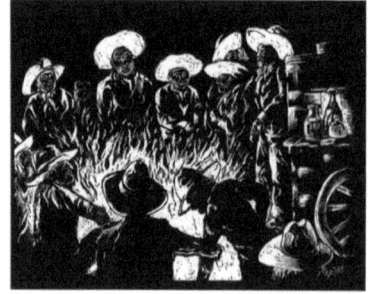

The OL WEST SERIES
SCRATCHBOARD ART

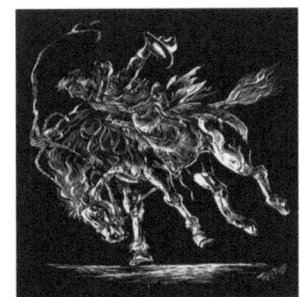

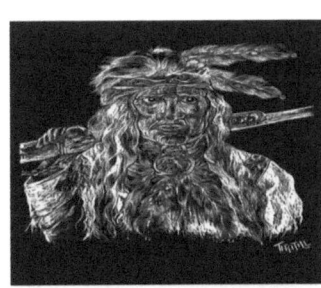

THE OL' WEST

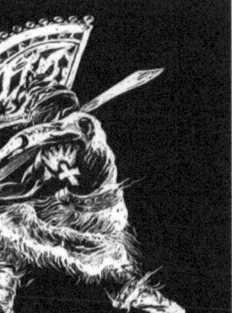

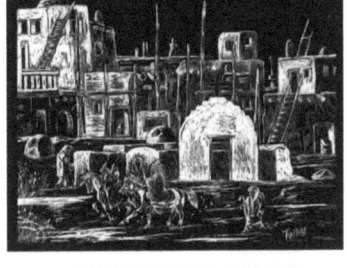

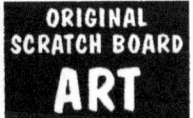

ORIGINAL
SCRATCH BOARD
ART

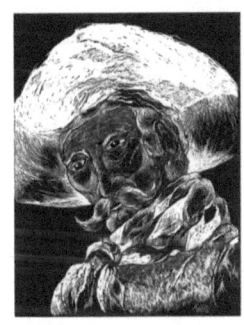

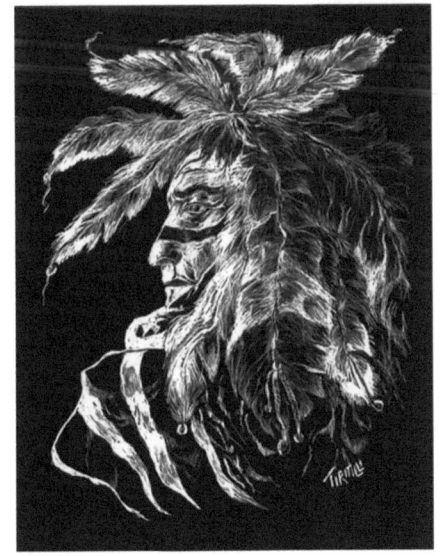

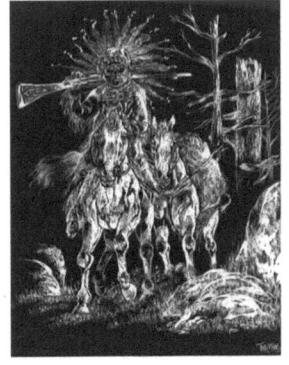

9

American Plains Defender

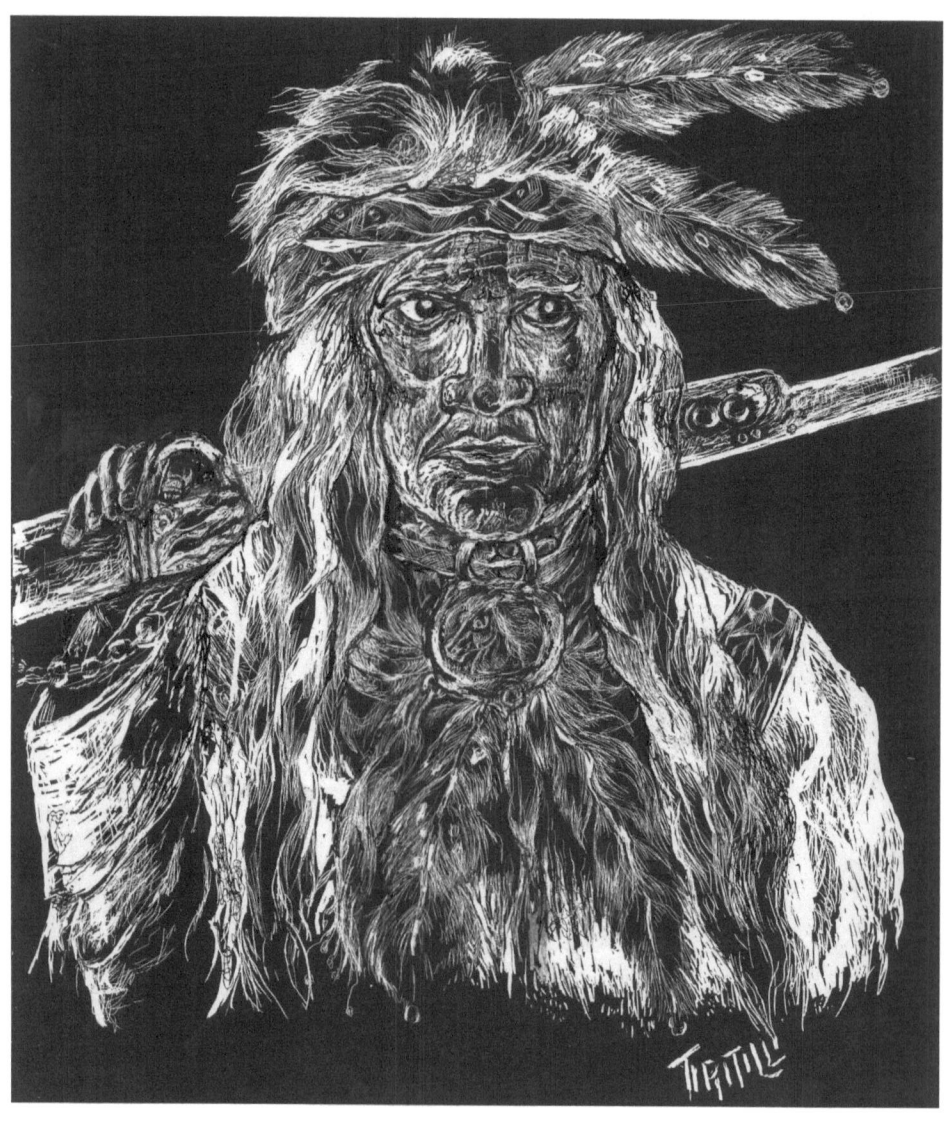

Crown Dancer

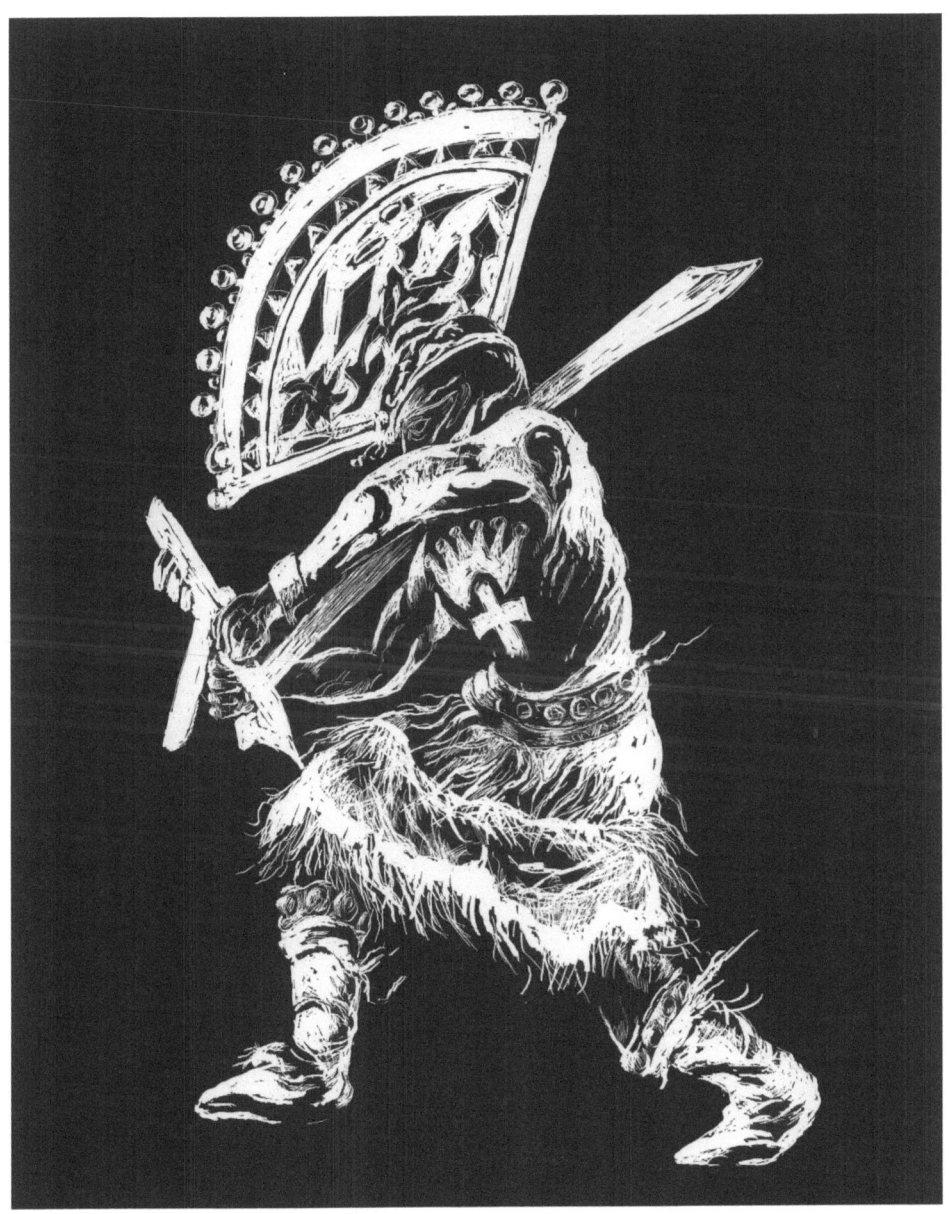

Echoes of Sunset

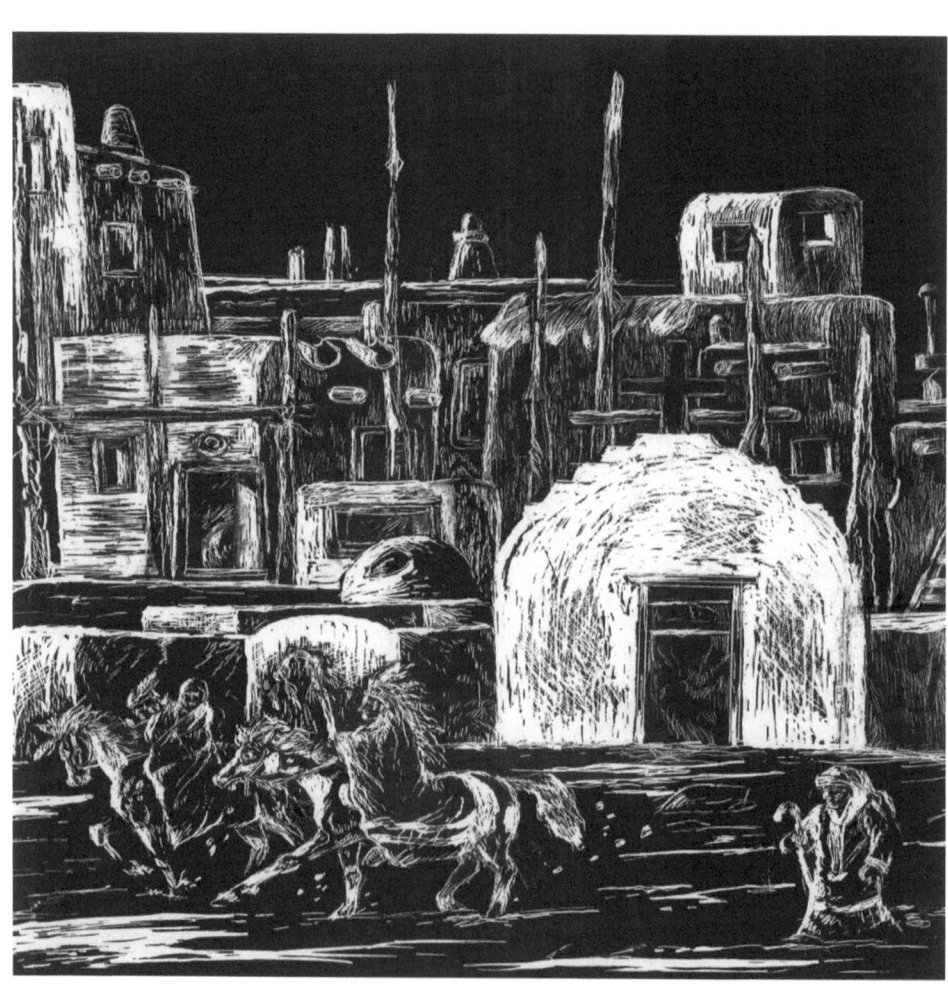

Holy Response

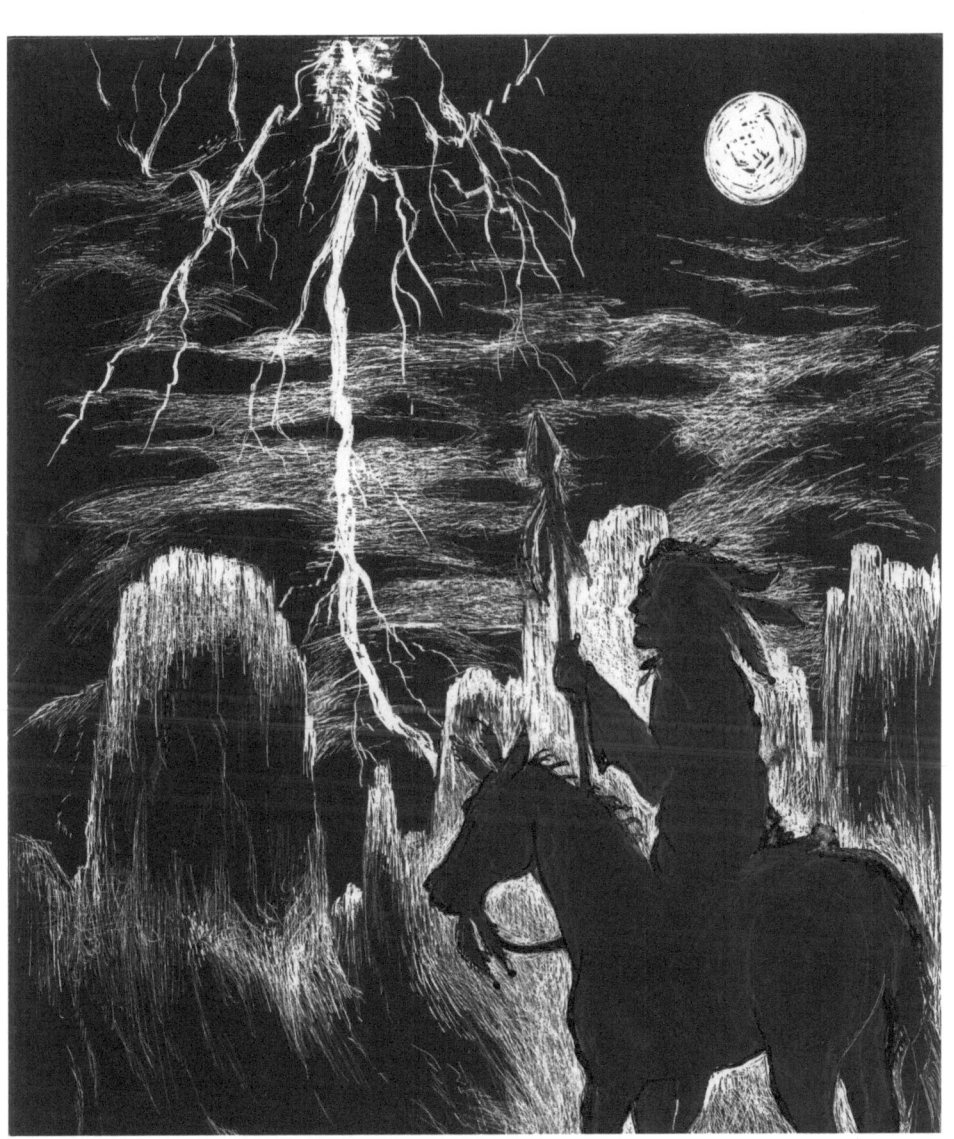

Holy One

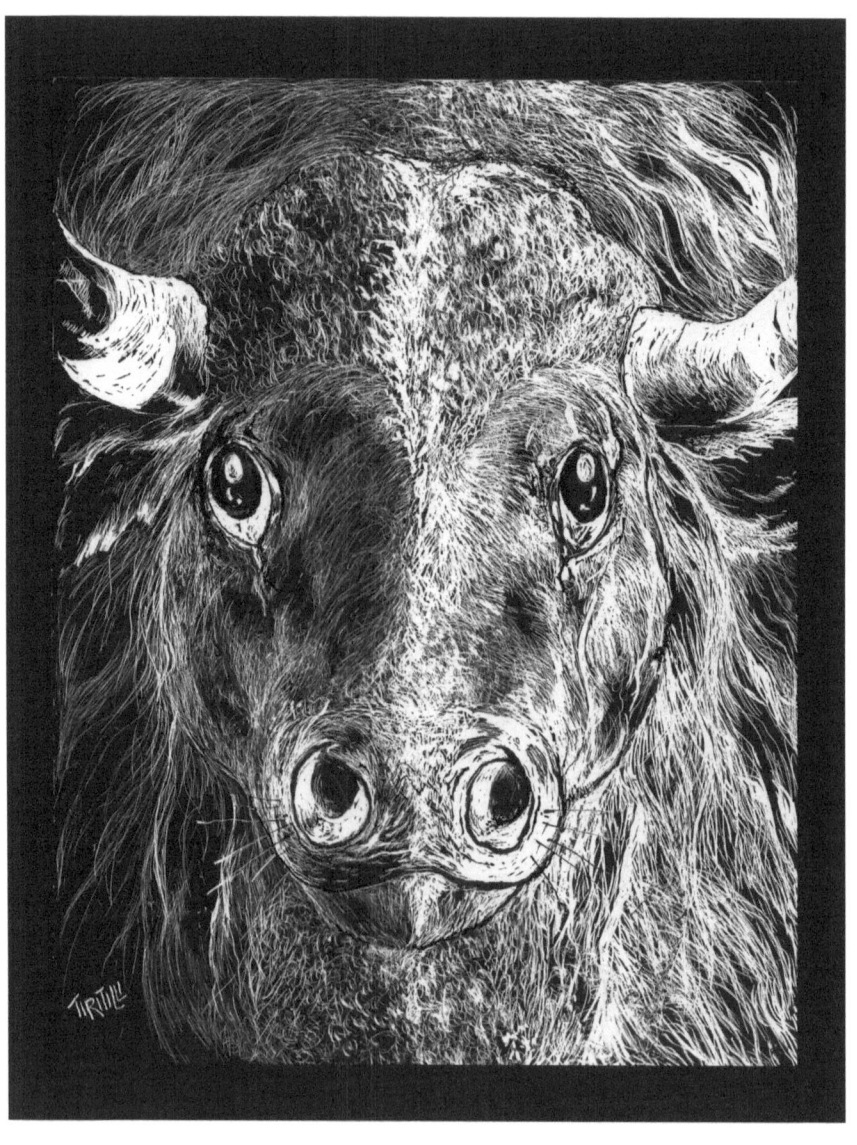

Lookin' for Trouble

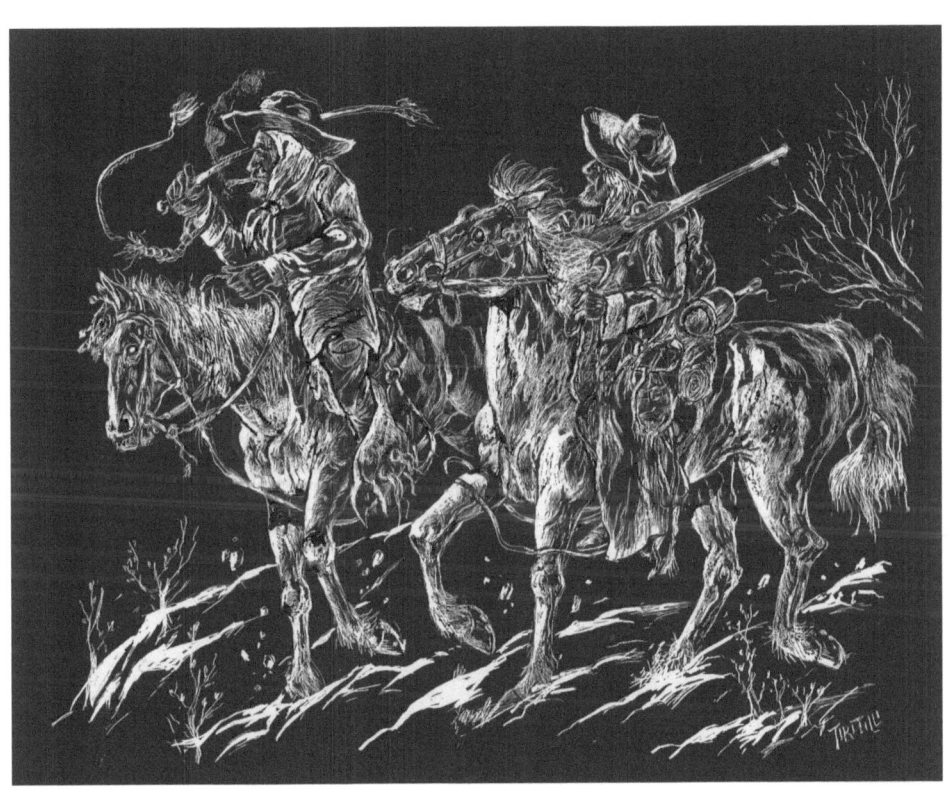

My Land My Home

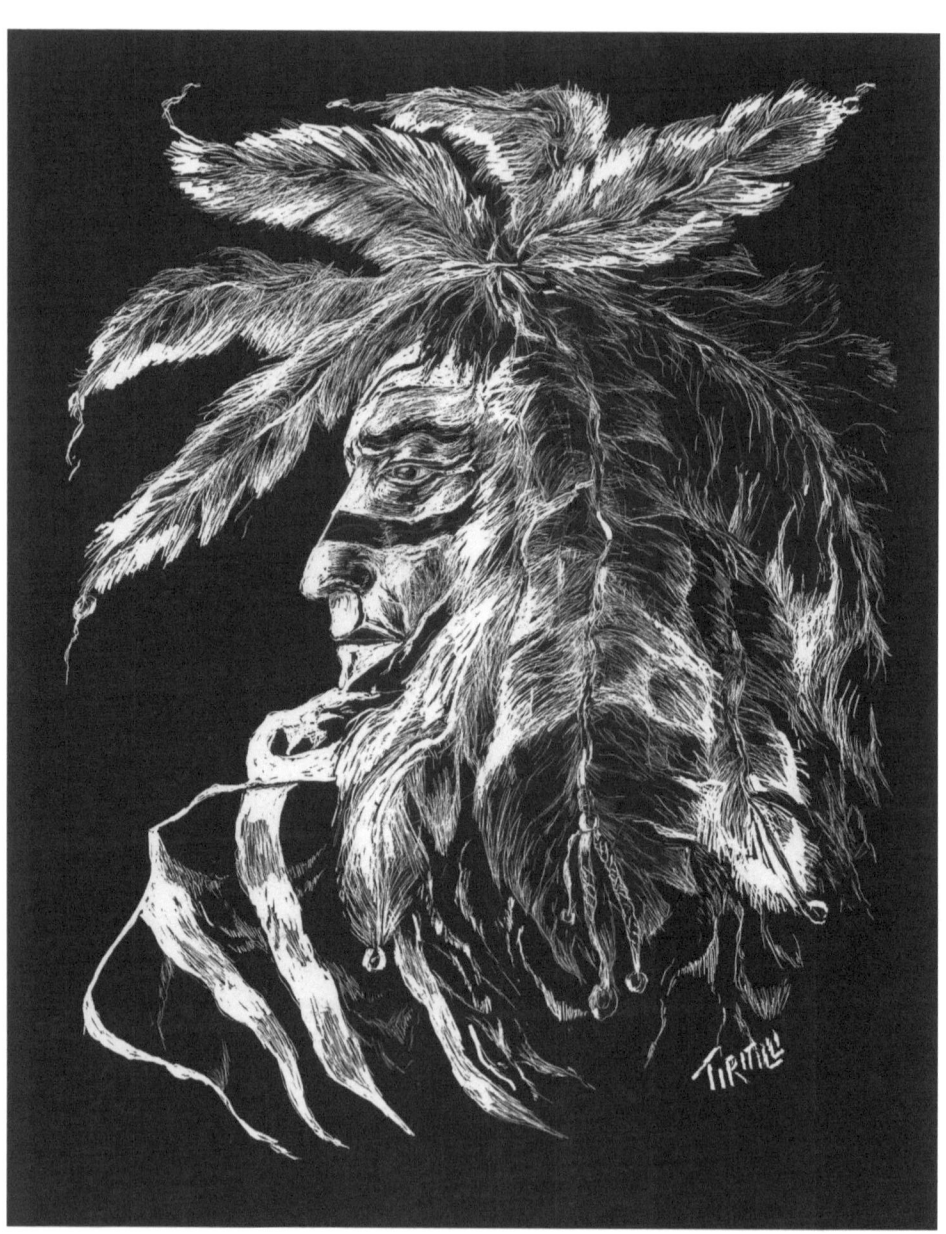

Indian Brave

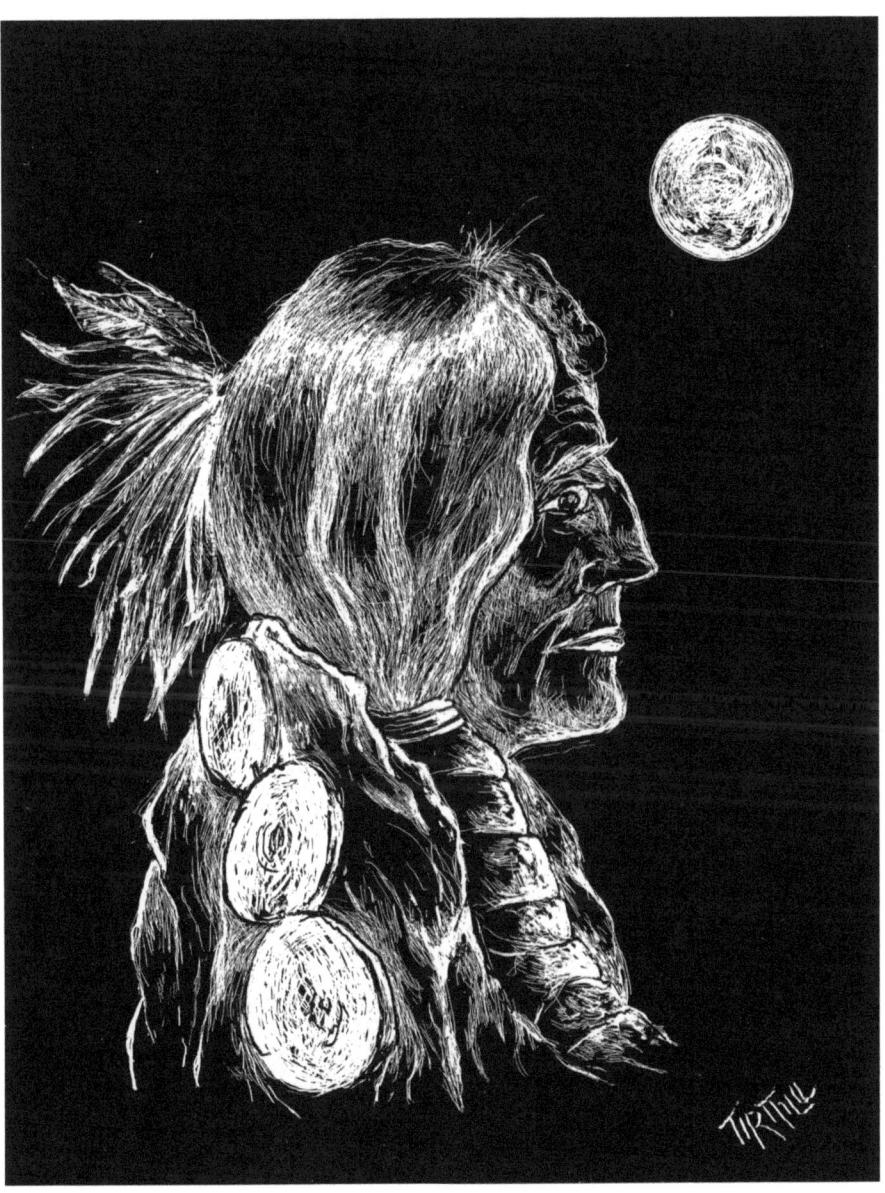

Squaw

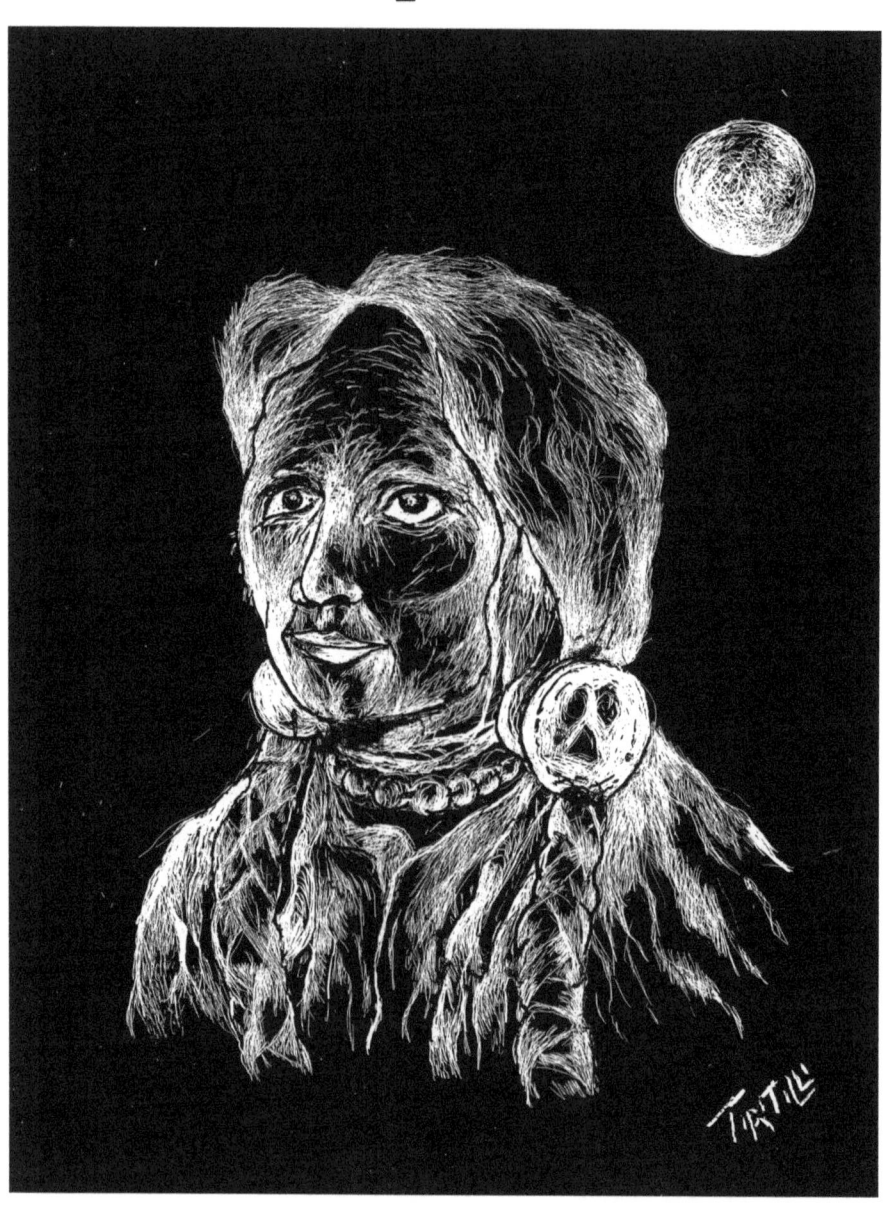

Aditya

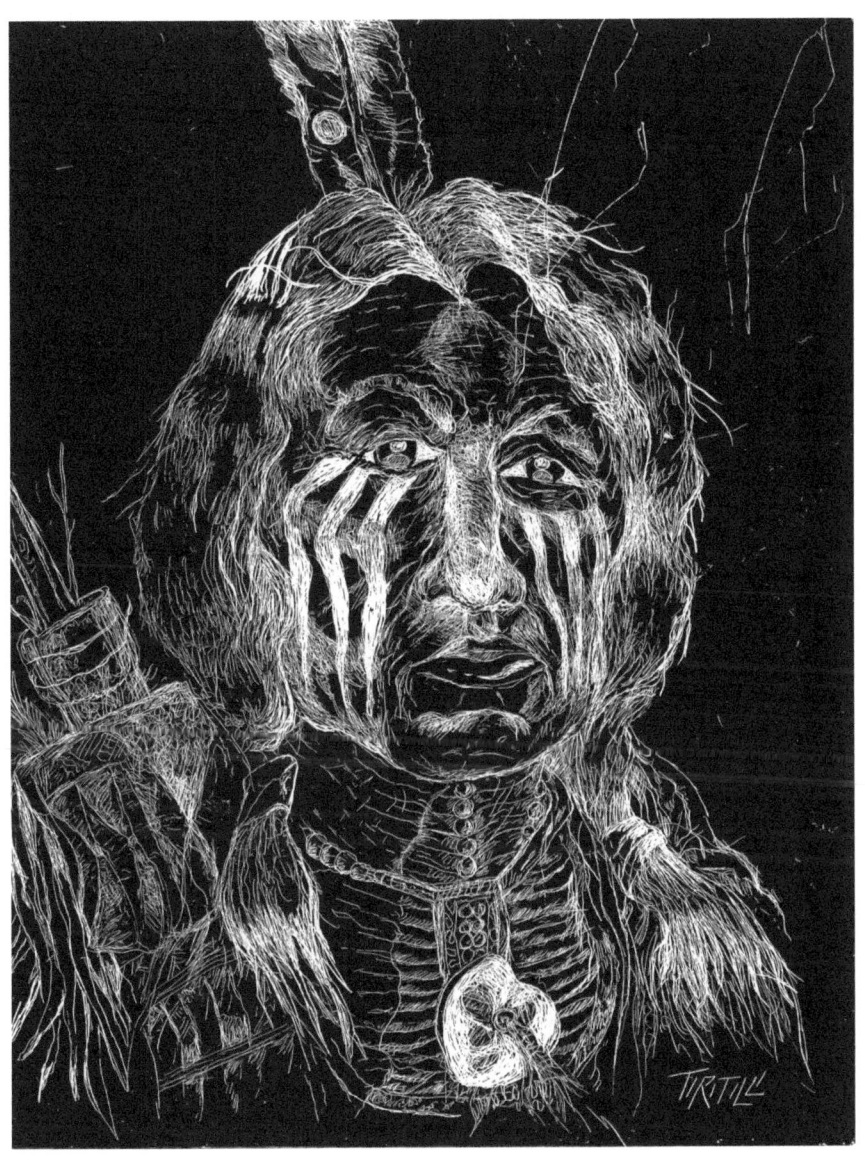

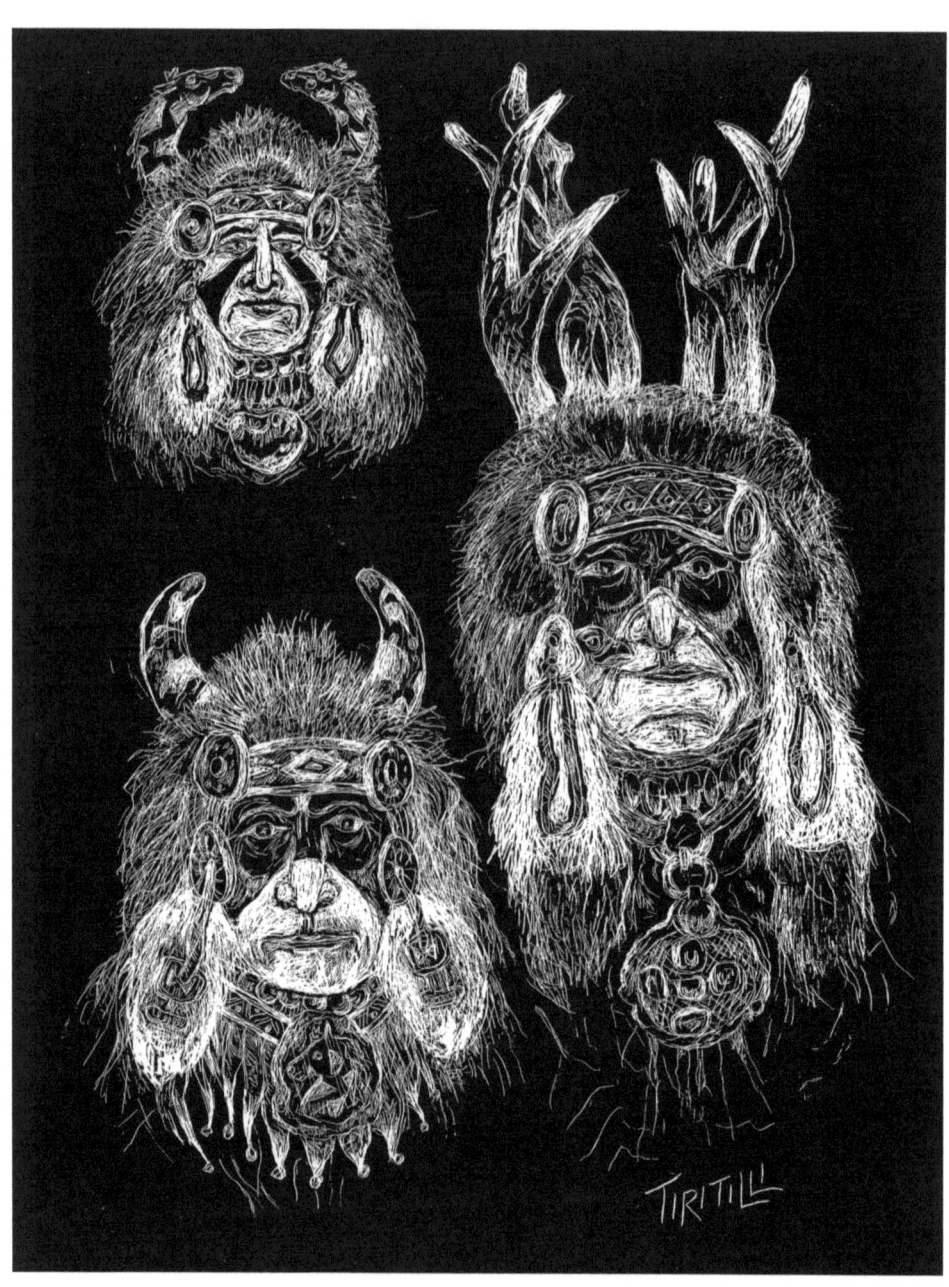

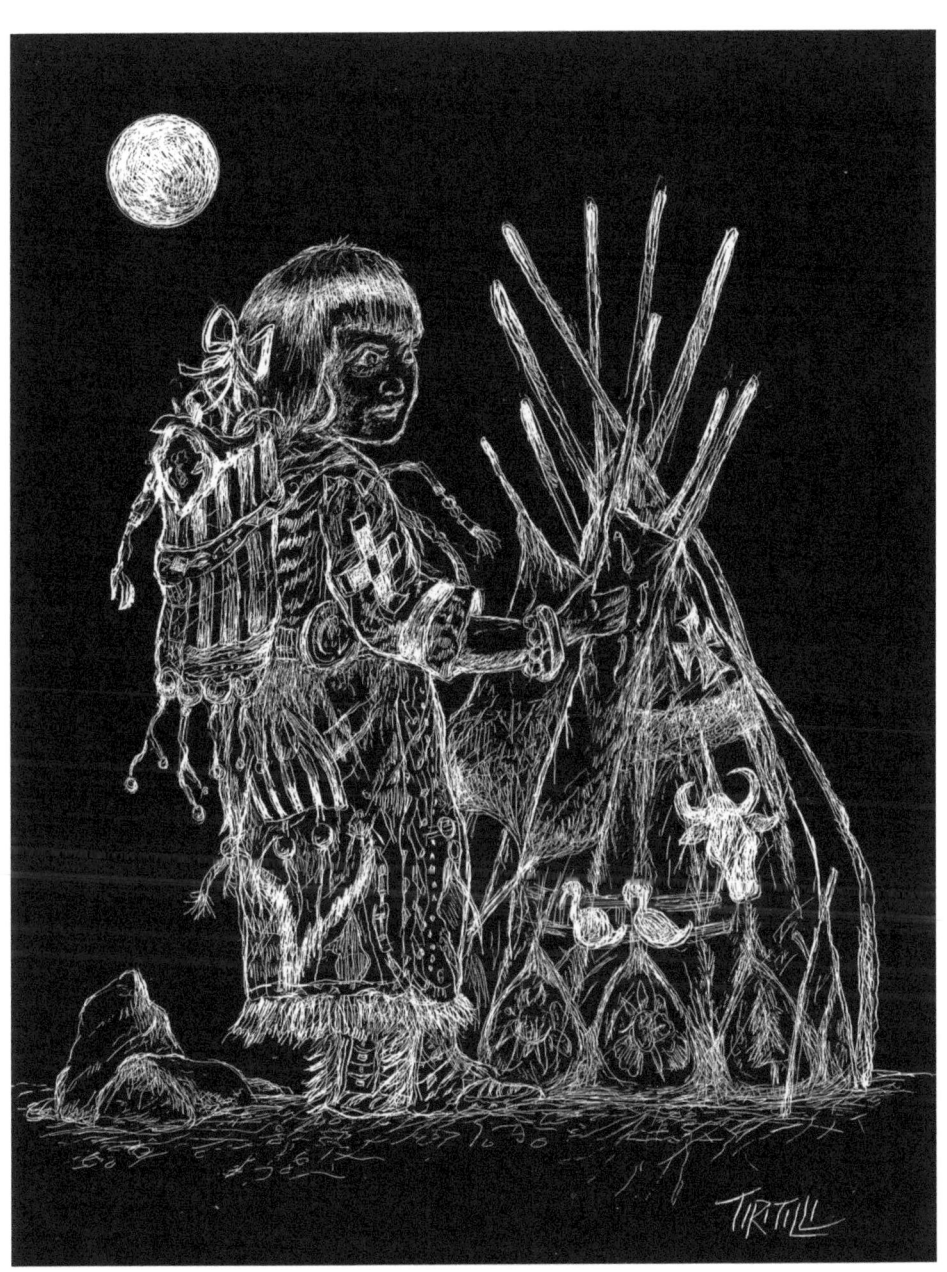

New Found Bounty

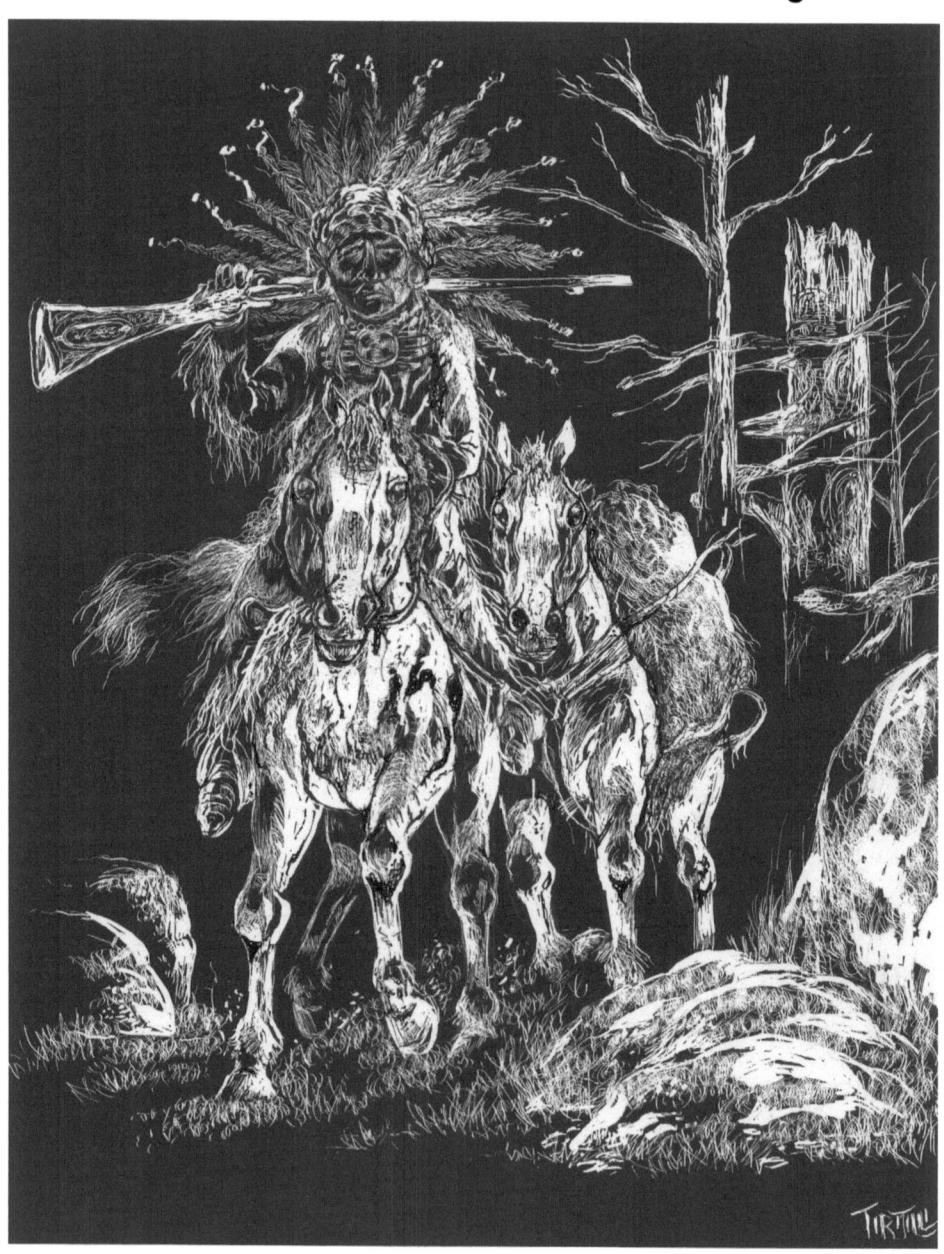

Indian Warrior

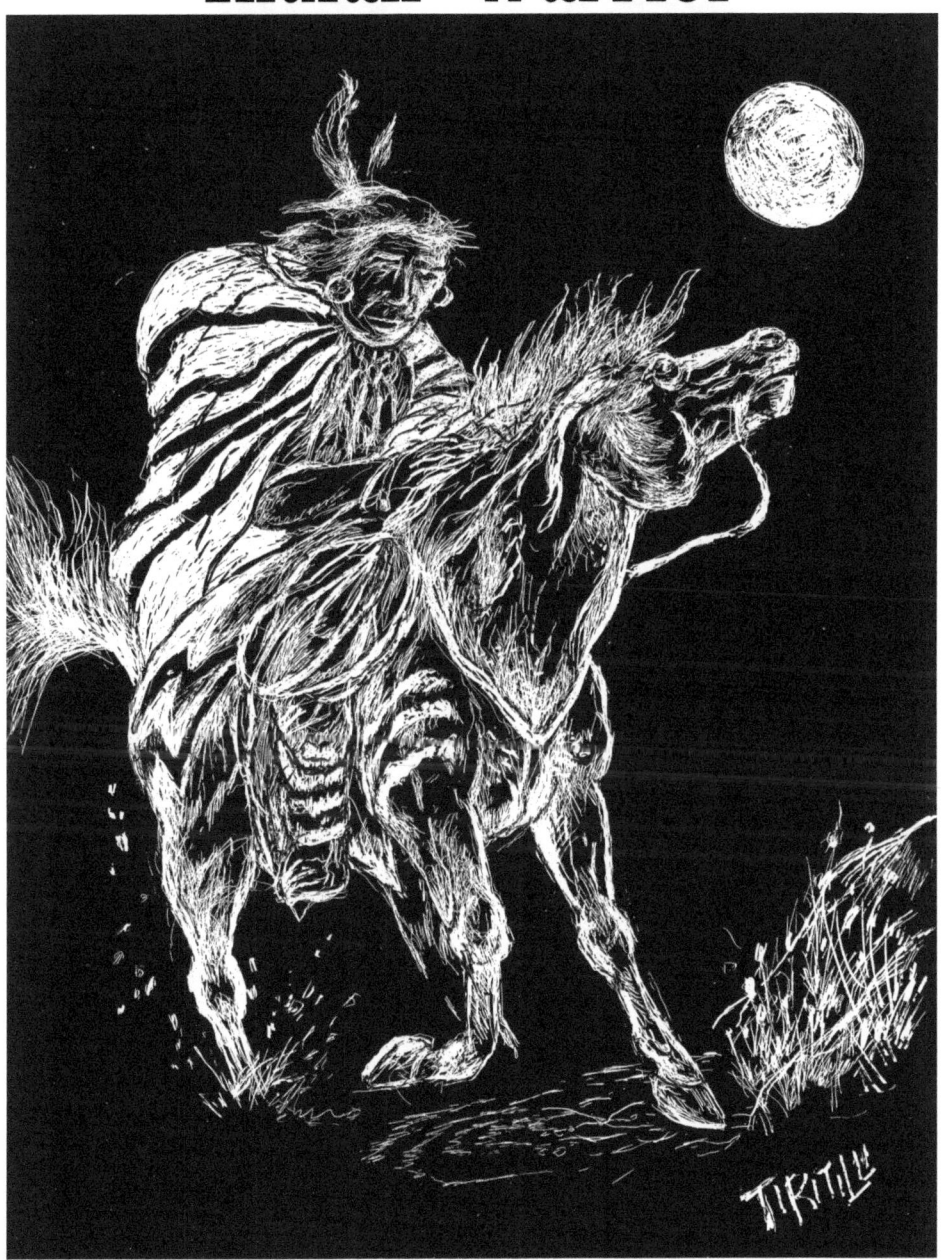

Sentenels of Yesterday

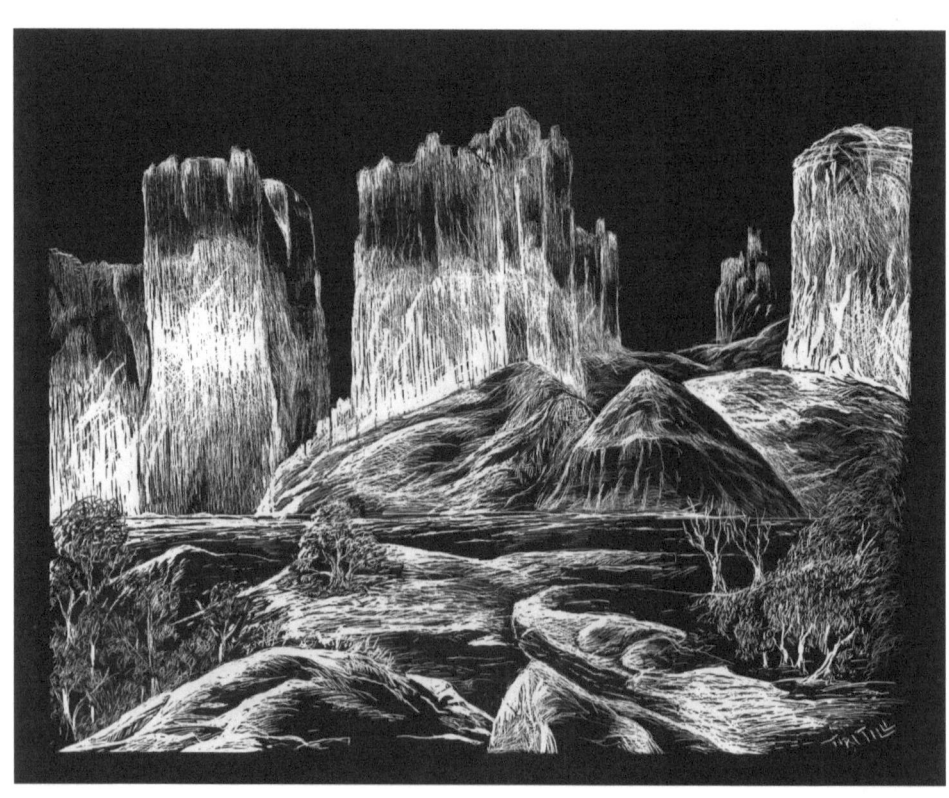

Sod Buster

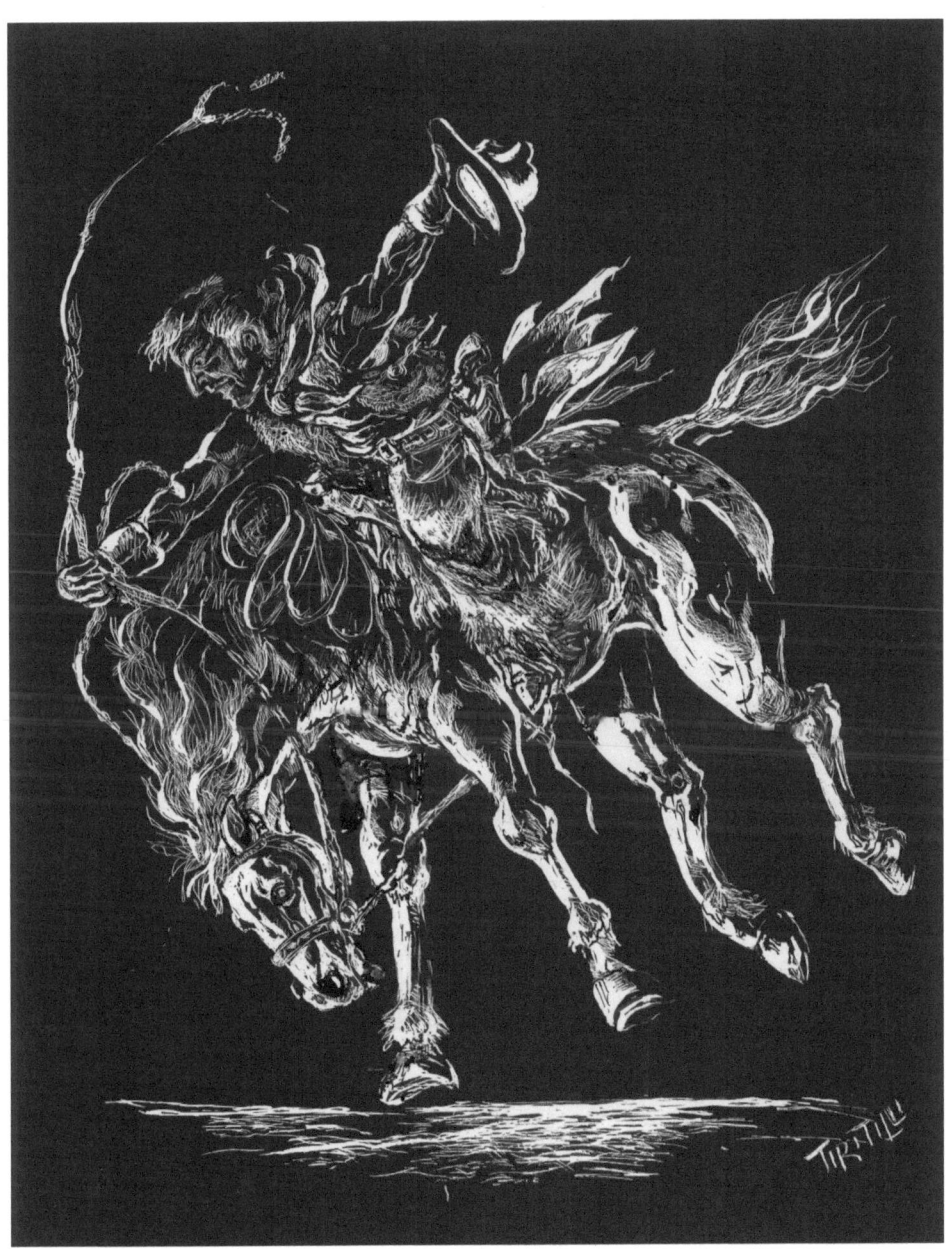

Soul of Matter

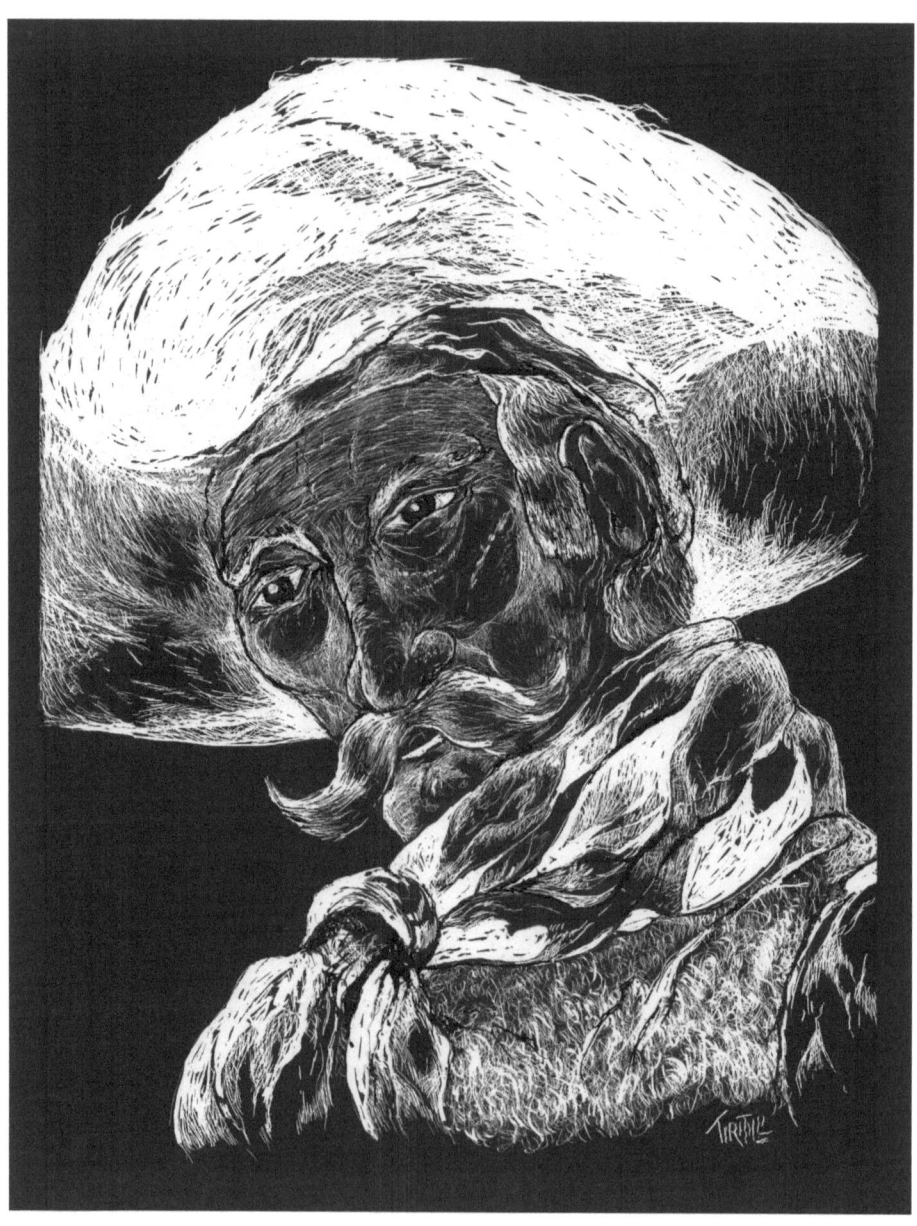

Strange Companions

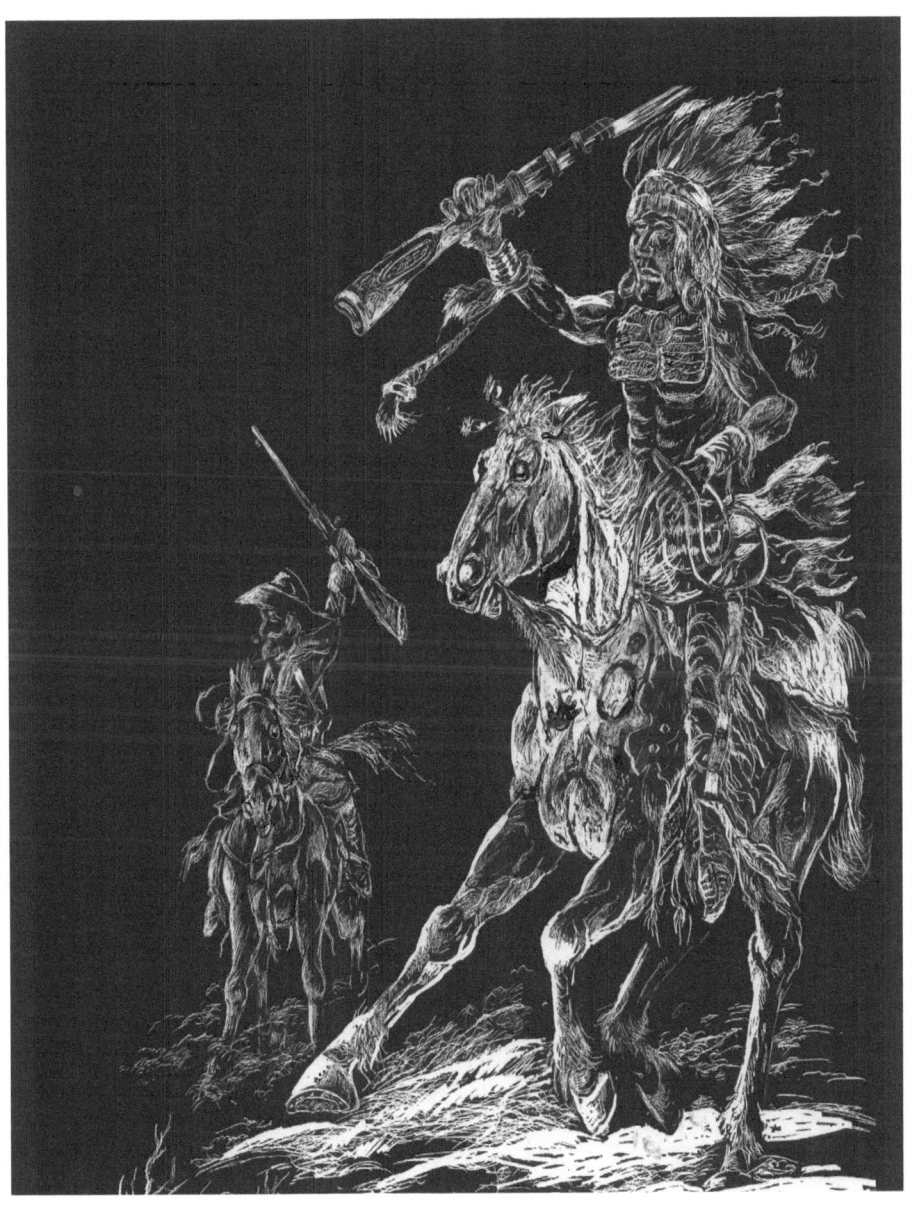

Tall Tales

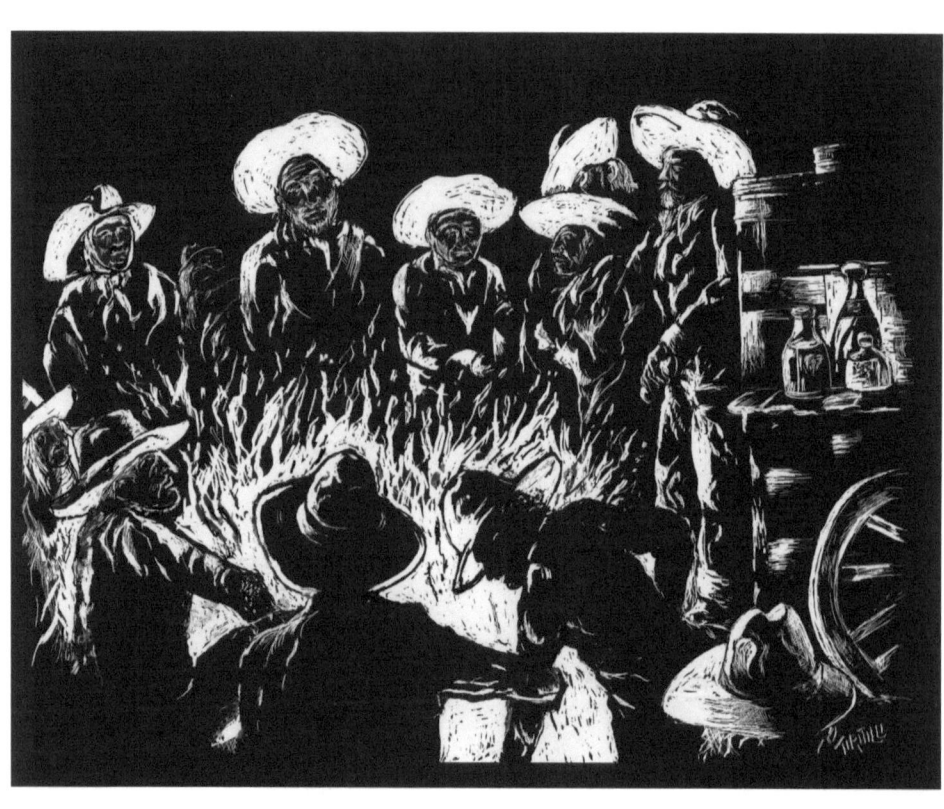

First Round-up

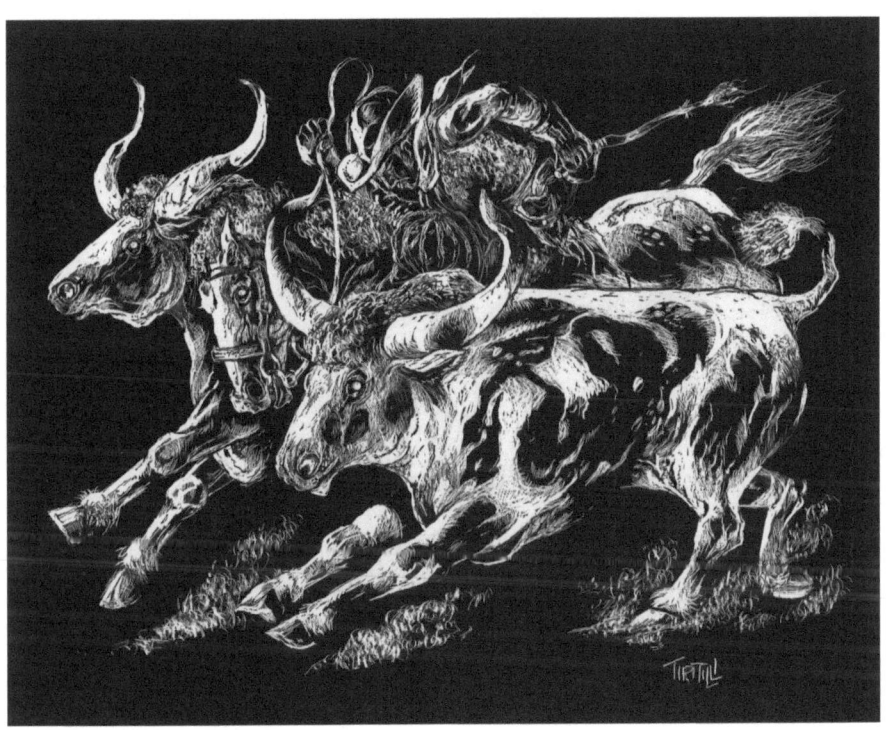

First Round-up II

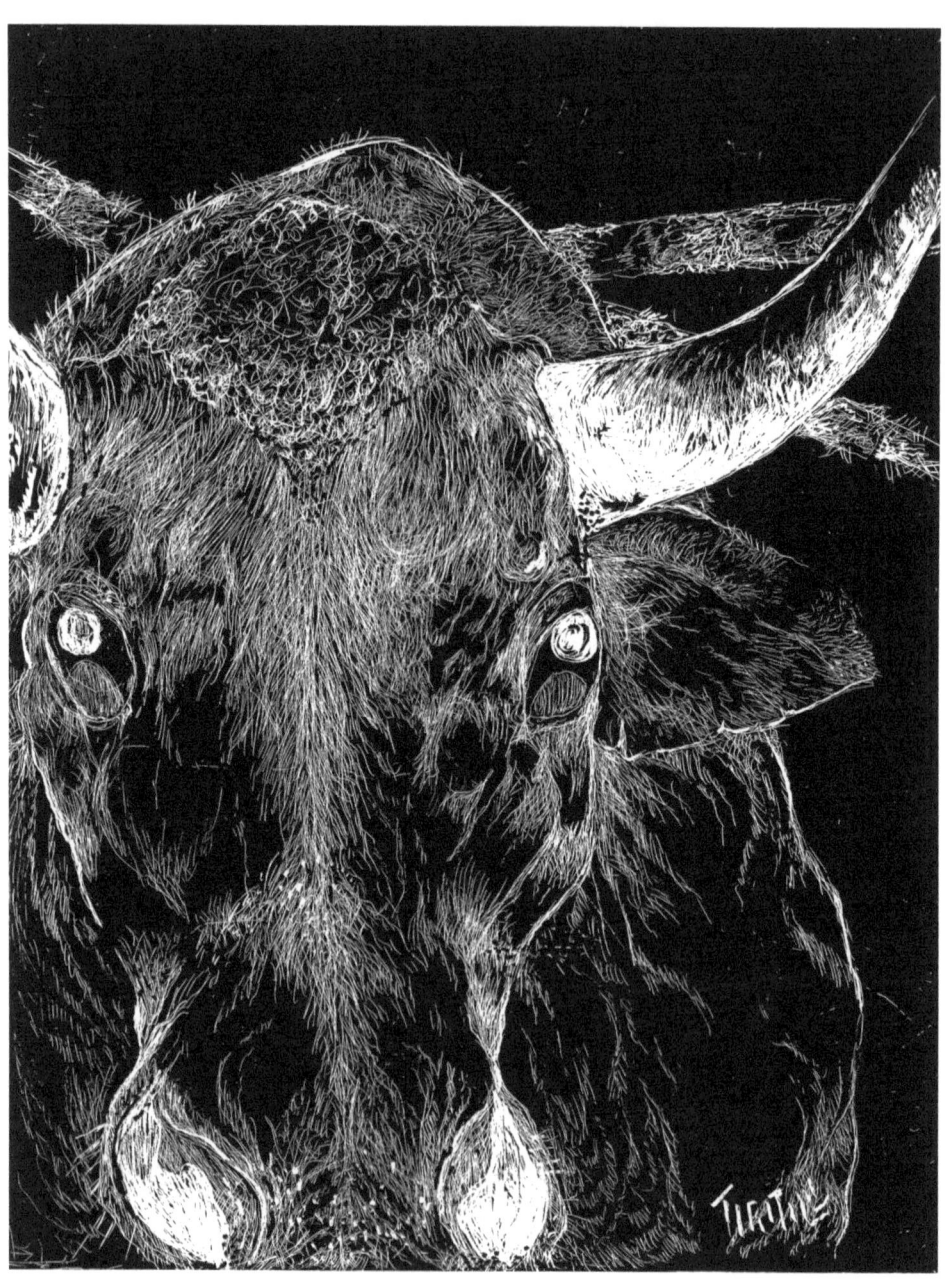

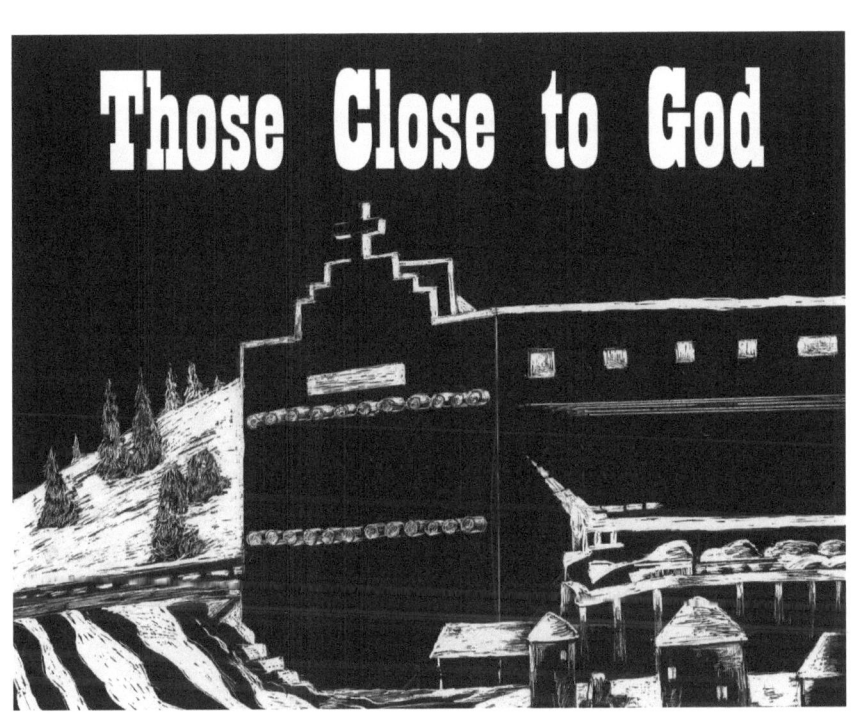

Those Close to God

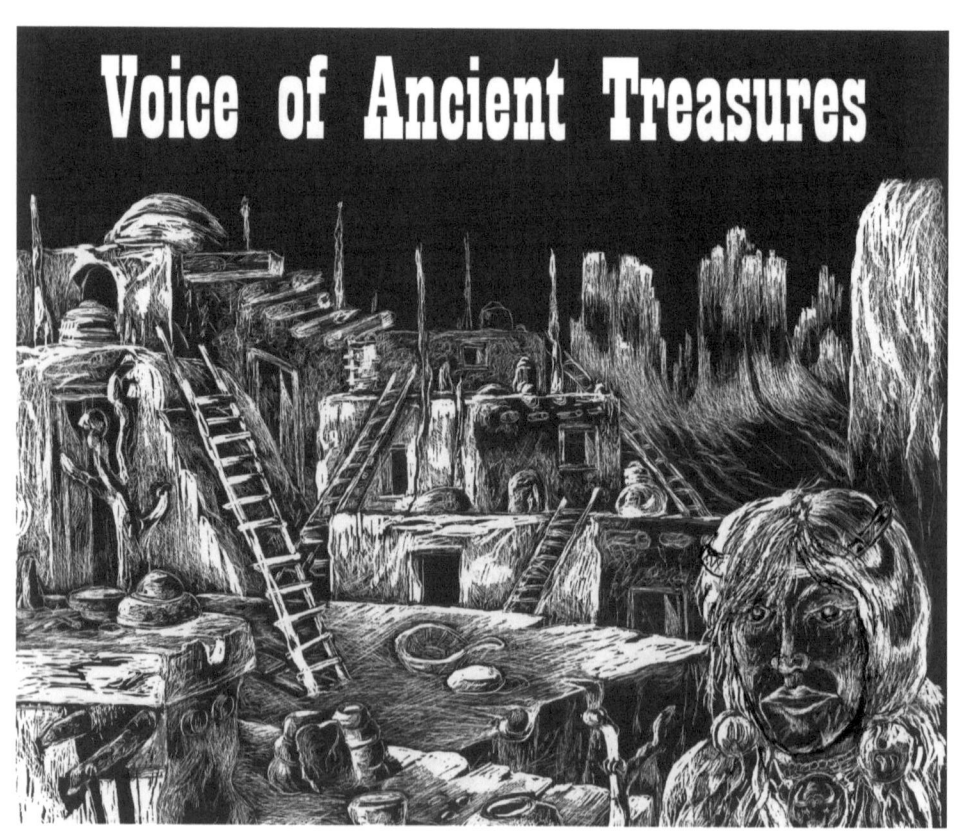

Voice of Ancient Treasures

Warrior's Best Friend

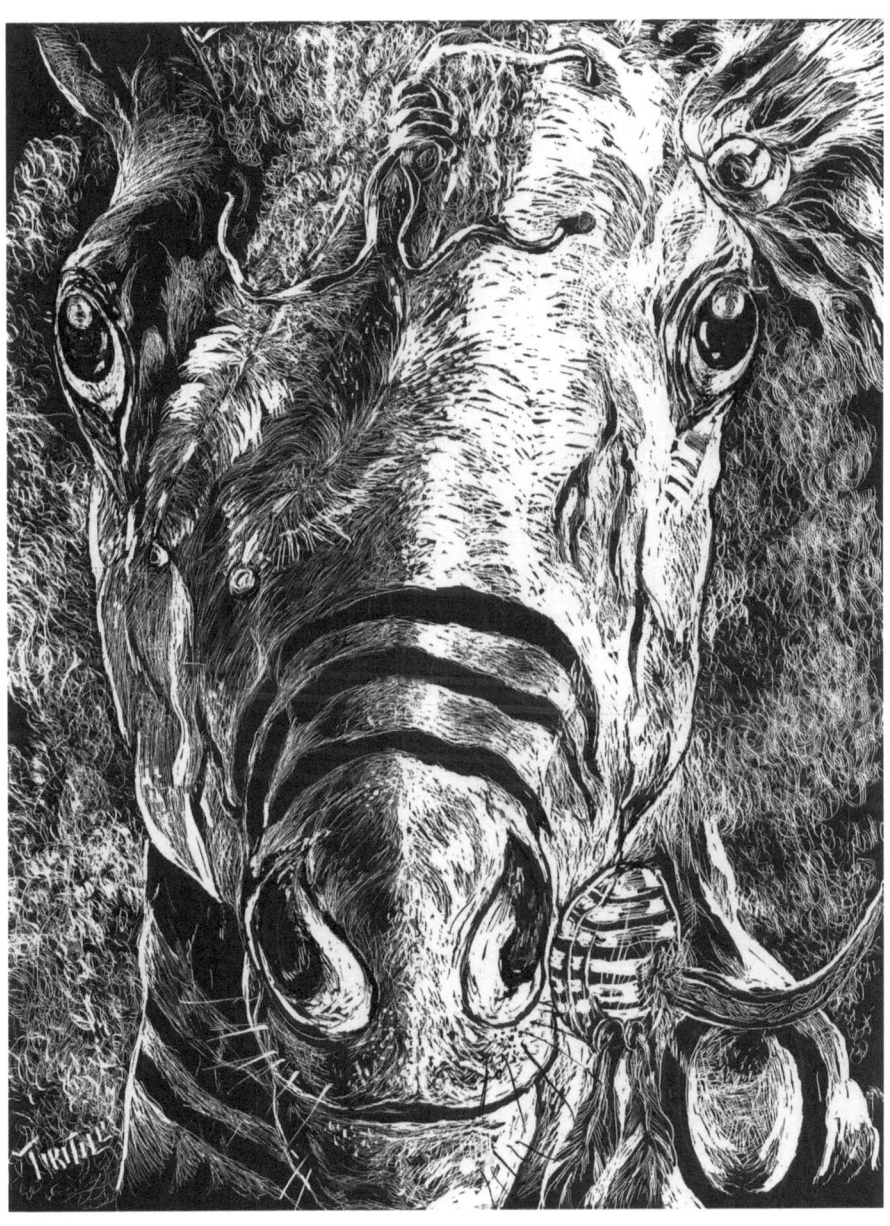

Other Scratchboard Art

The Plot

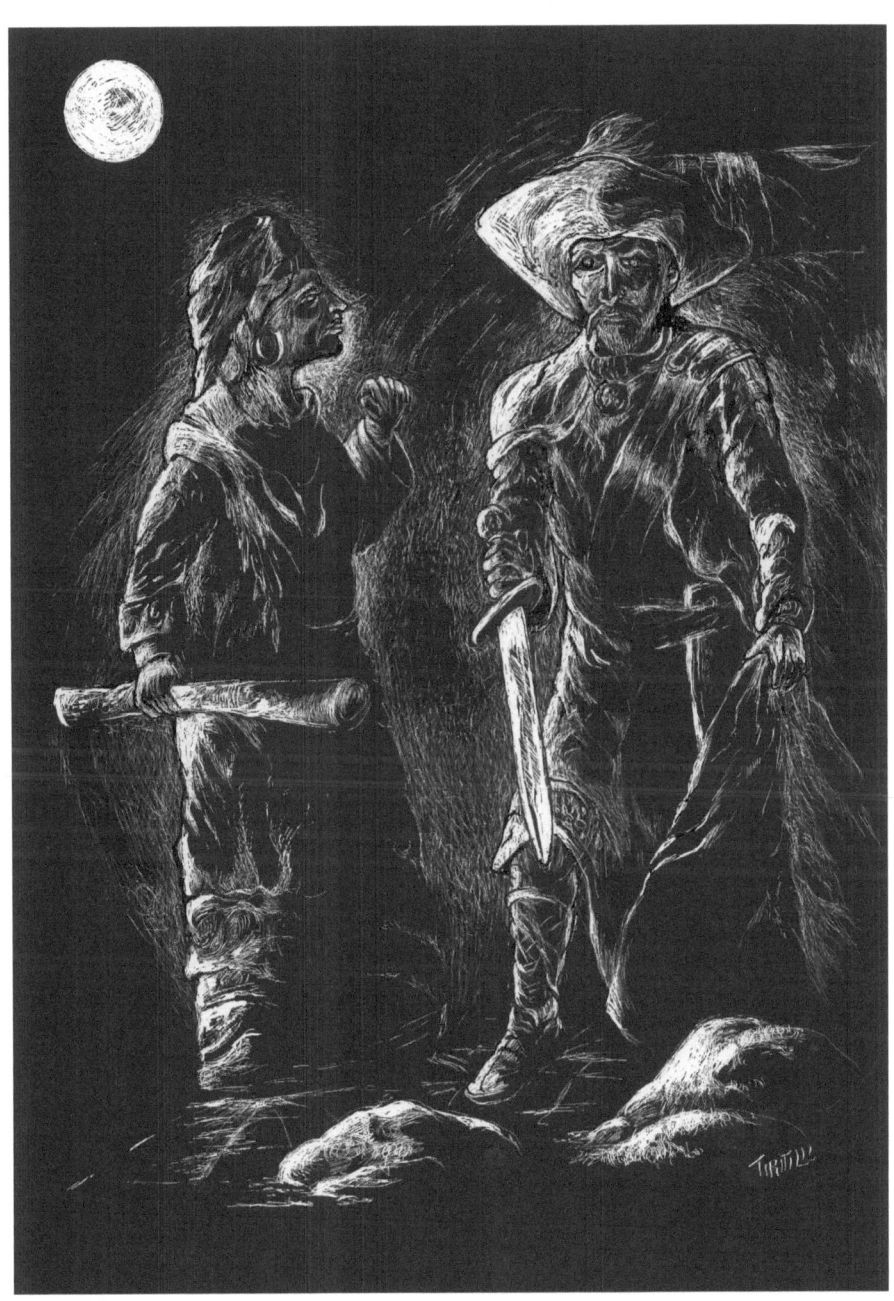

Mug

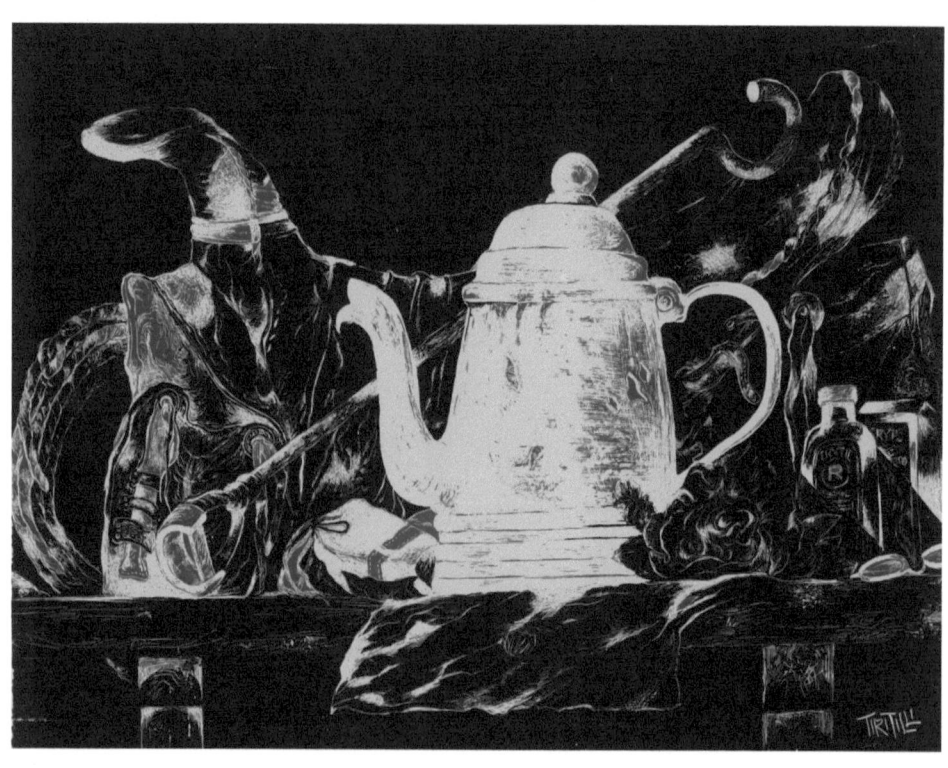

My Desert My Home

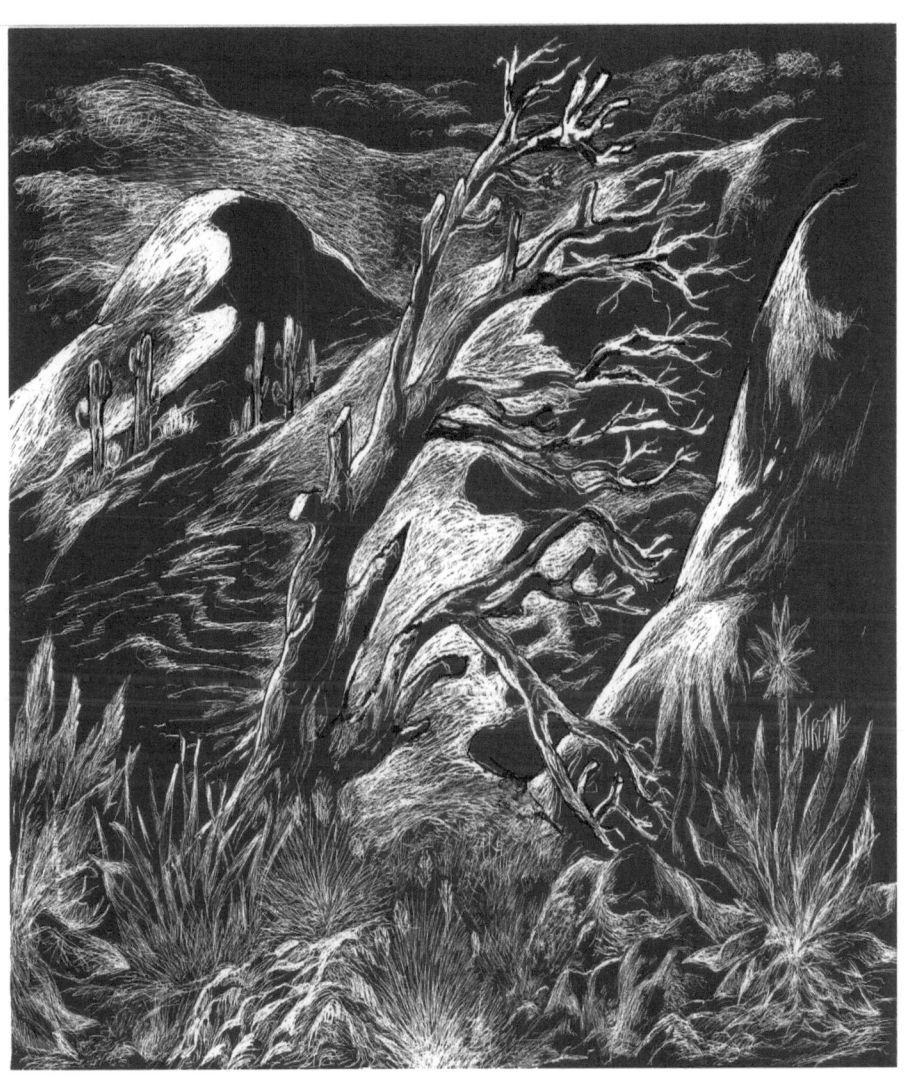

Indoors

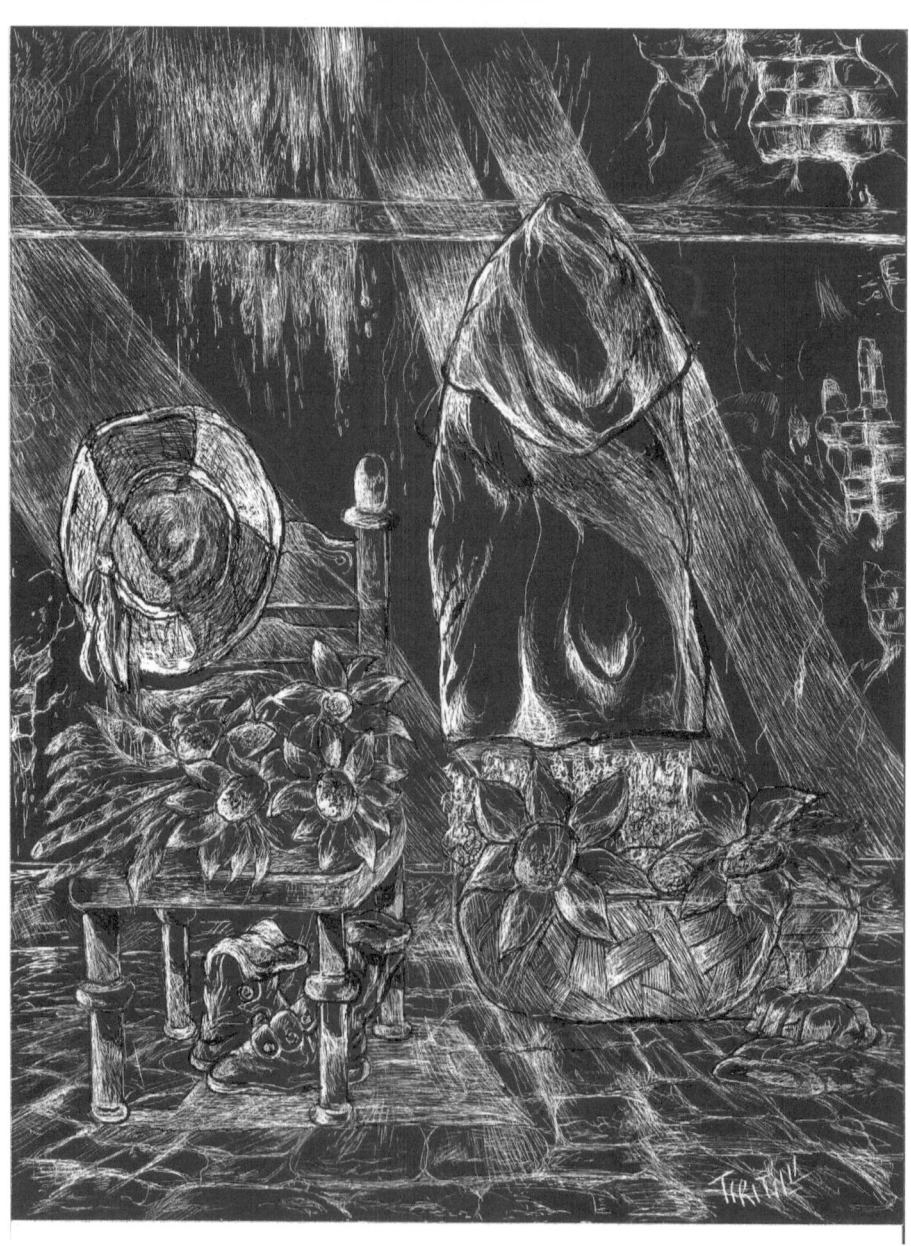

Dragon

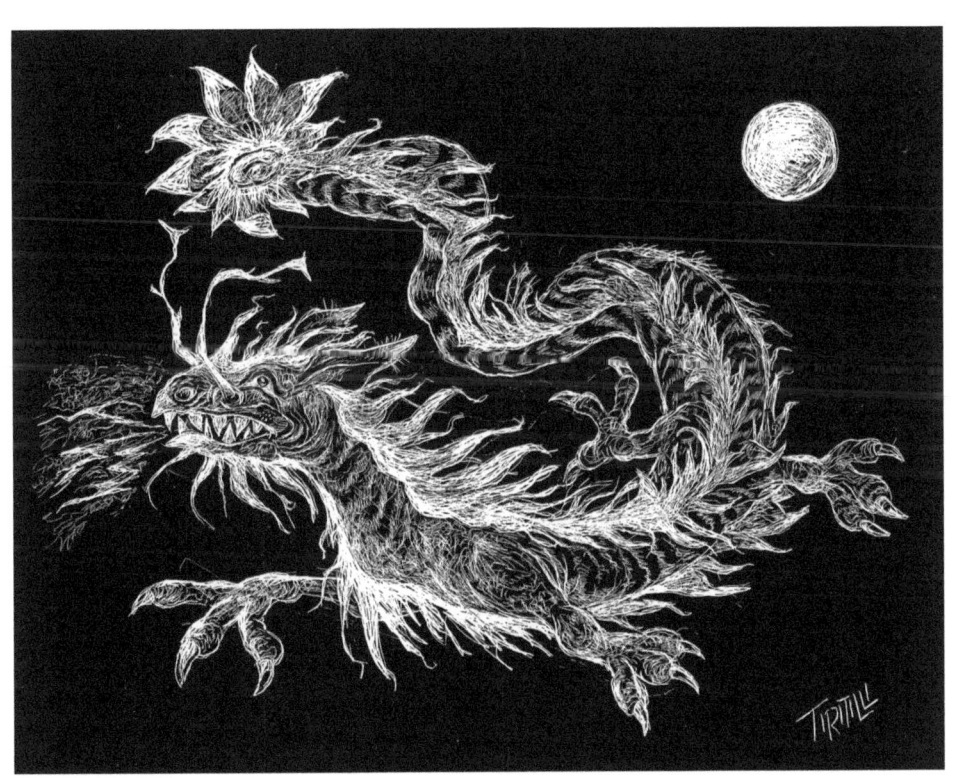

Lucky Dragon

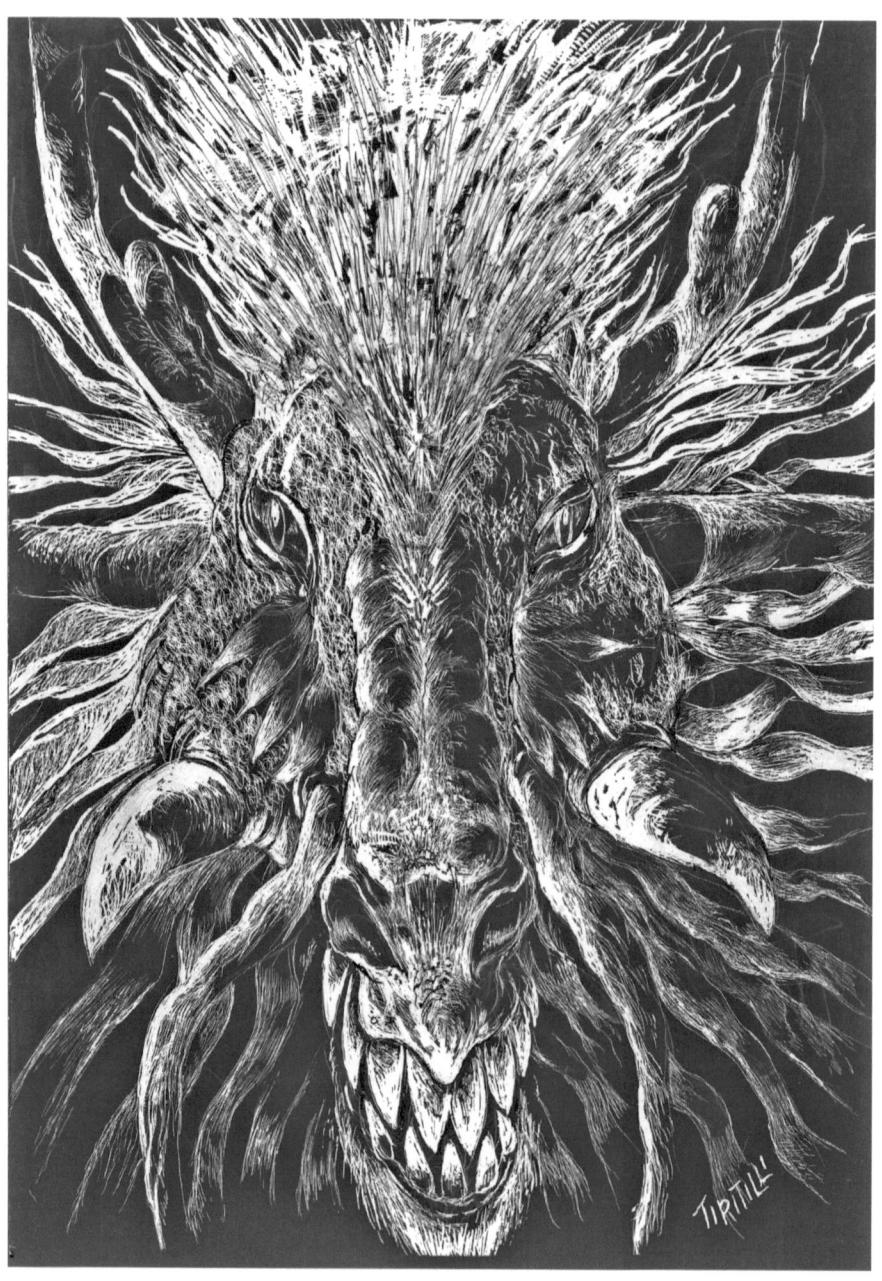

Zombie Mombie

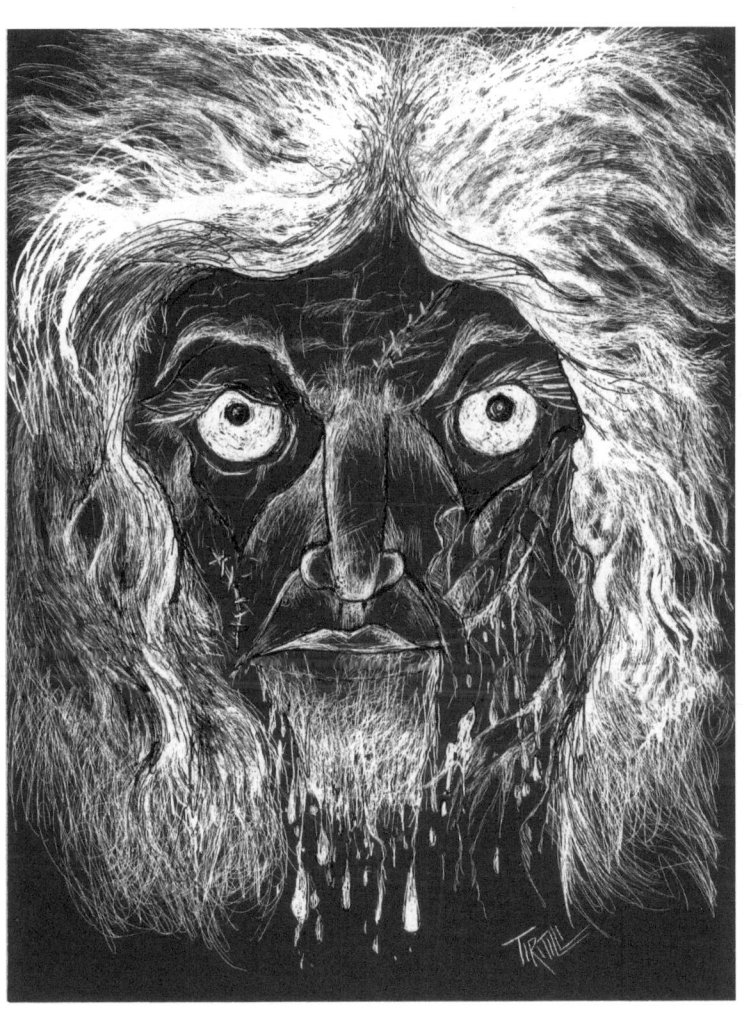

Moonlight Madness

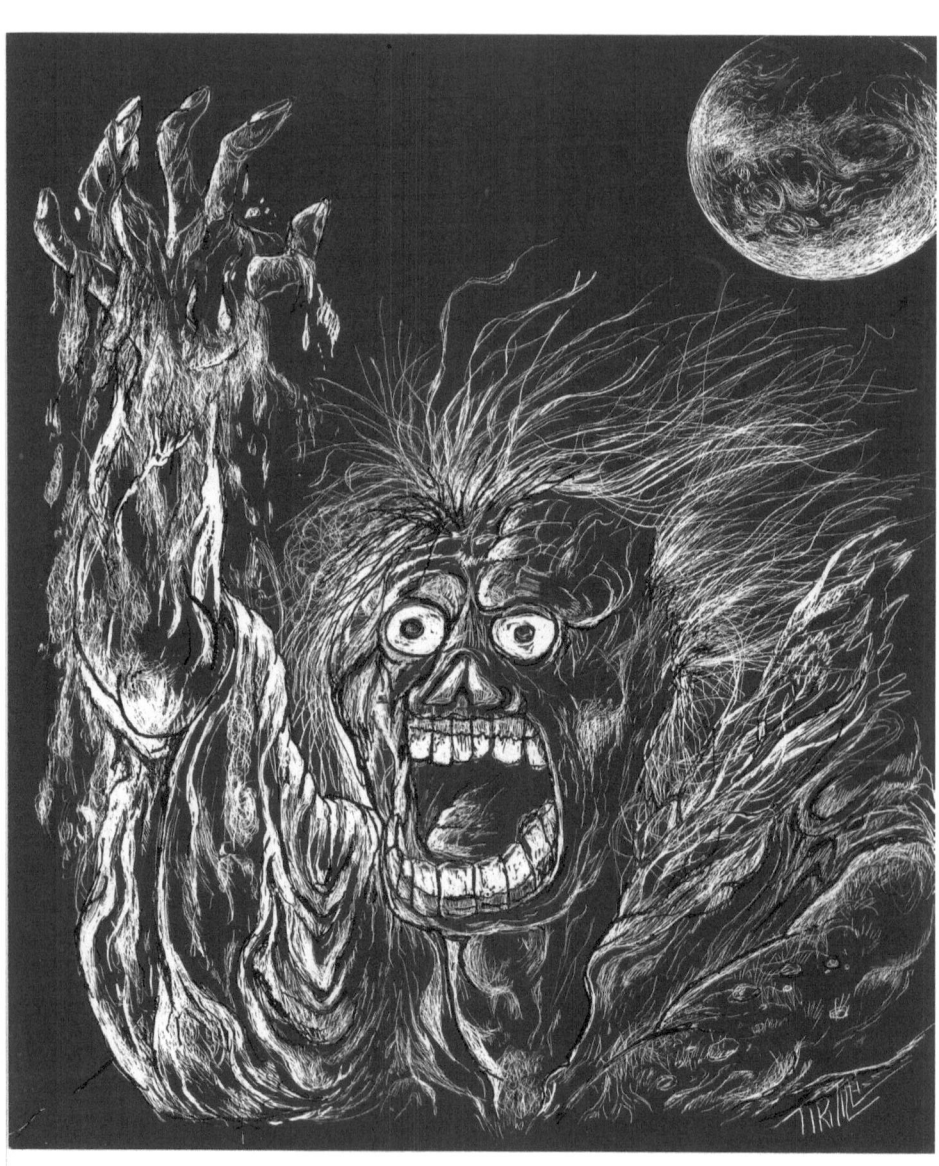

Big Horn

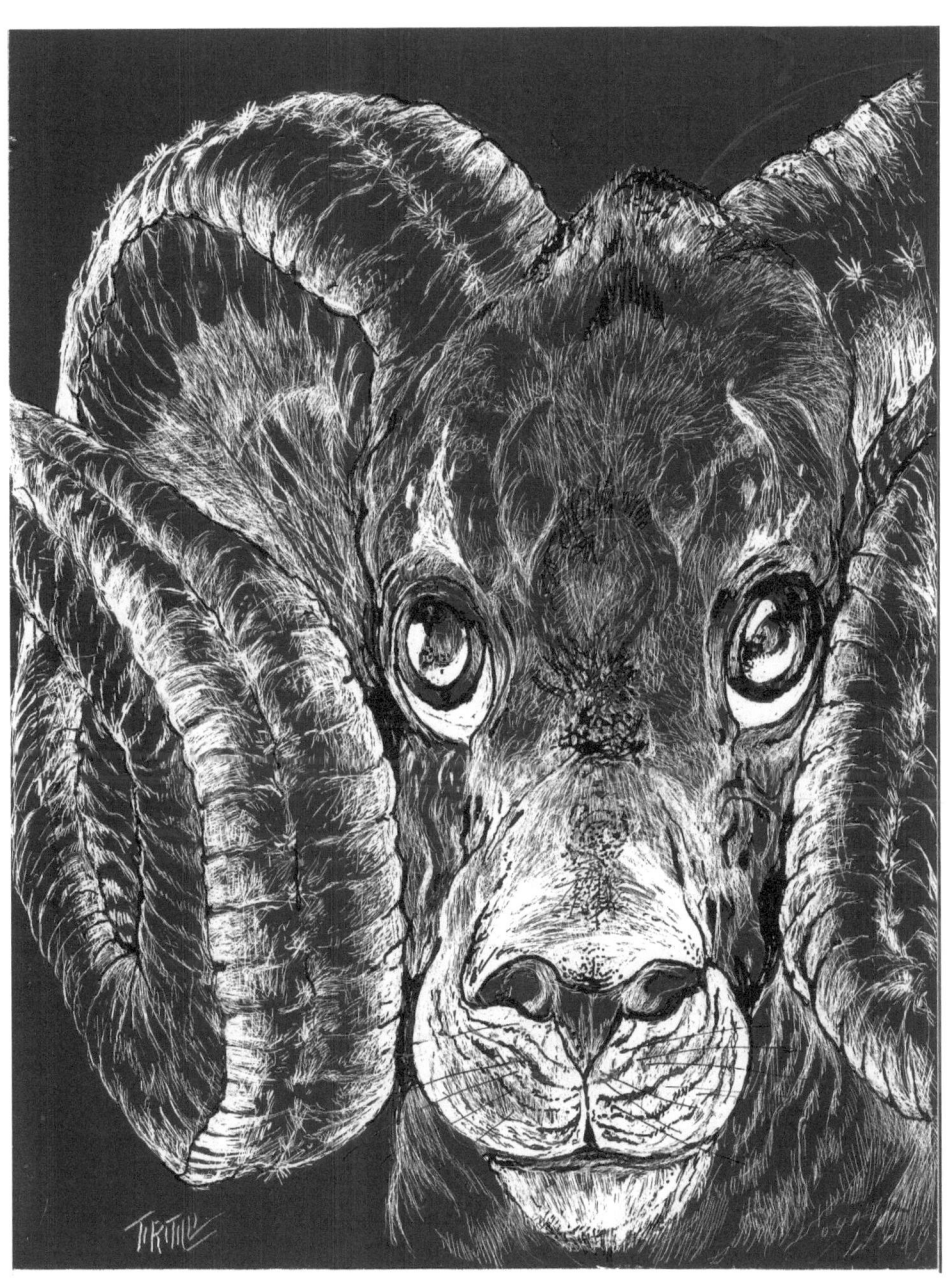

Zebras

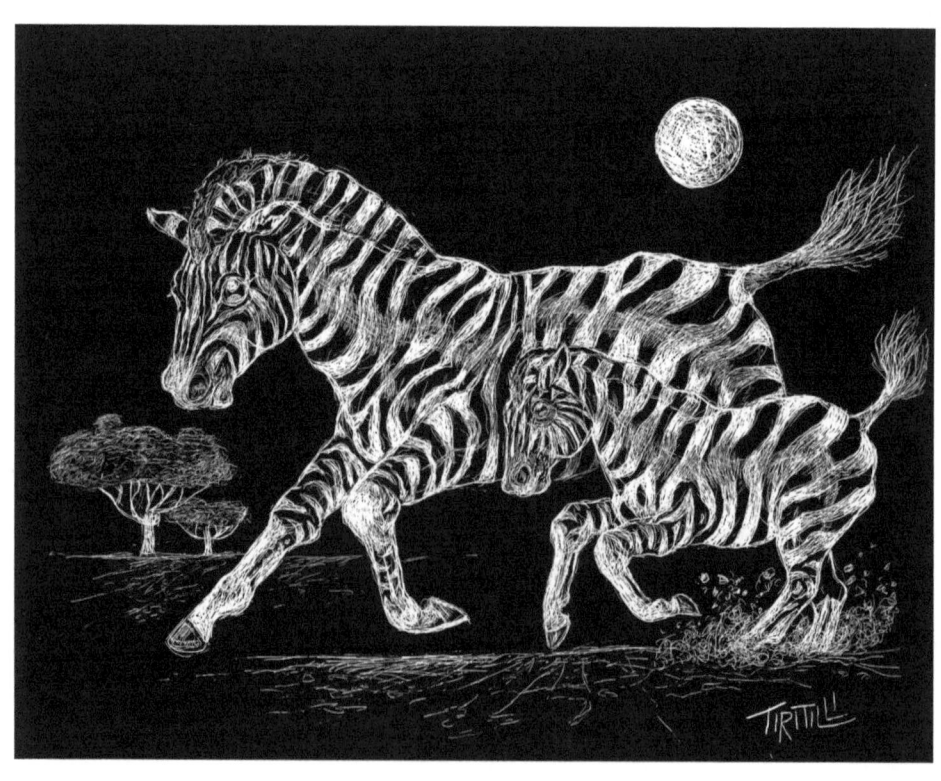

Life Well Lived

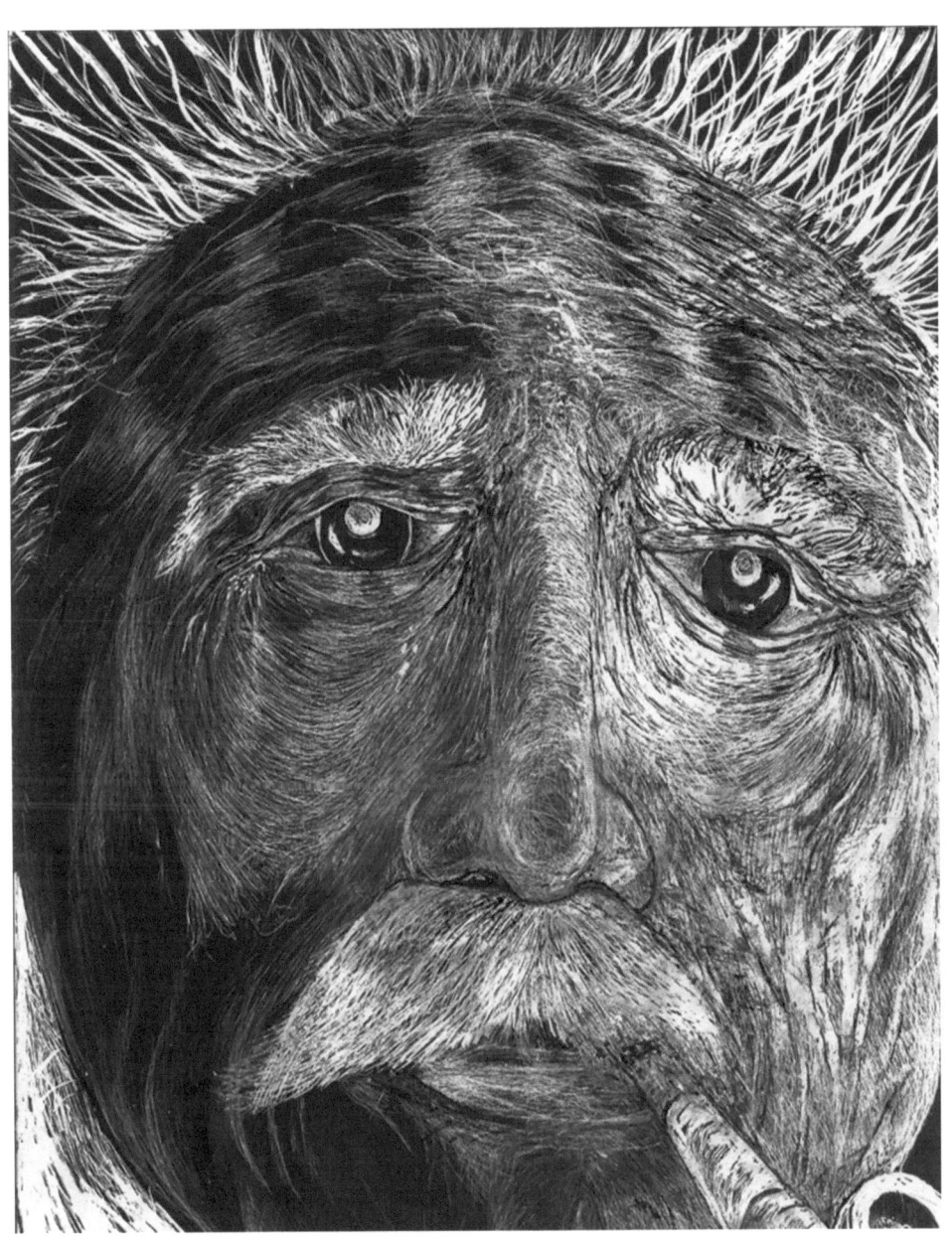

Lighting Candle

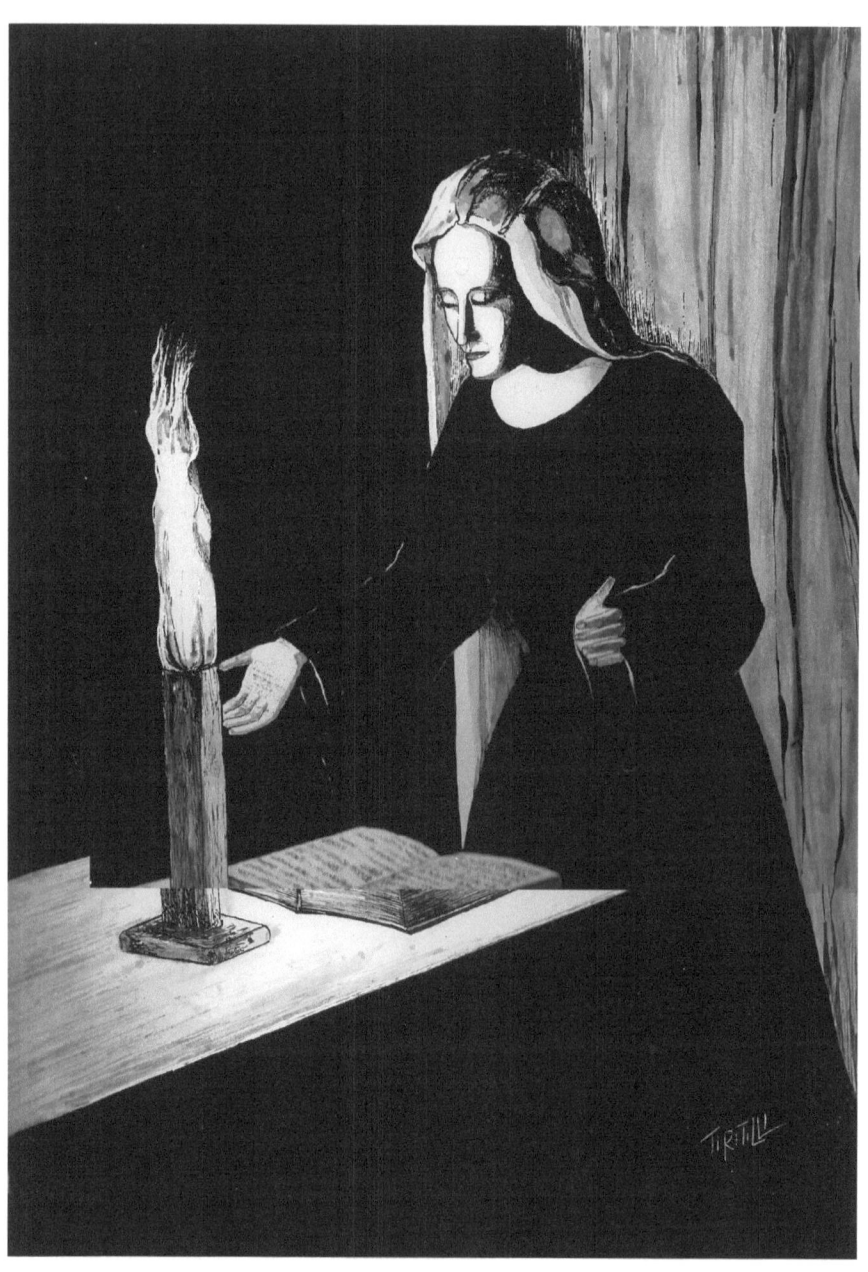

Lonely Sentinel

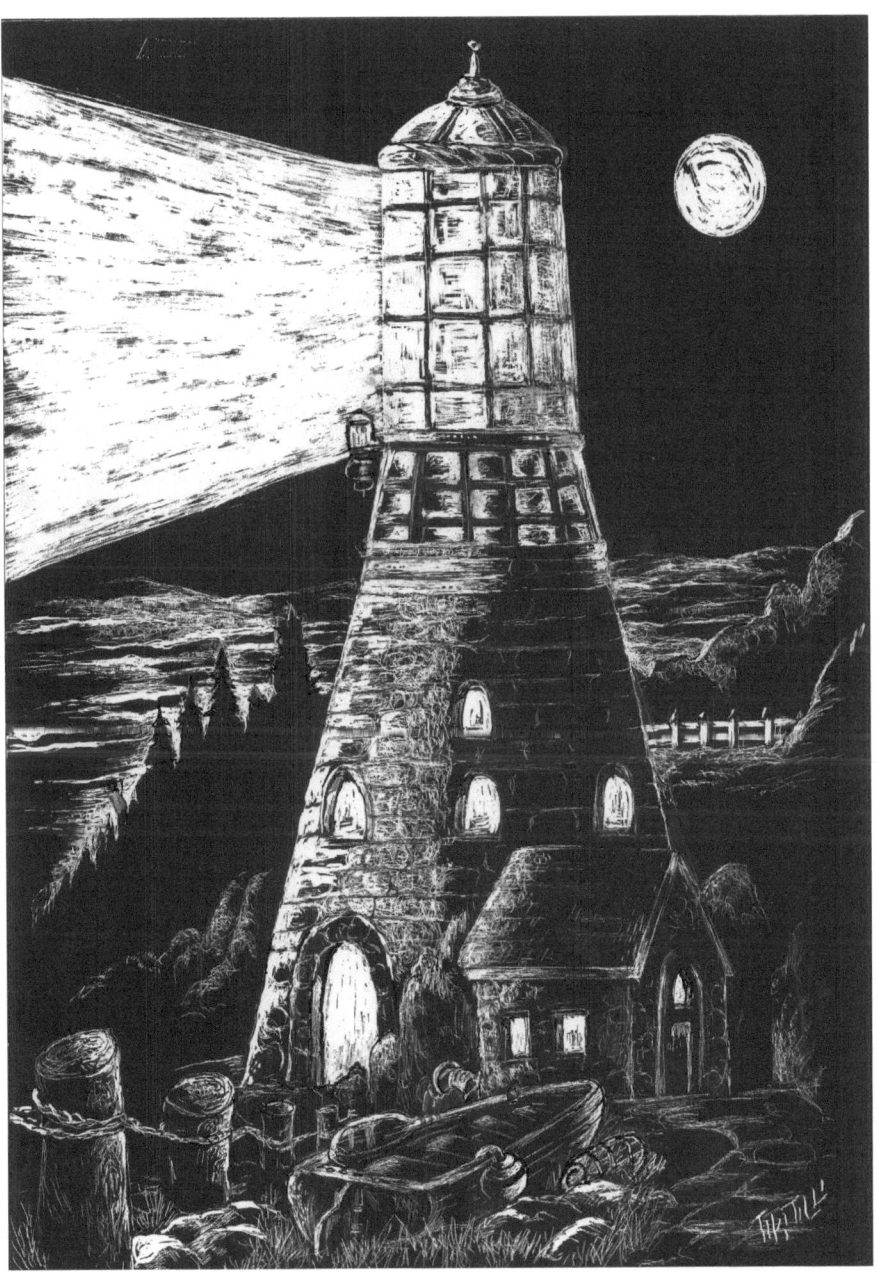

Light of Life

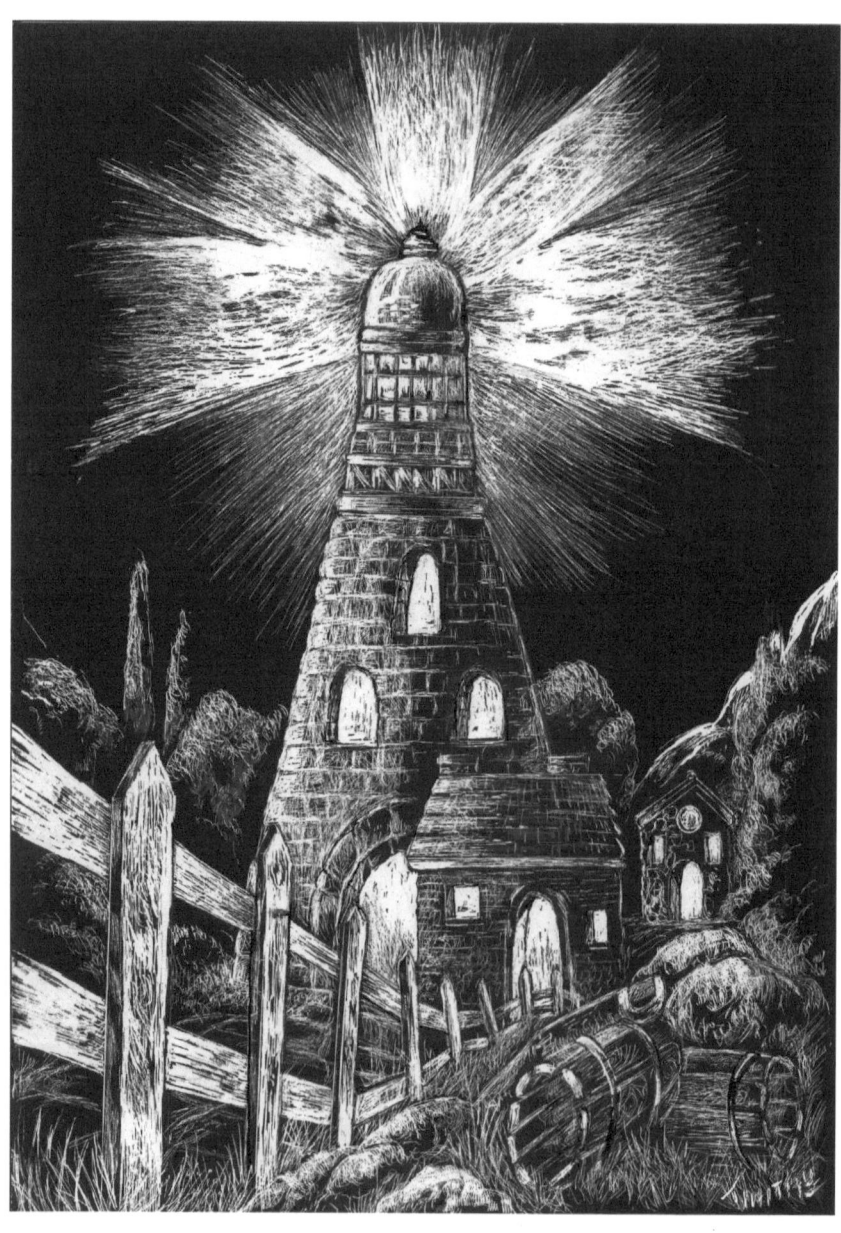

Mountain Man

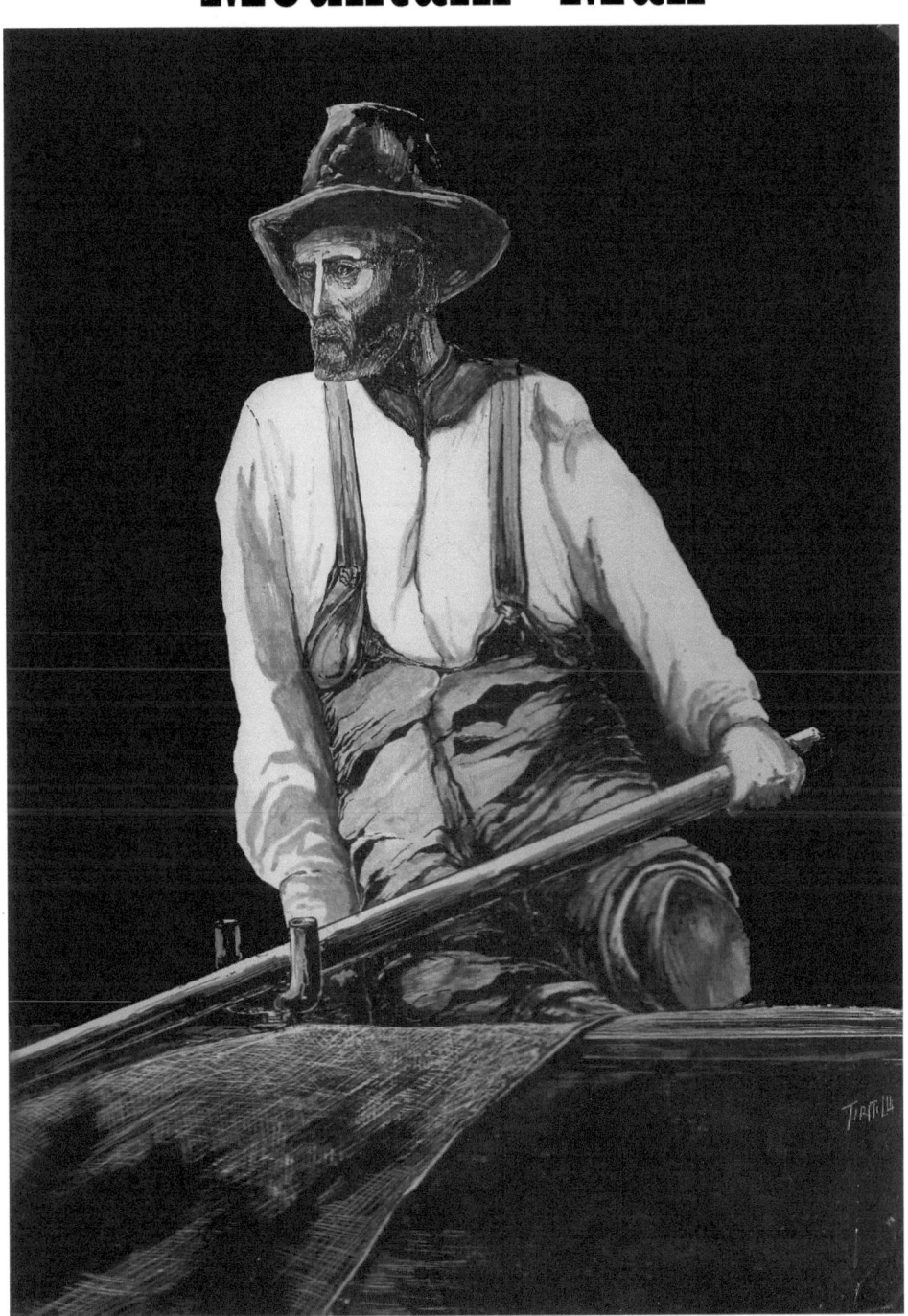

Gladiator

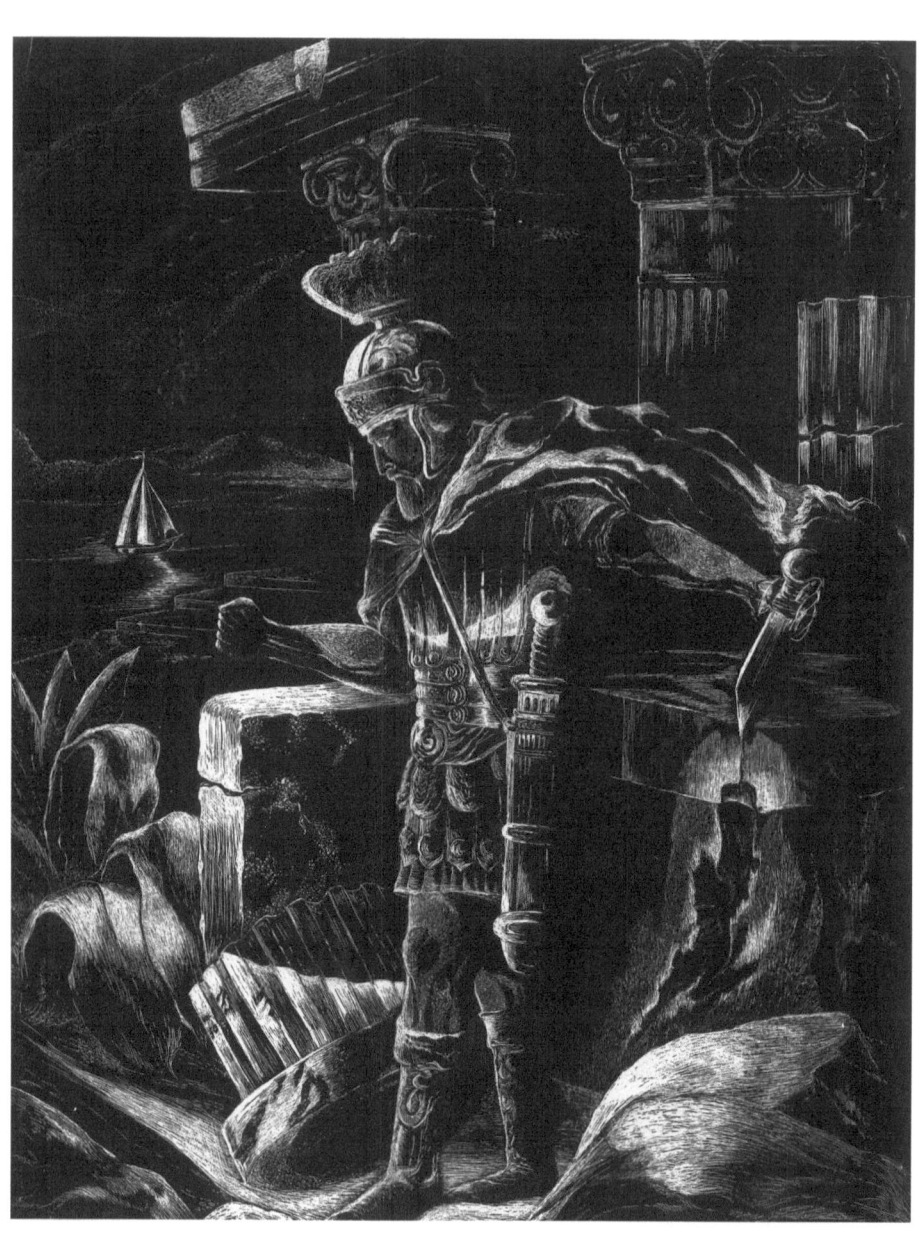

Horses

Chariot Race

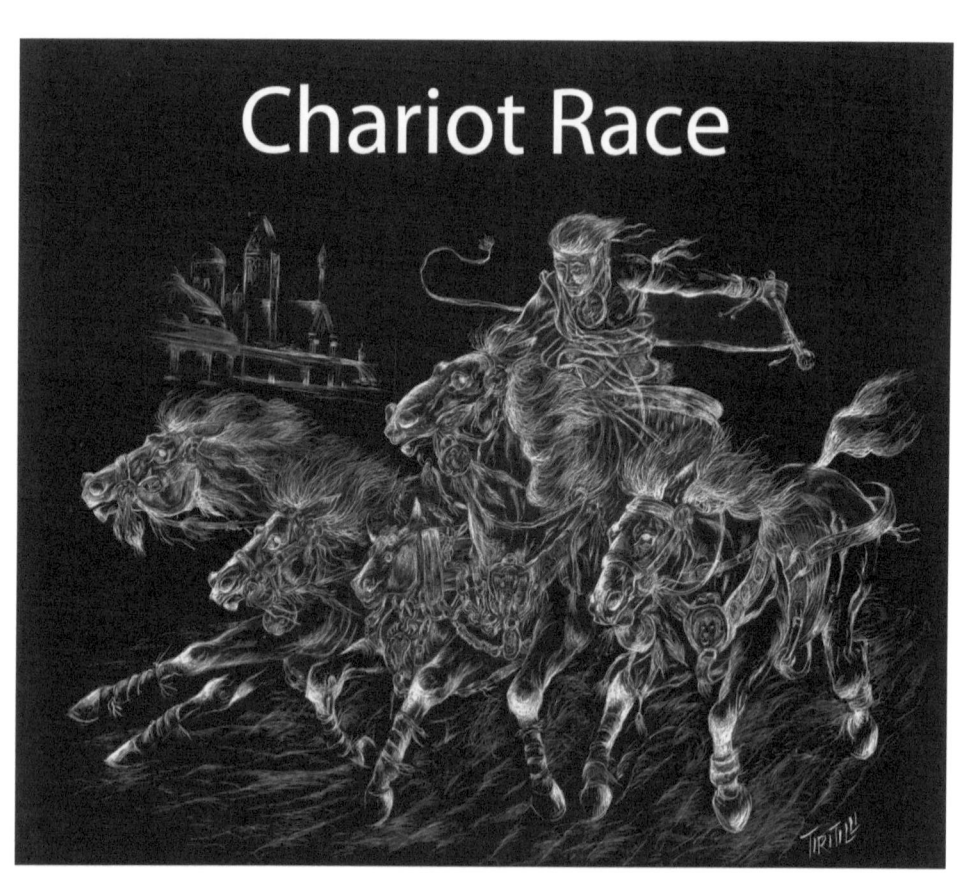

Forward!

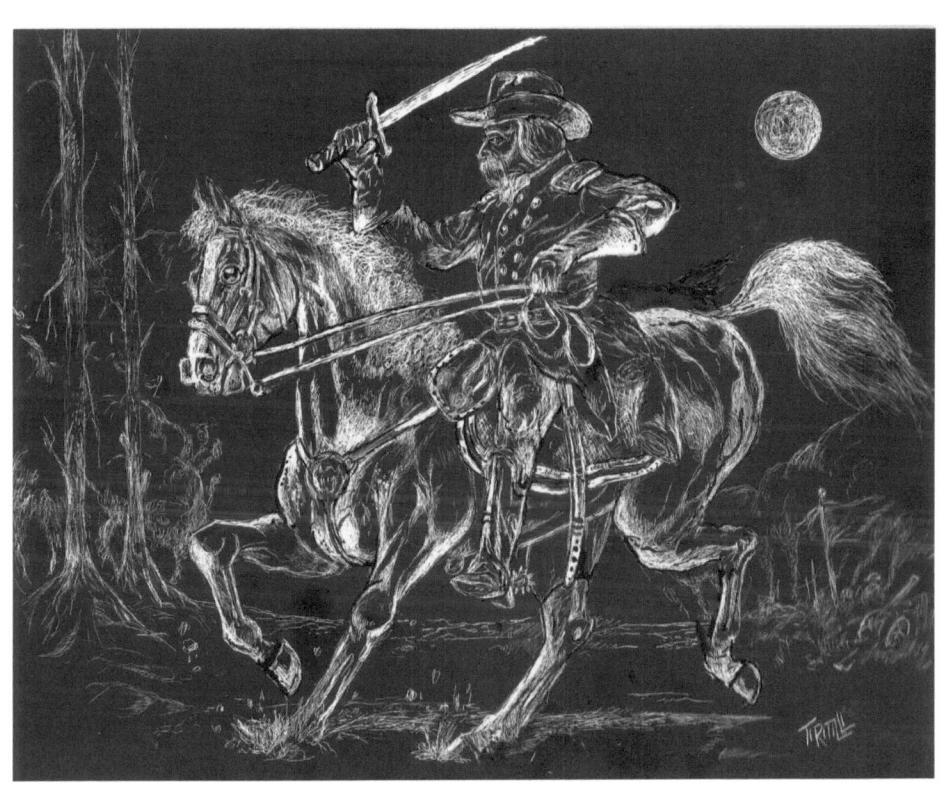

Horseman

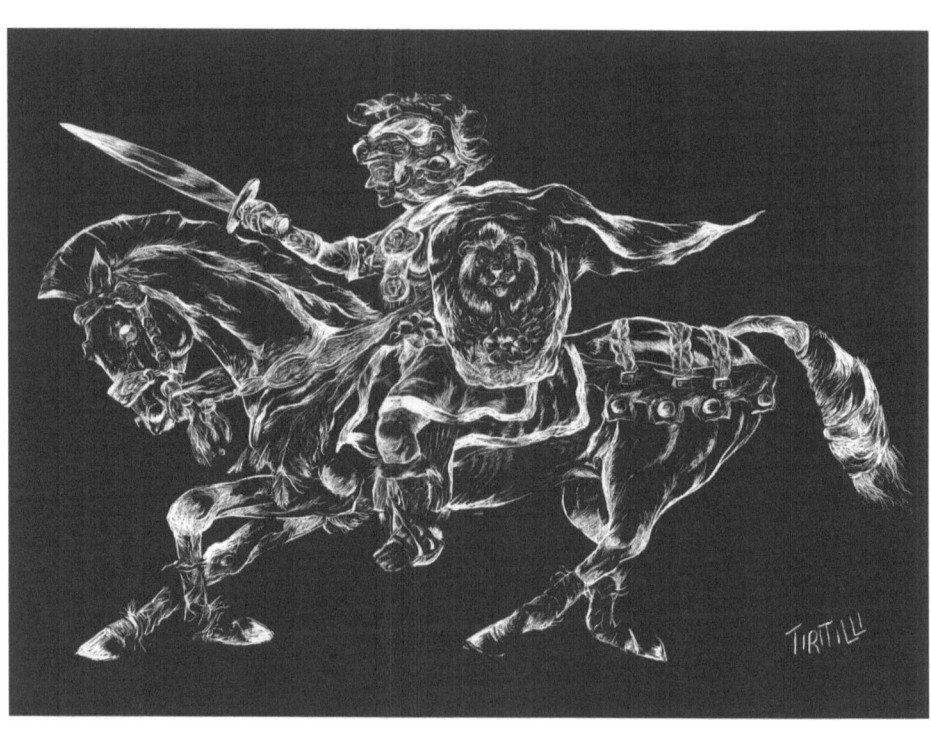

Morning Glory

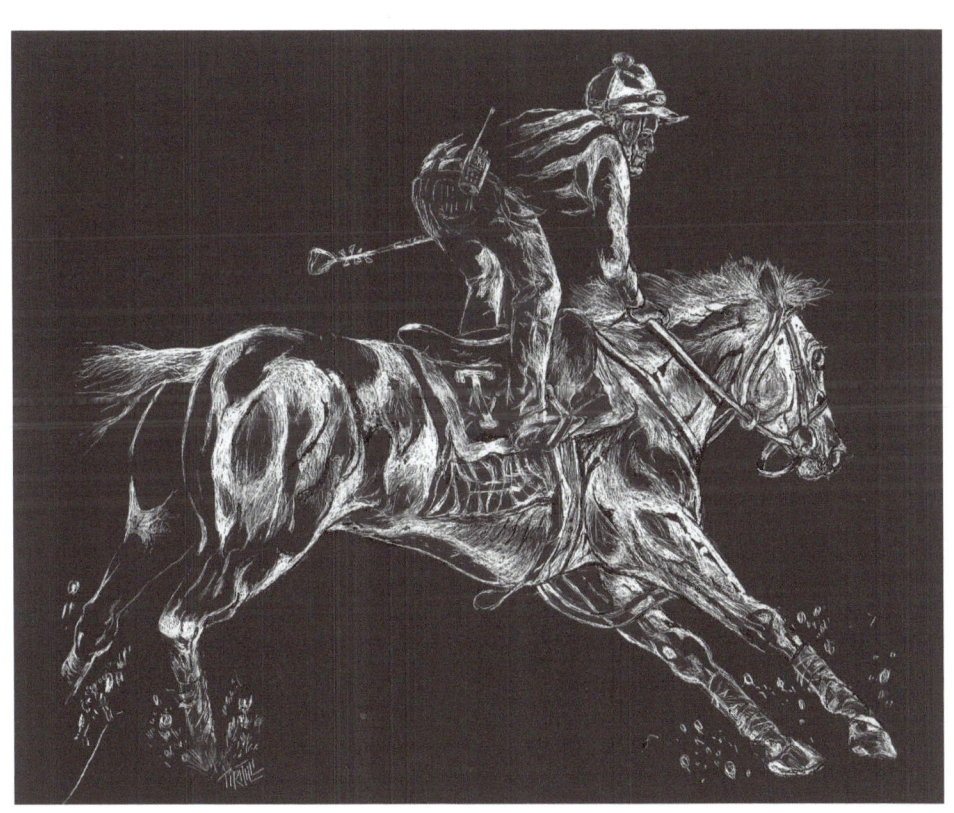

Bred to Run!

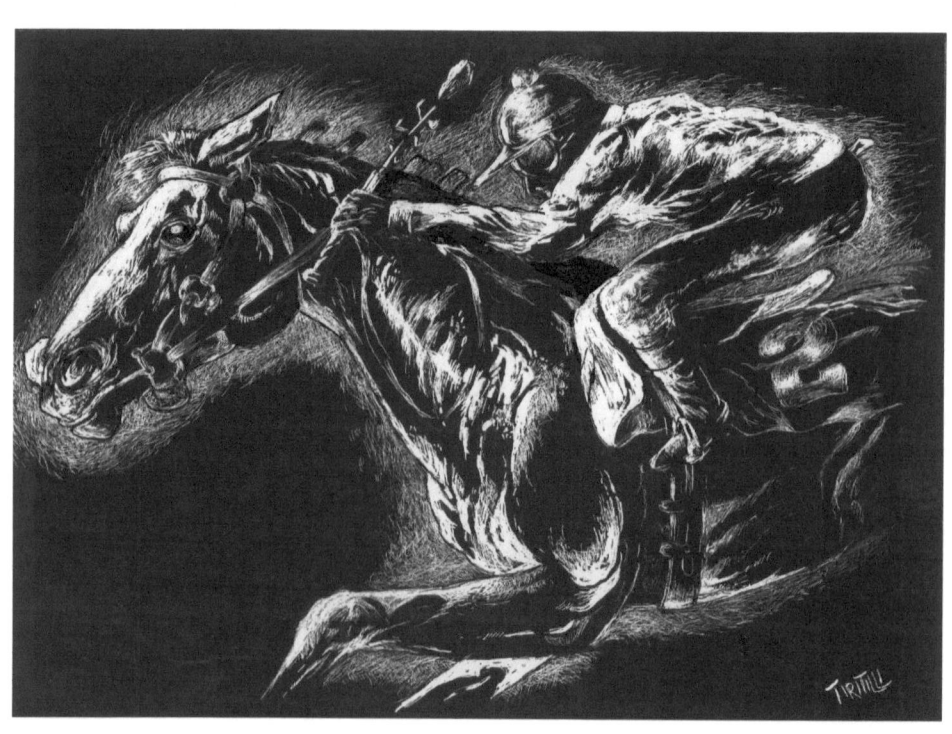

Silver

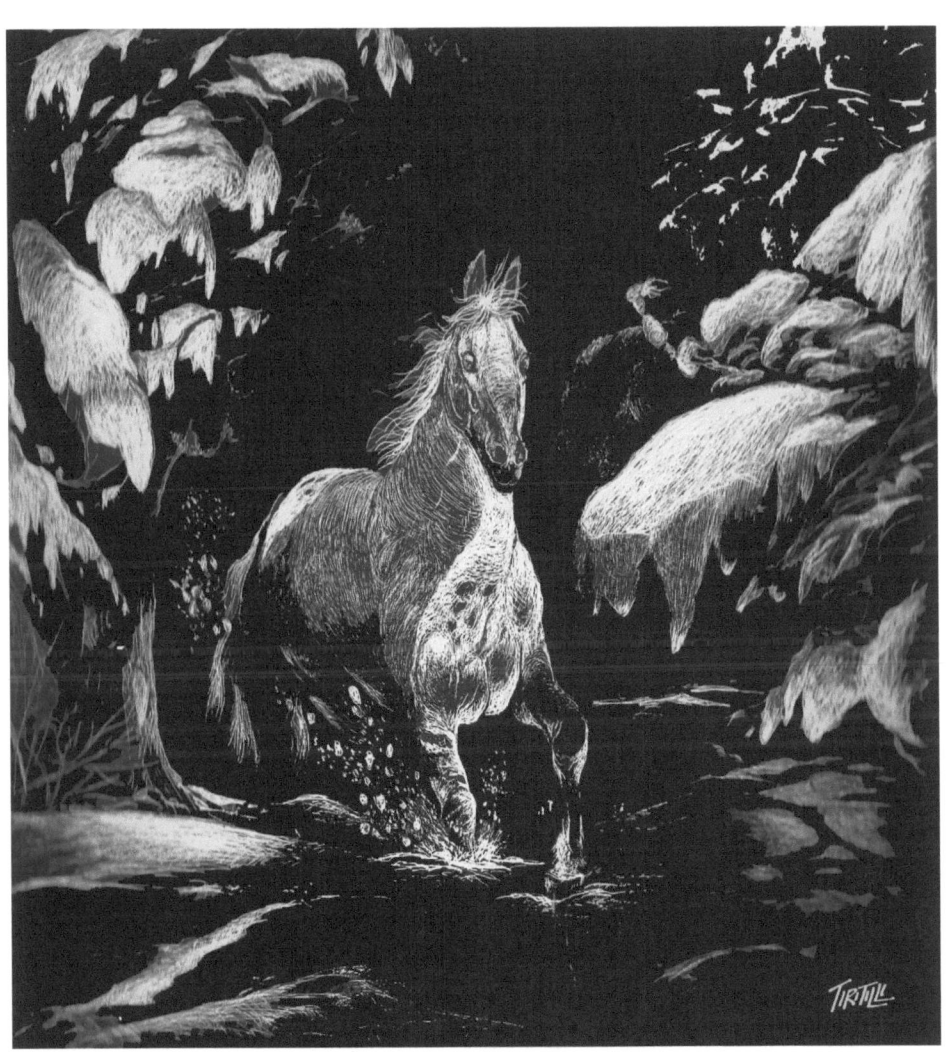

Horse 01

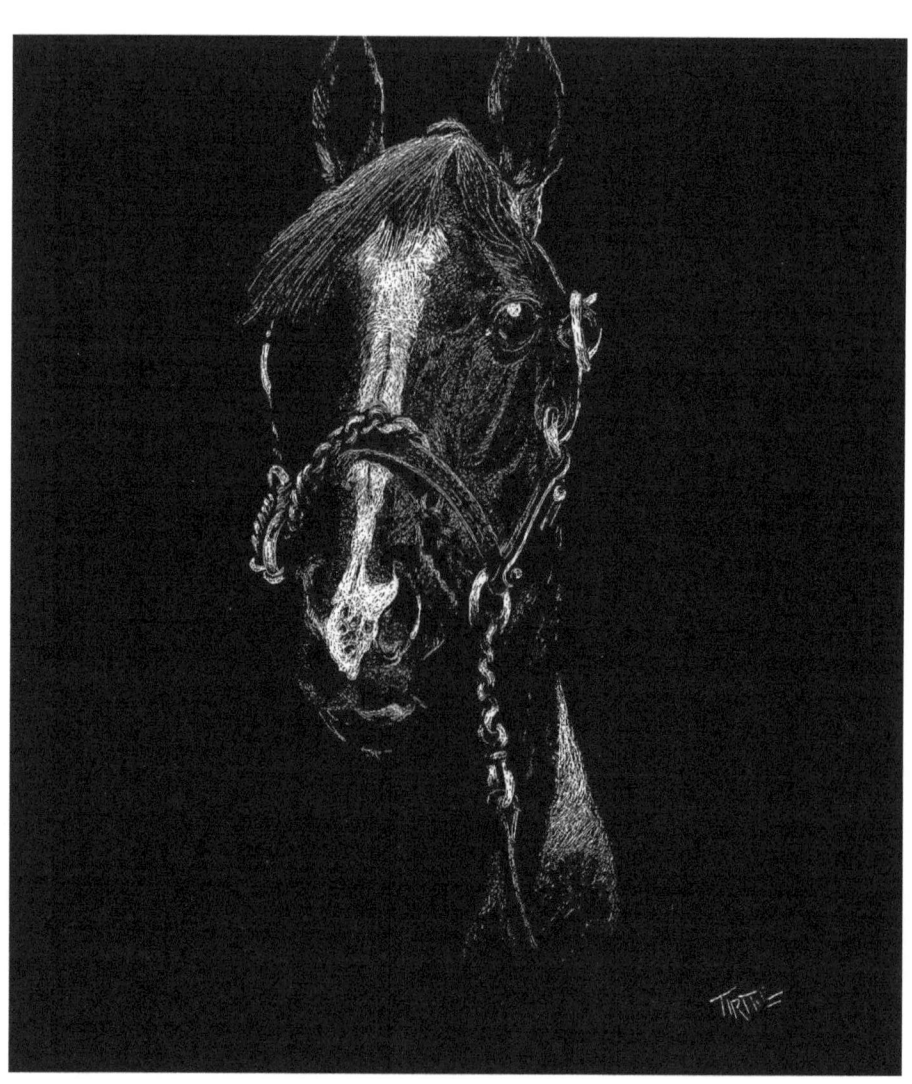

Horse 02

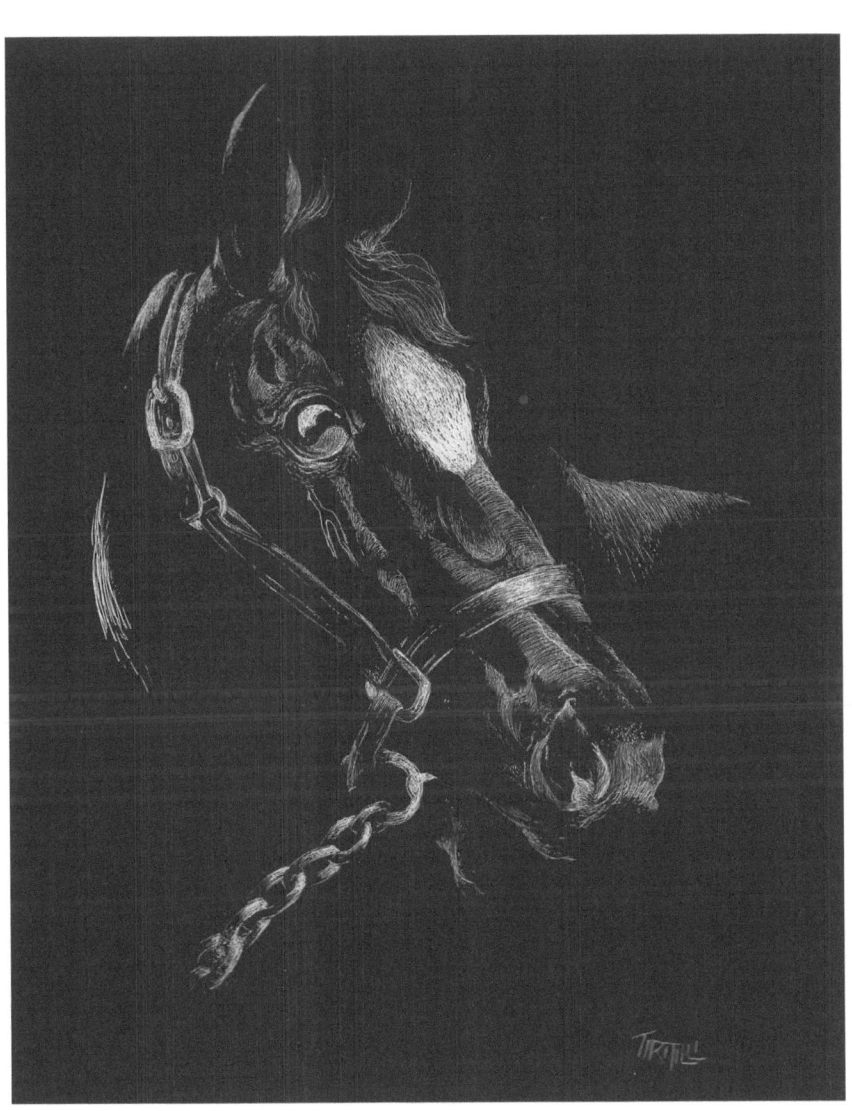

Horse 03

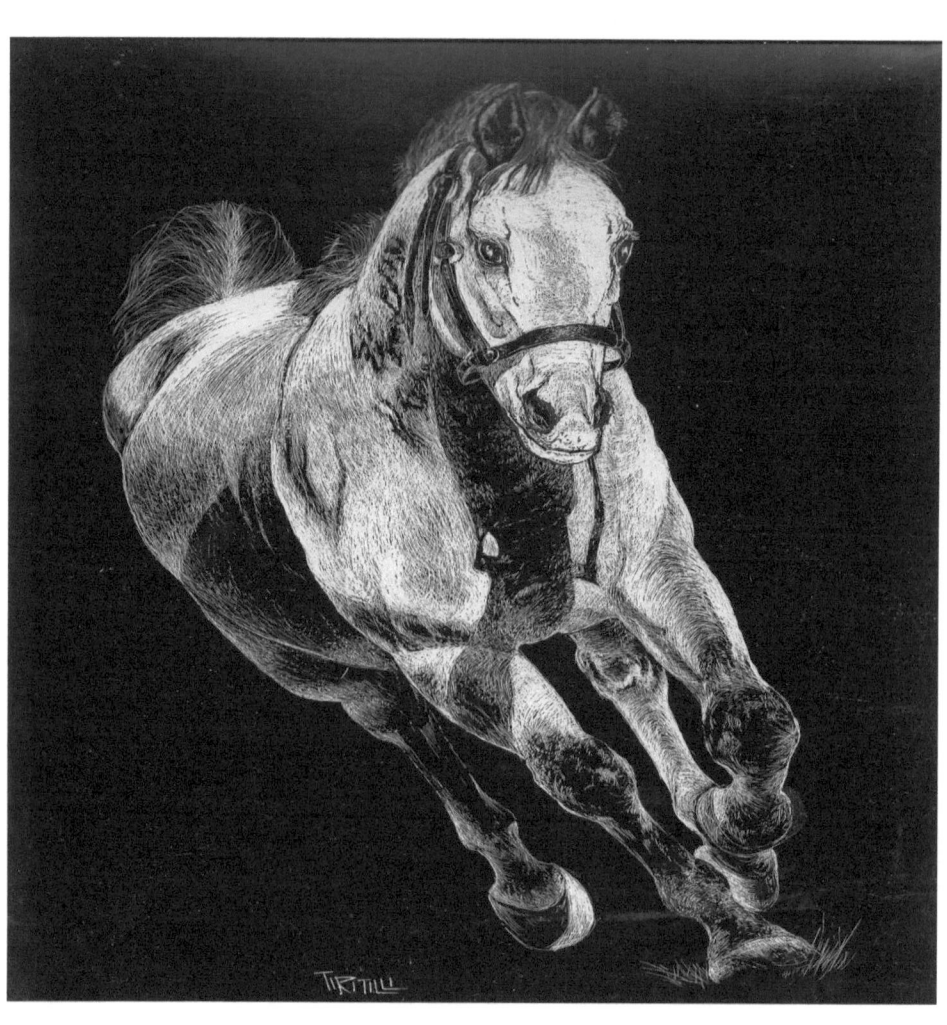

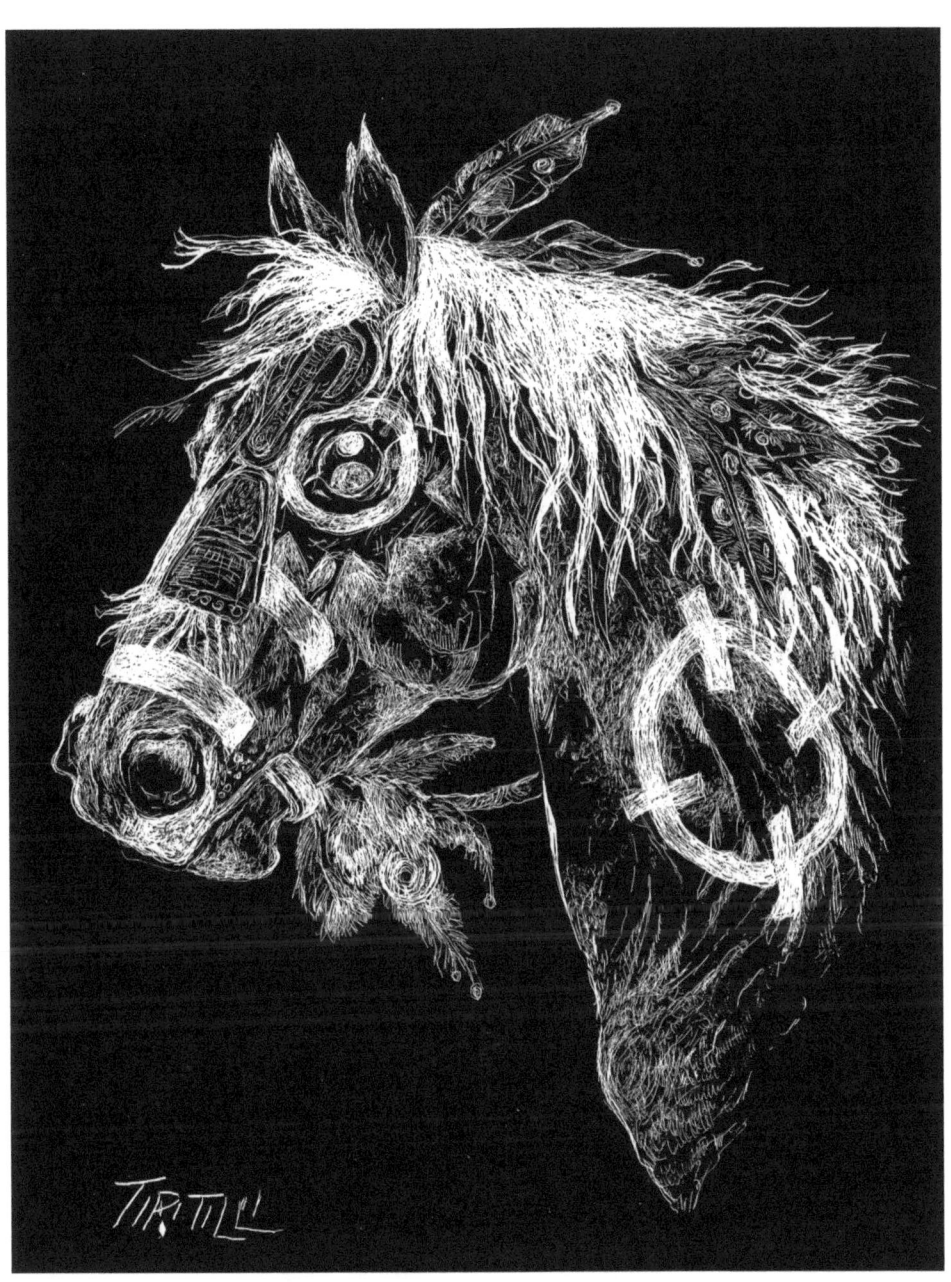

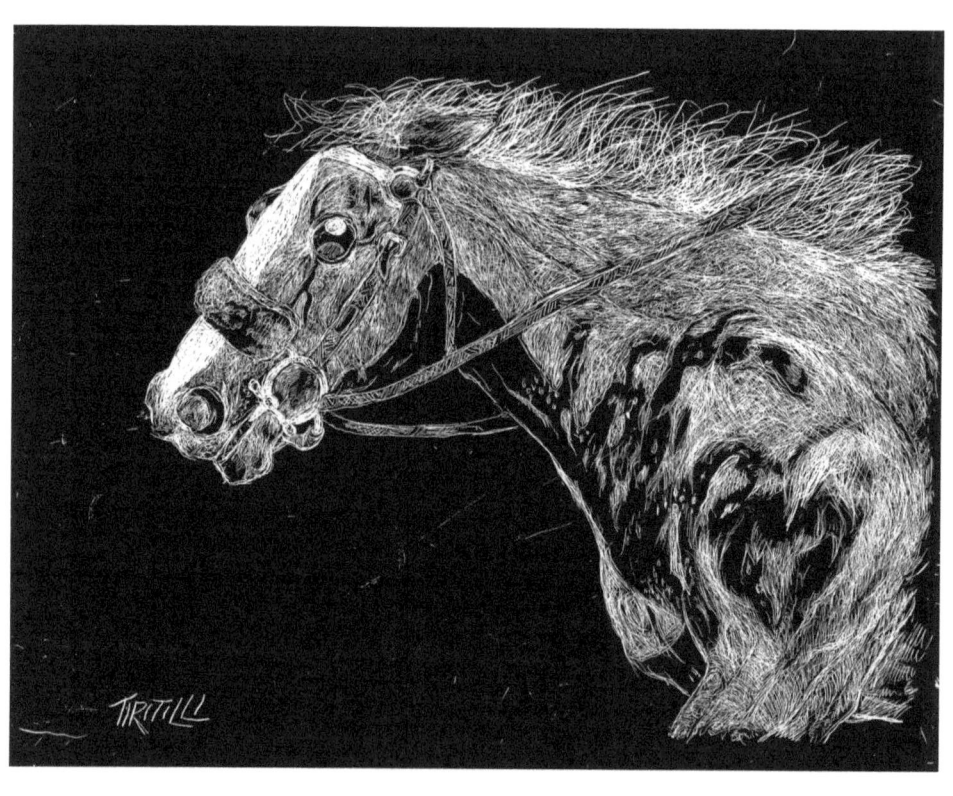

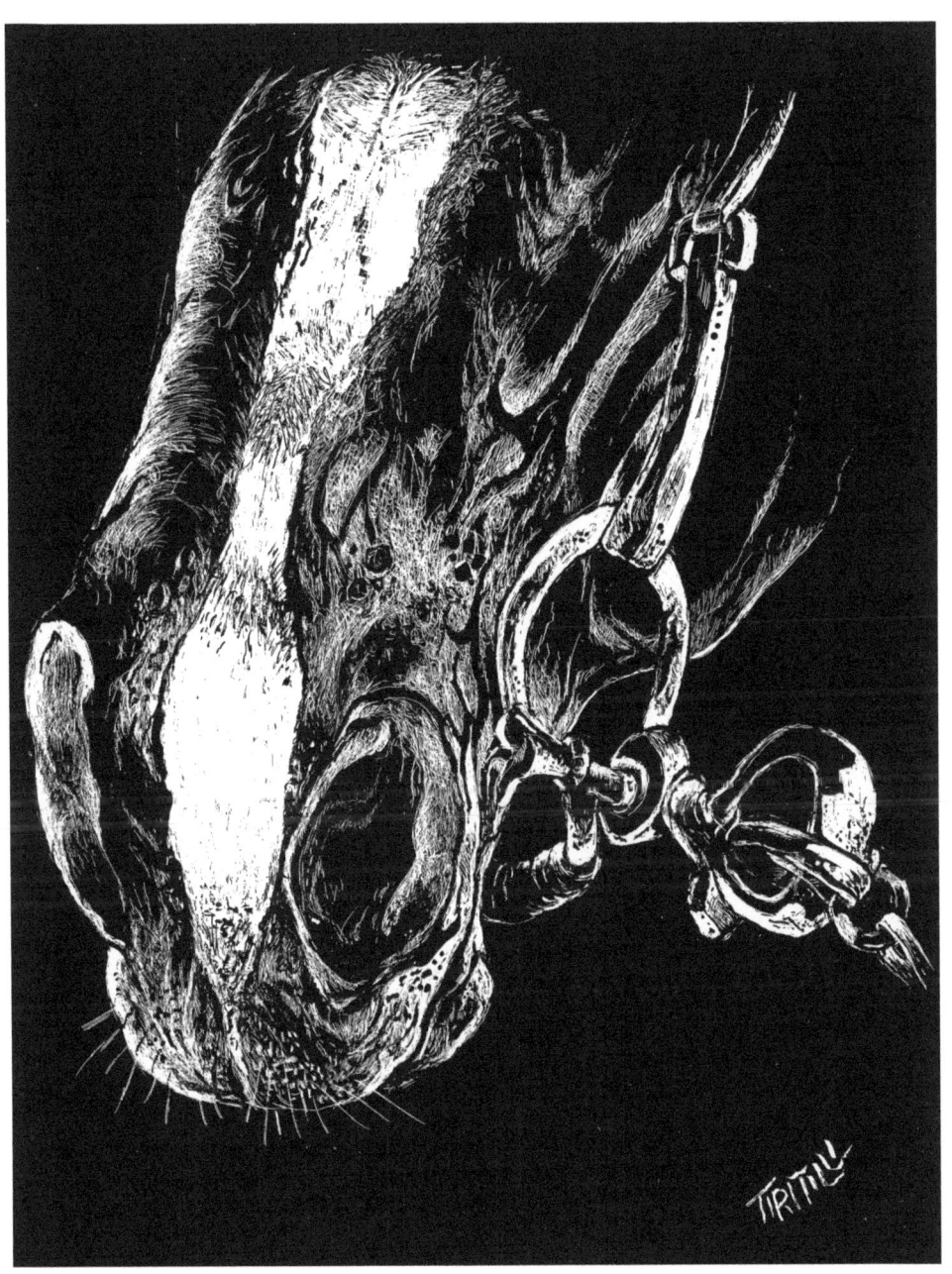

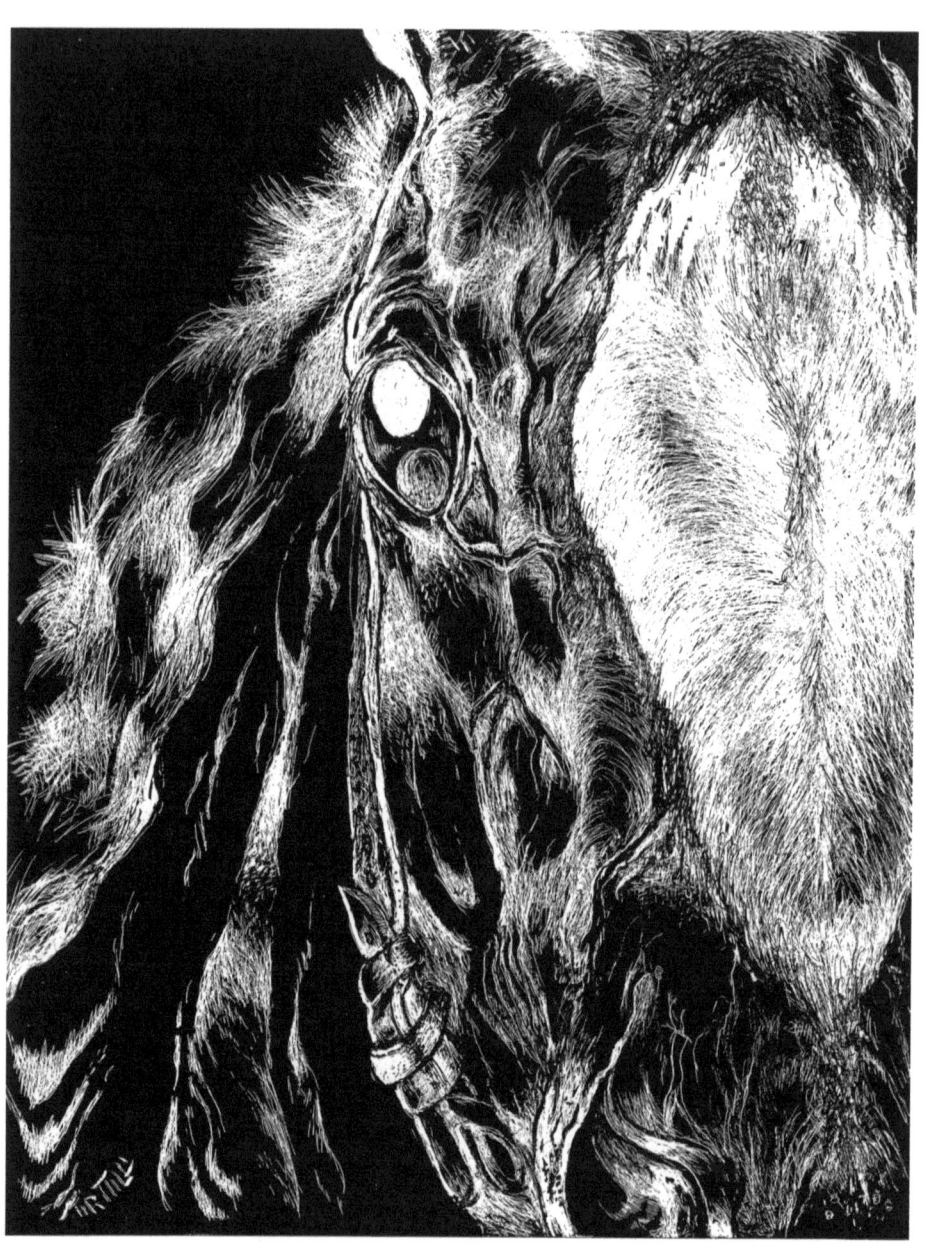

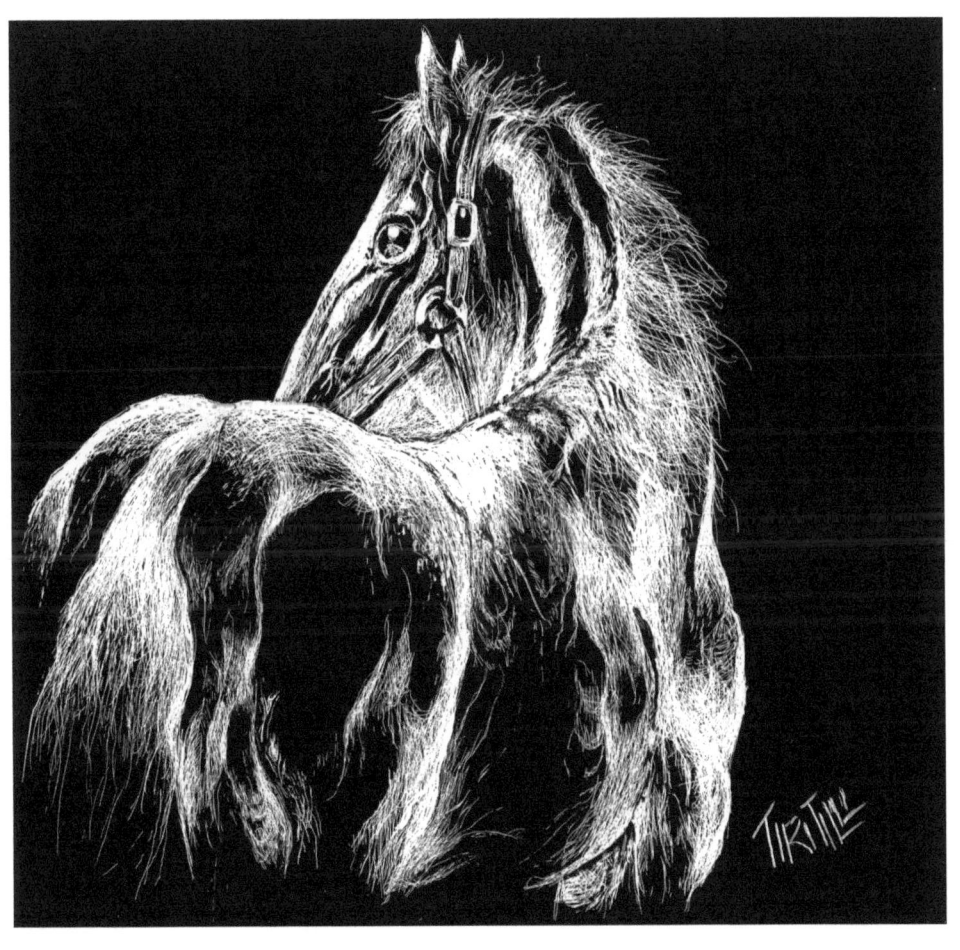

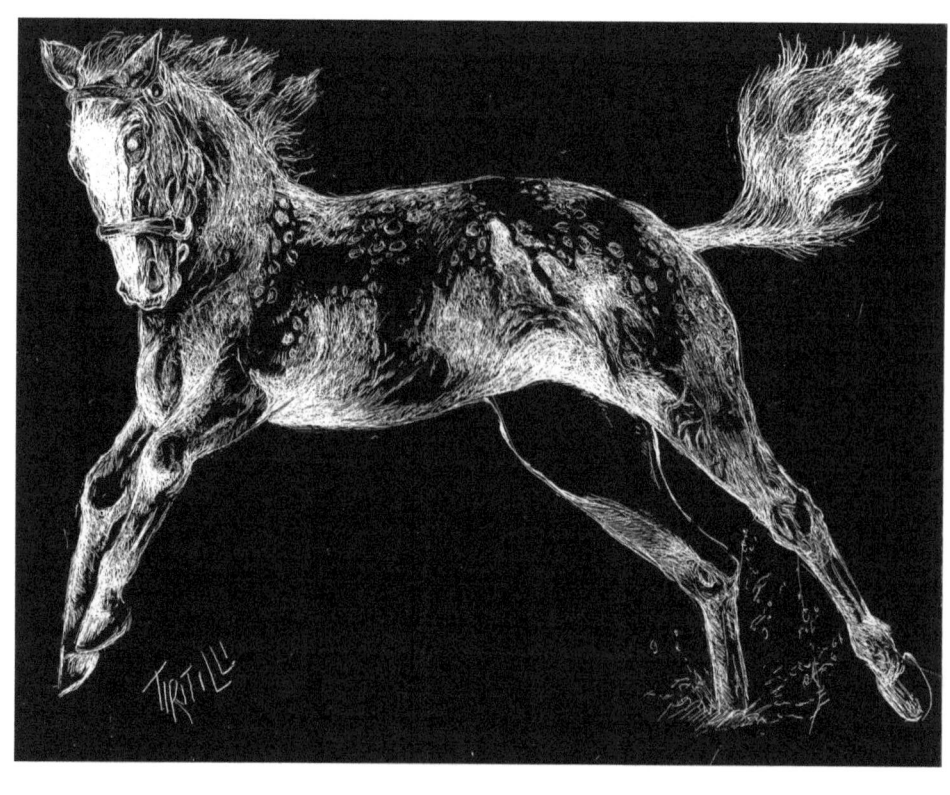

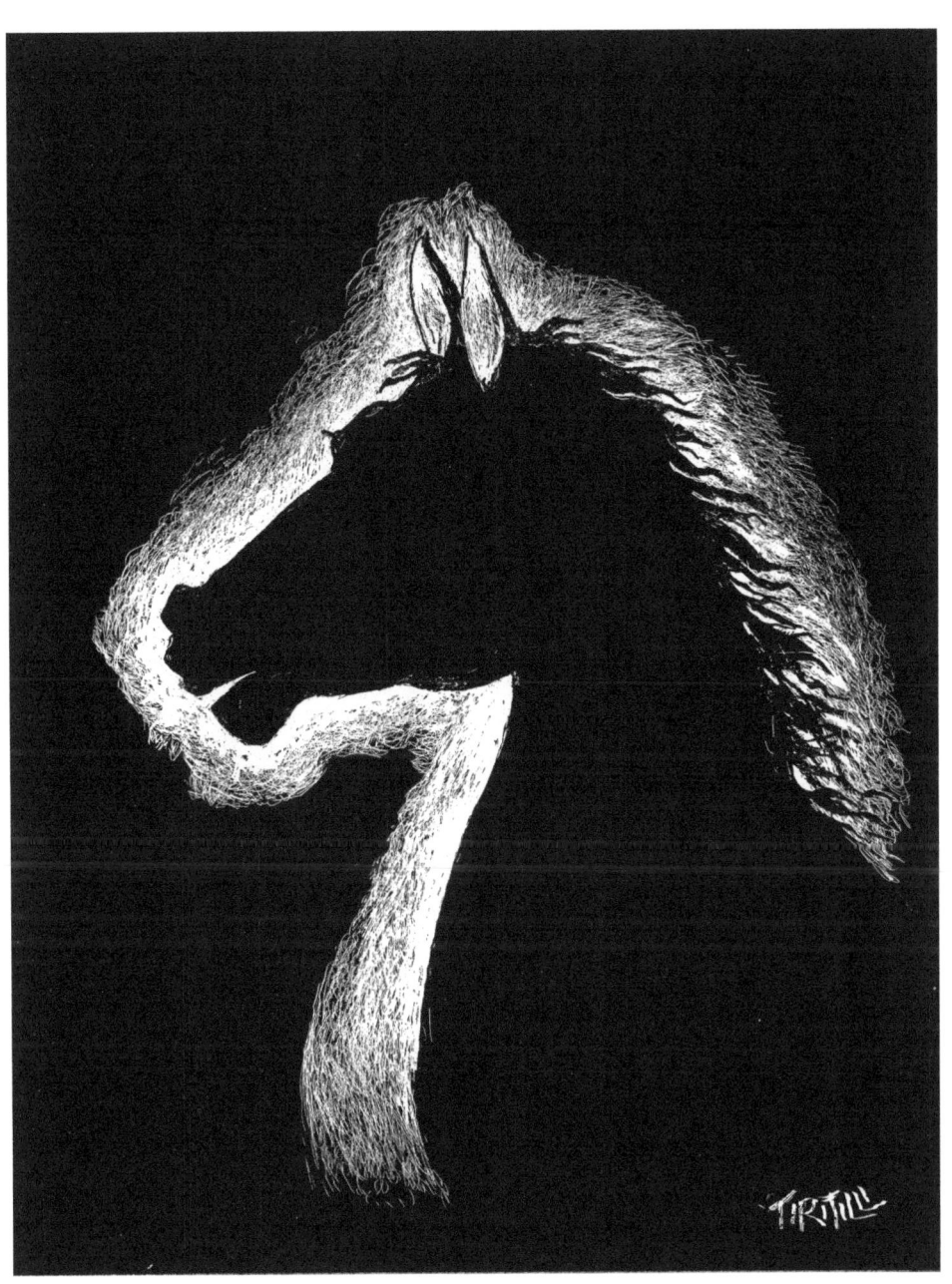

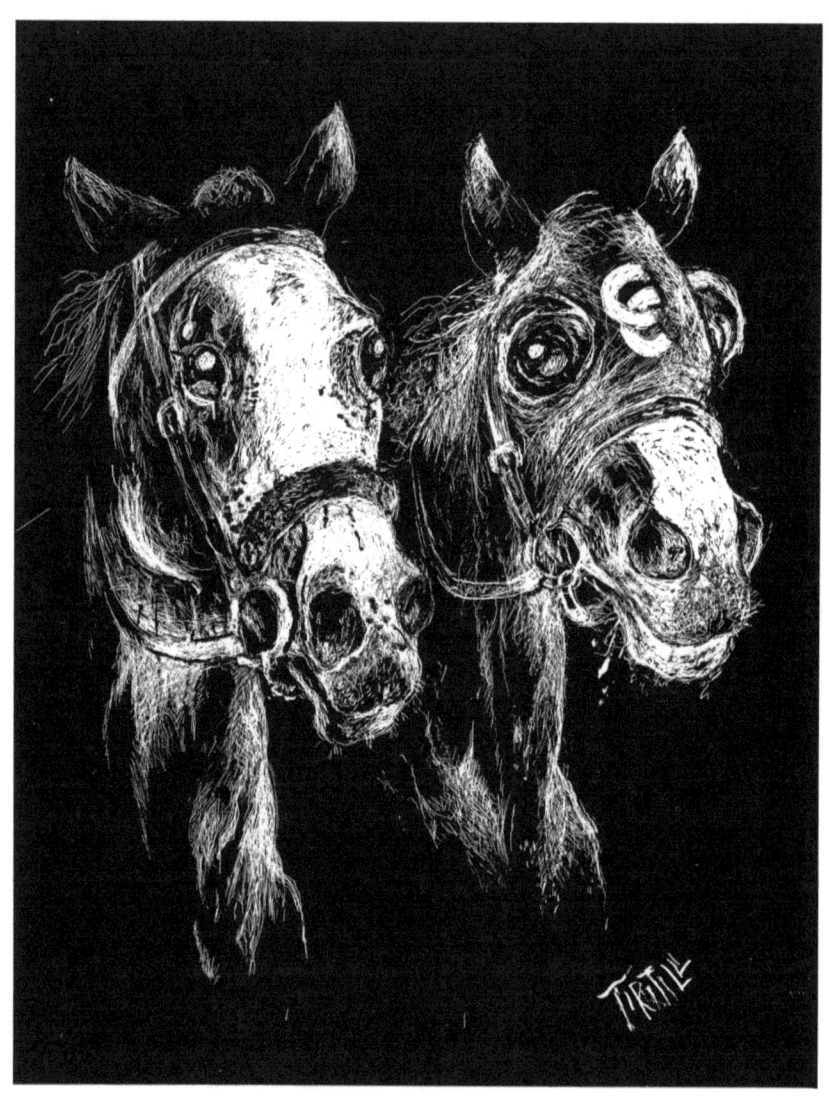

Polo 01

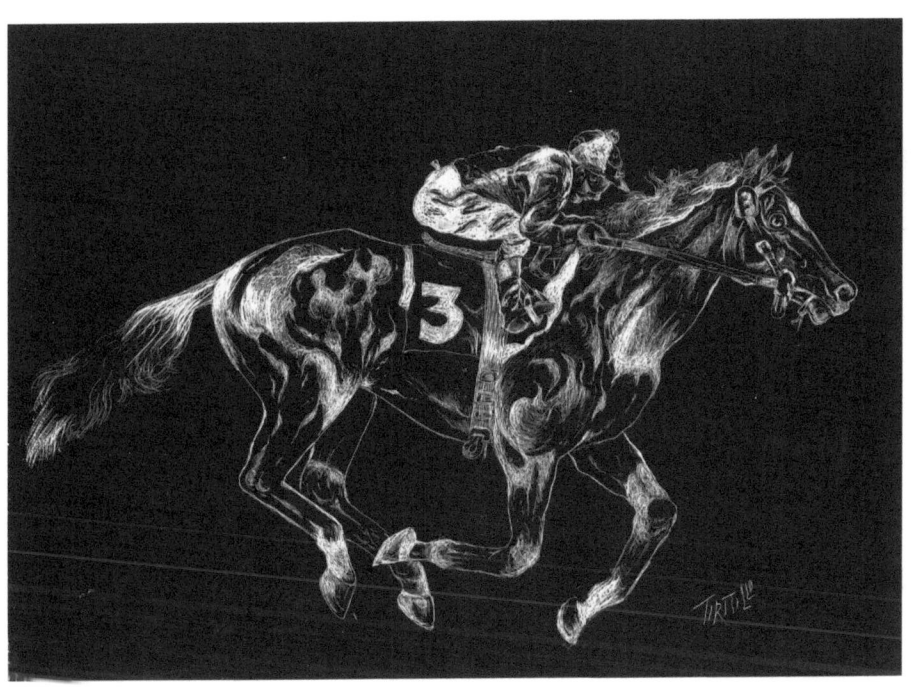

Polo 02

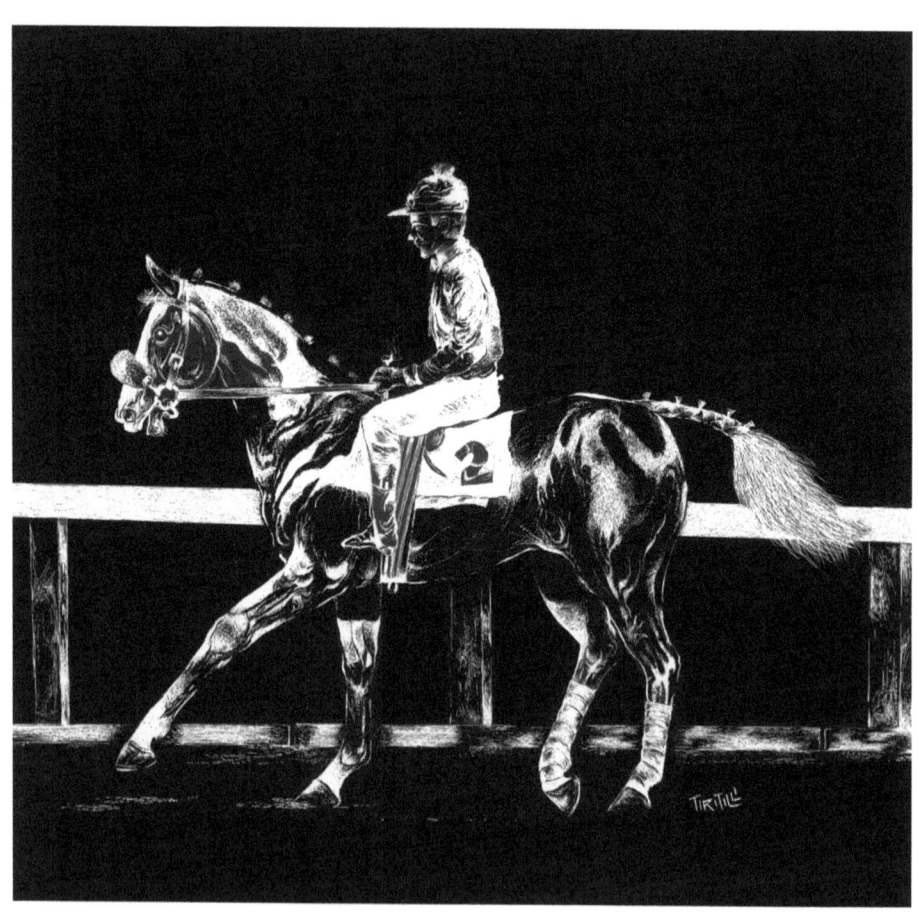

Dogs and Cats

West of Westie

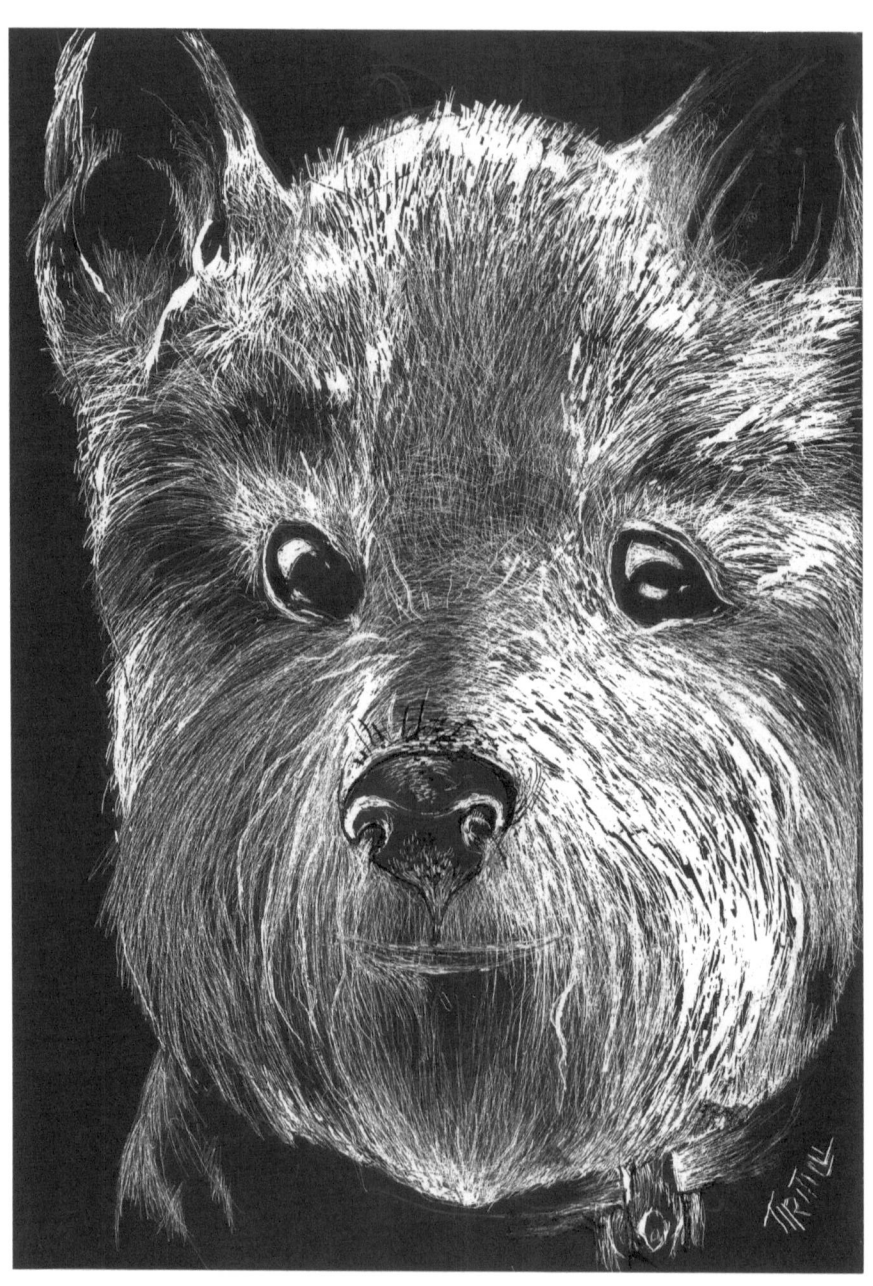

Puppy Love

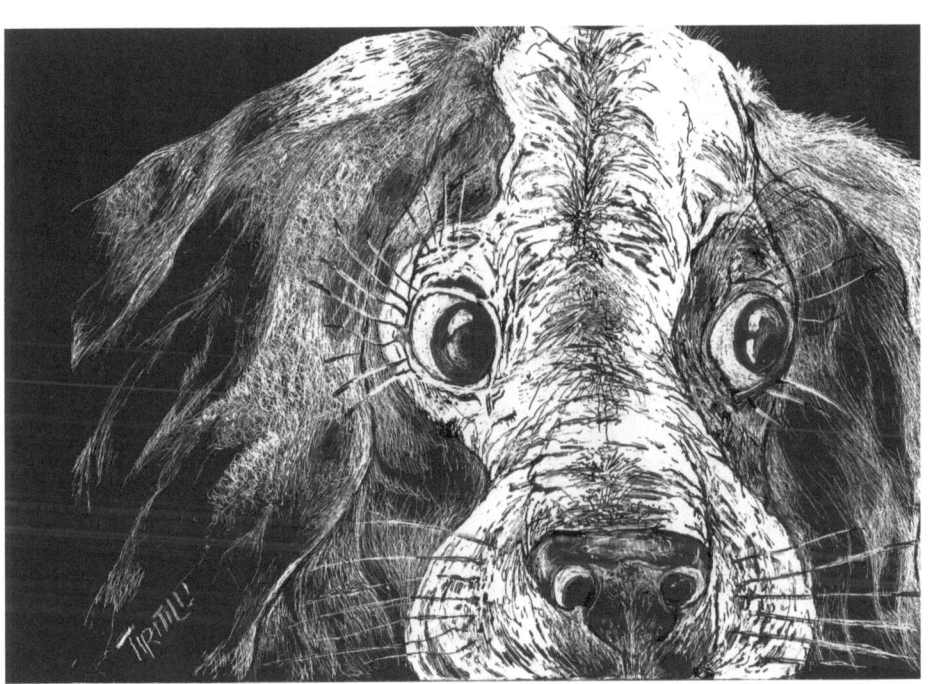

BOO TOO

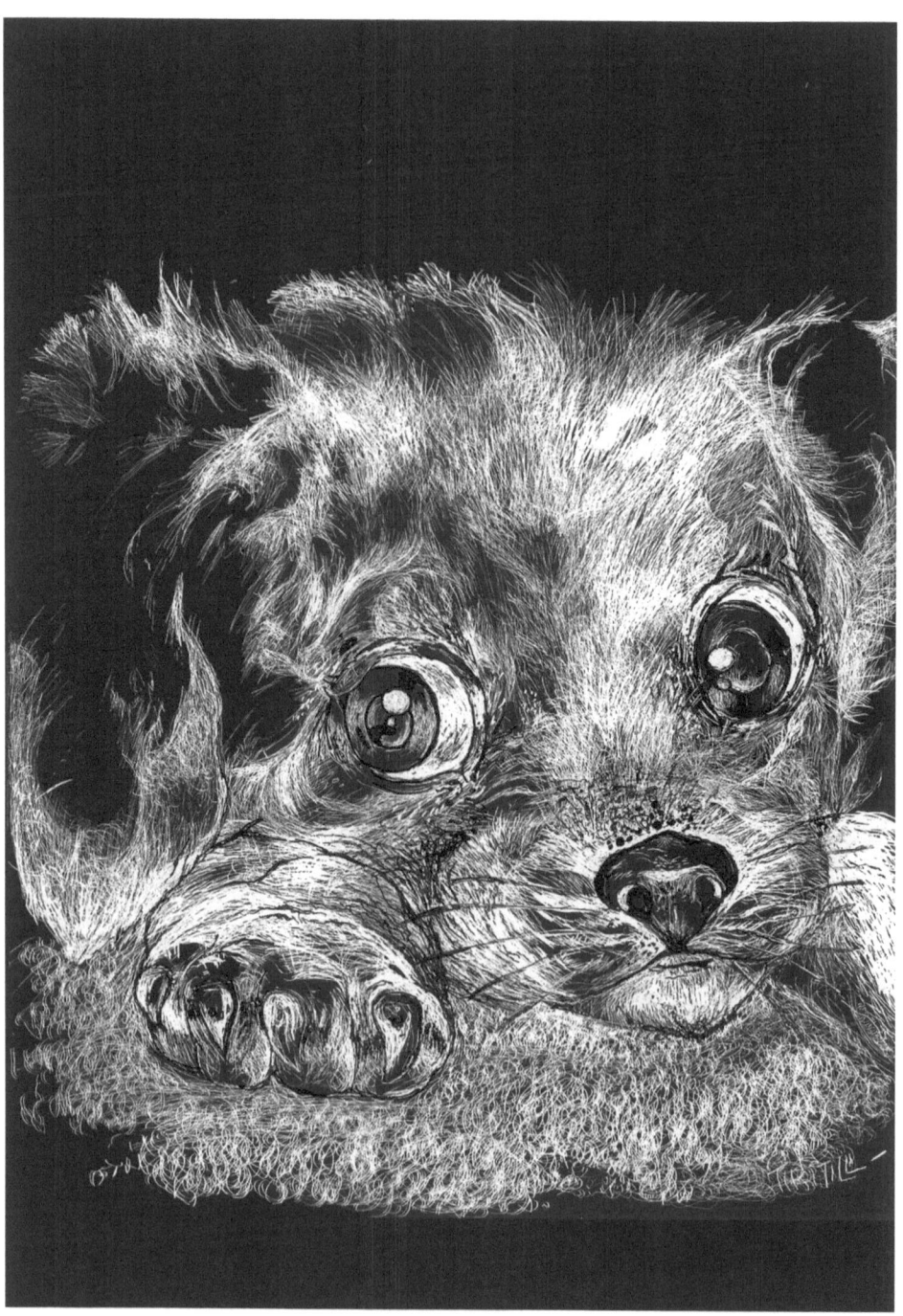

Boomley

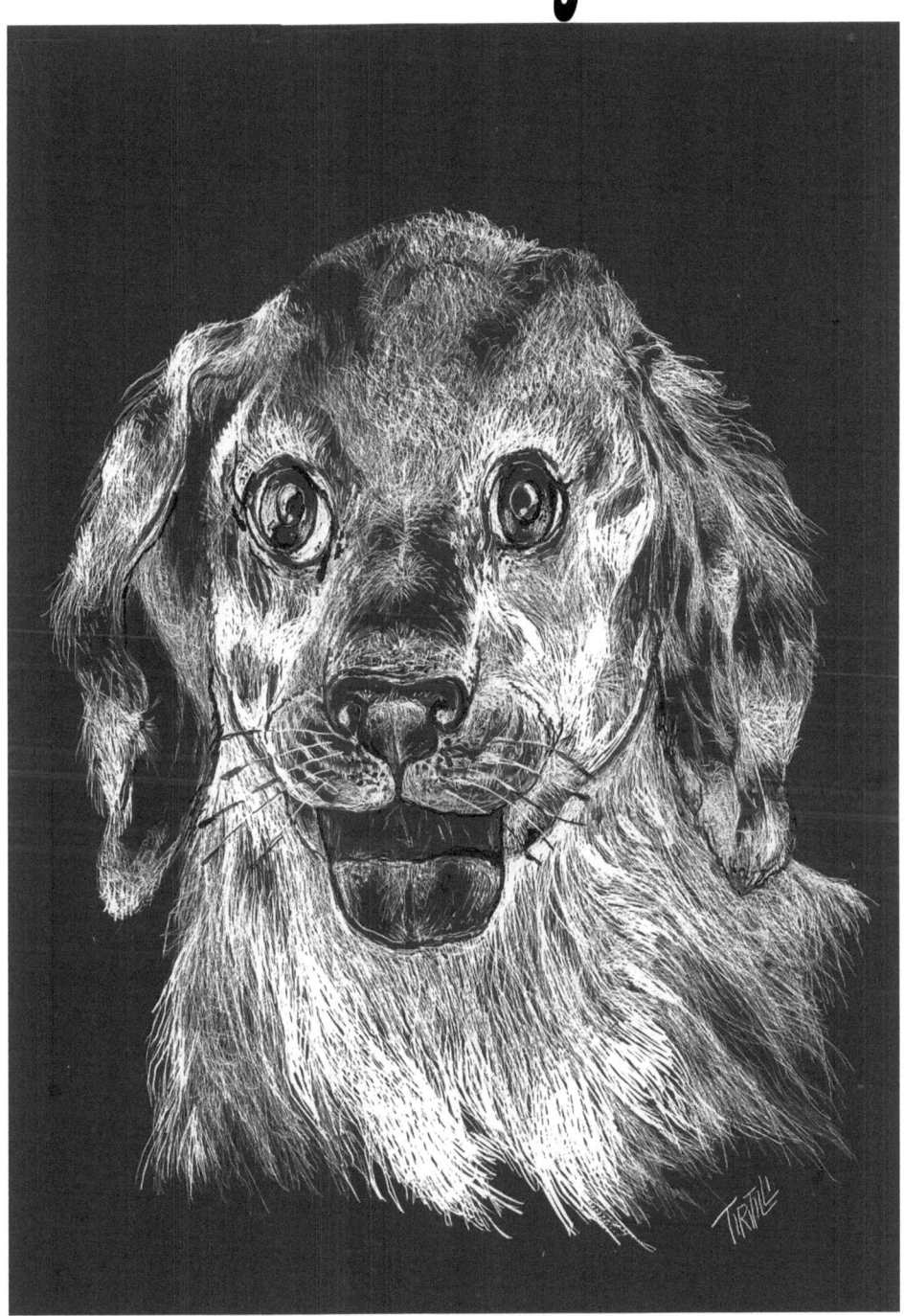

Divine Messenger

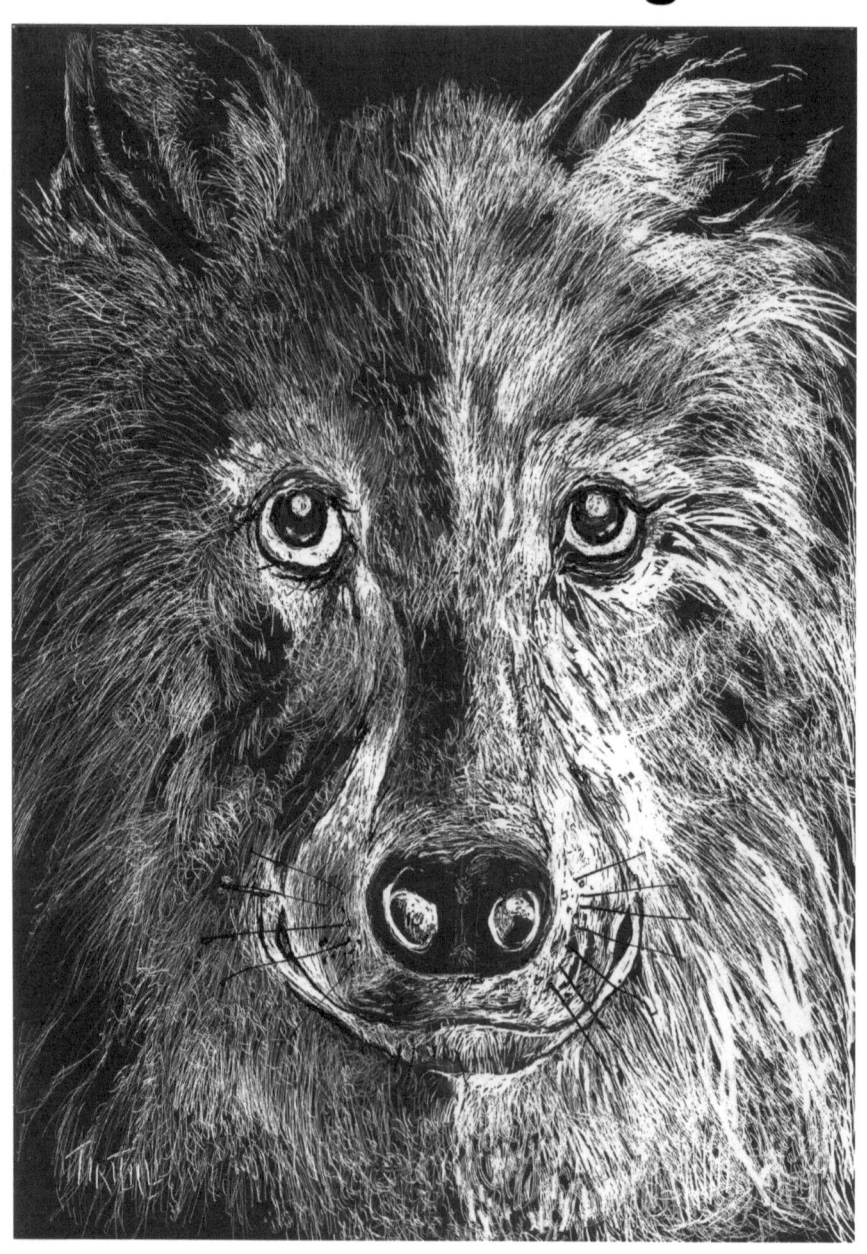

Boo Boo

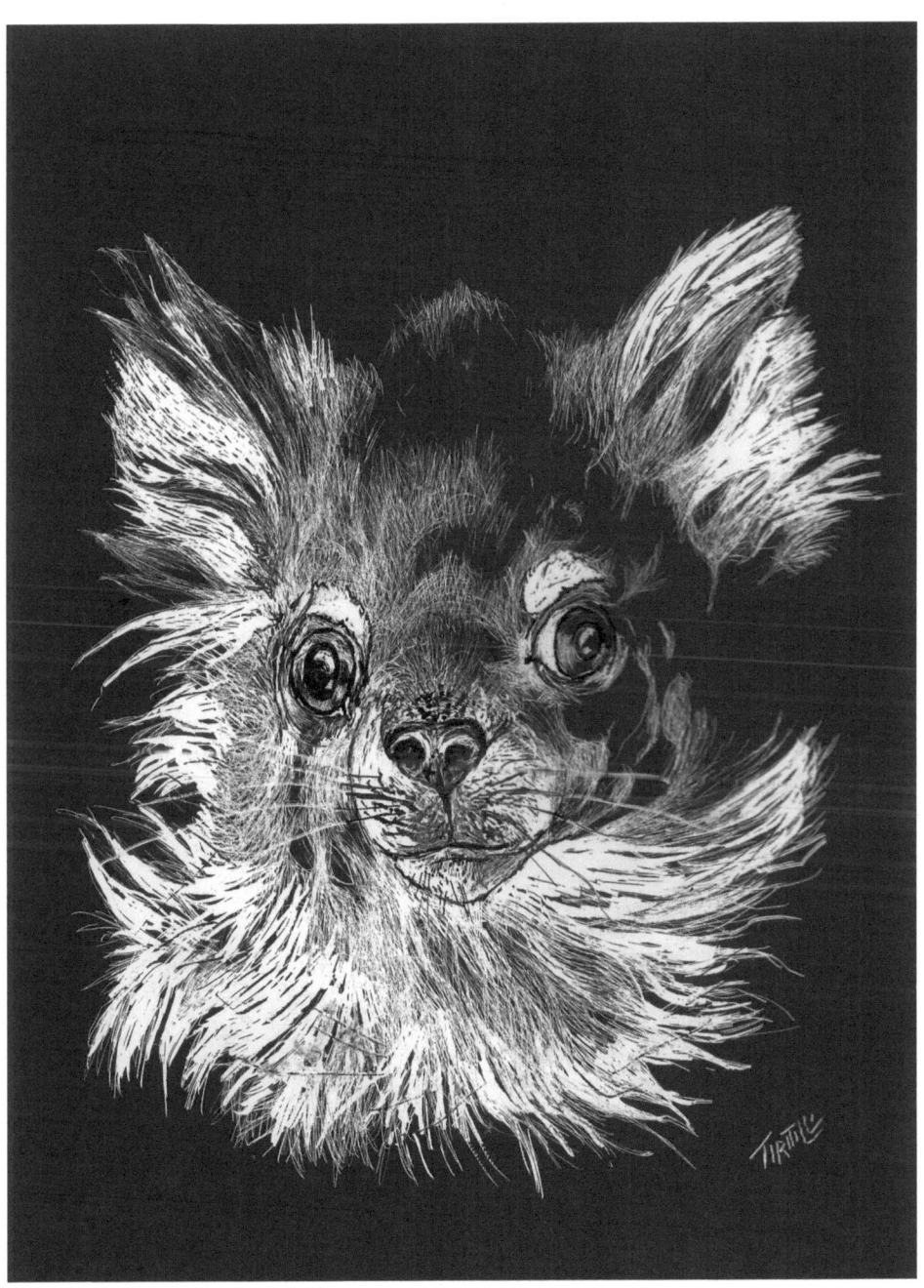

Cross-Eyed

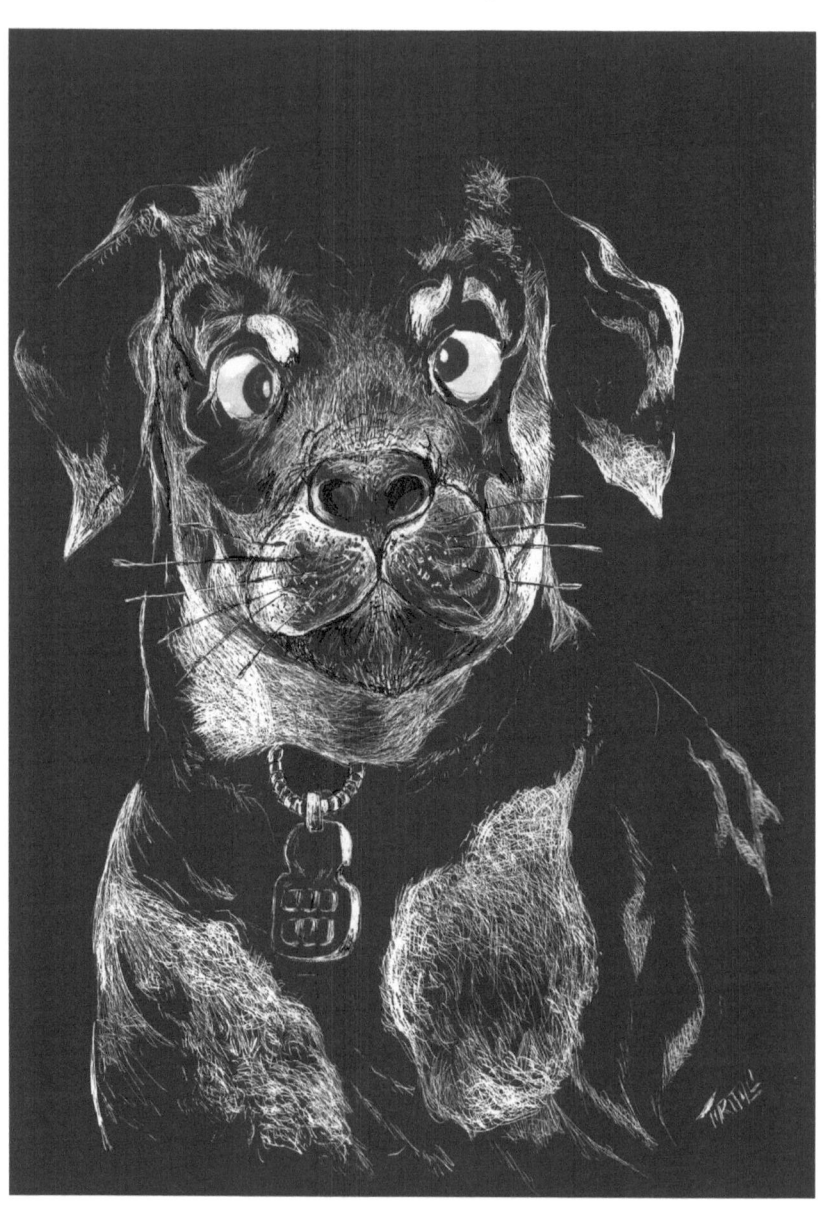

Lucky Dog

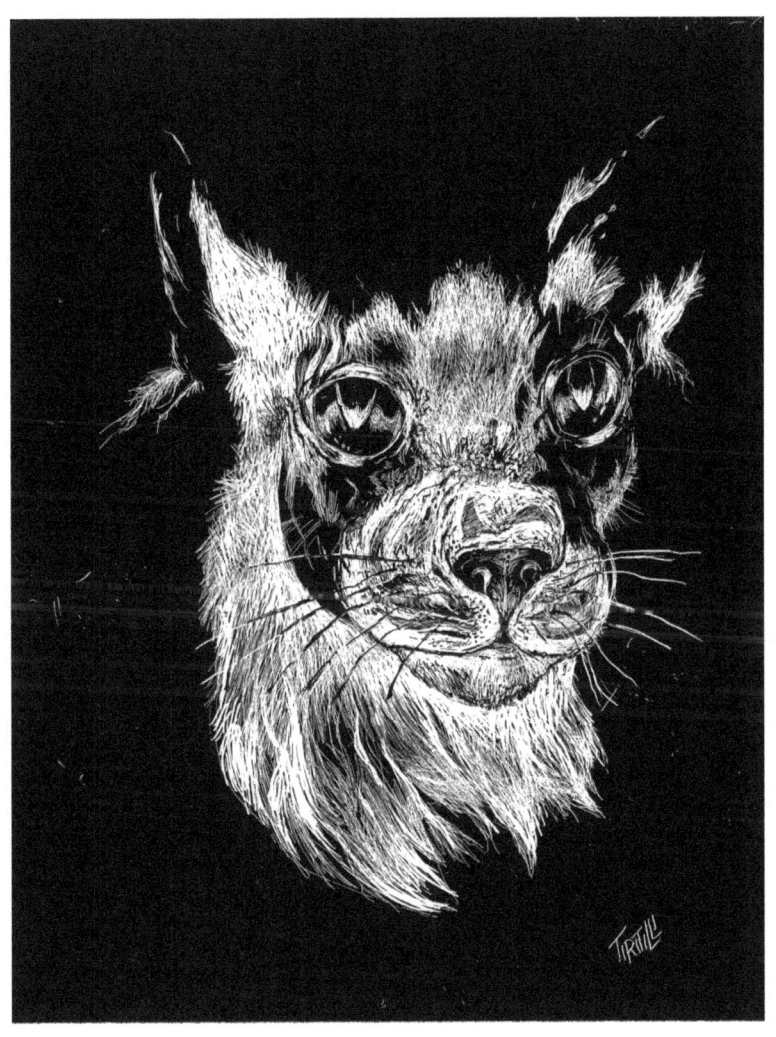

That Cat

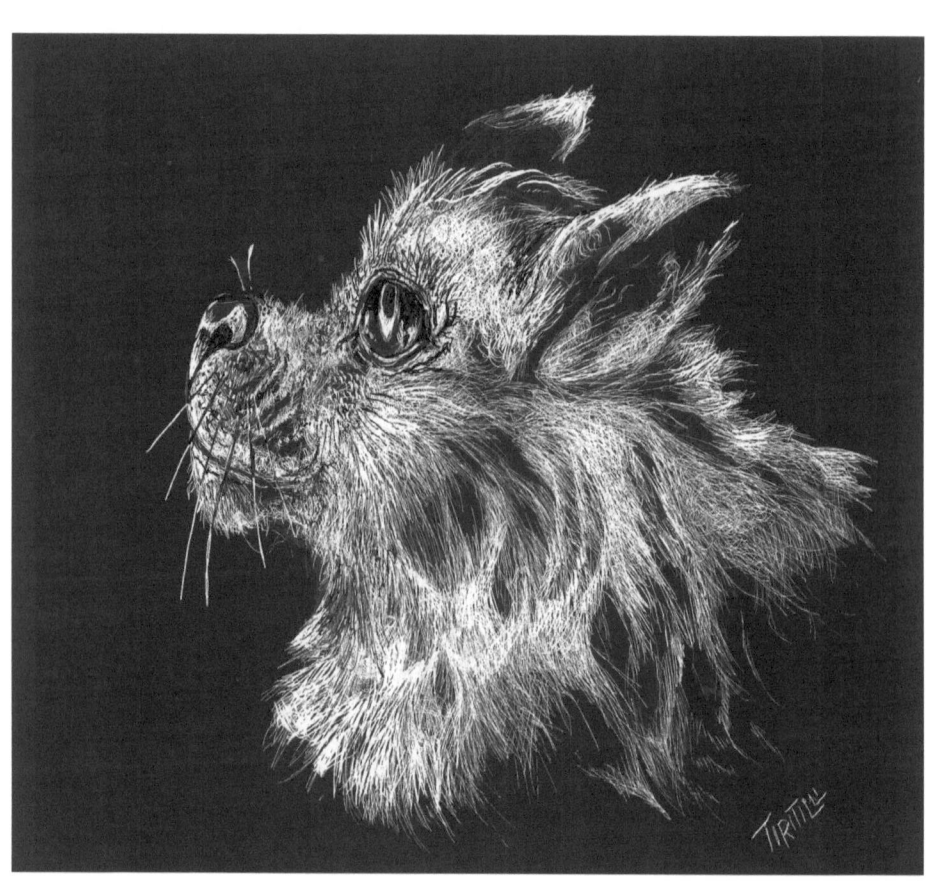

That Cat II

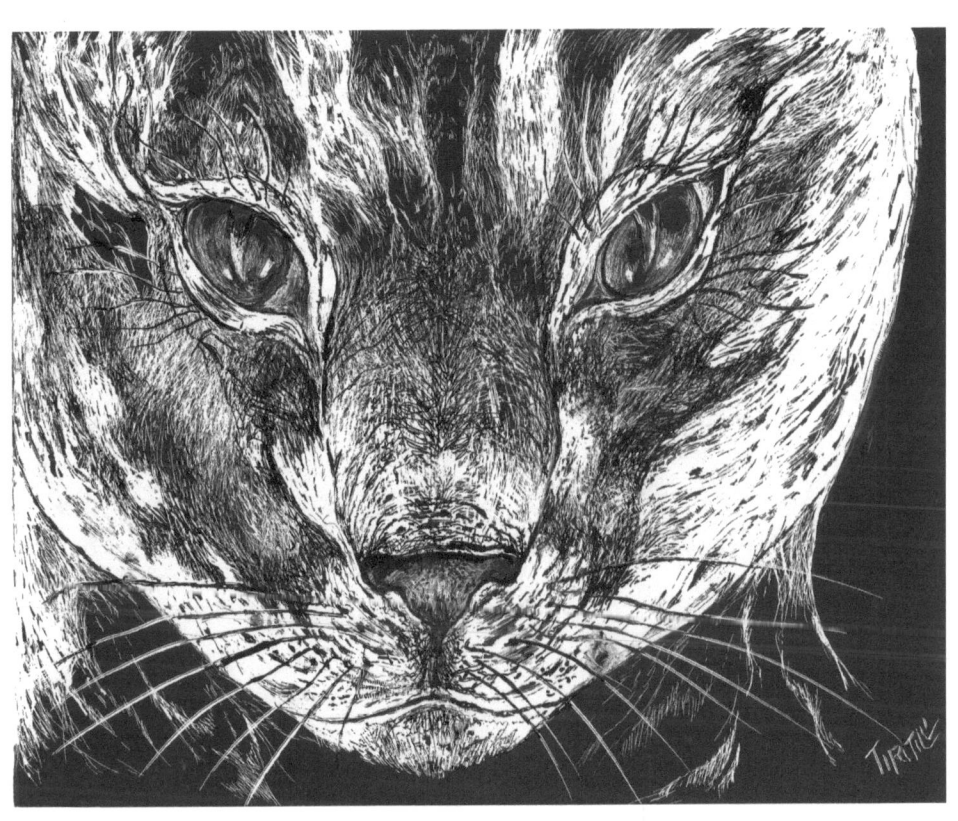

Spoiled One

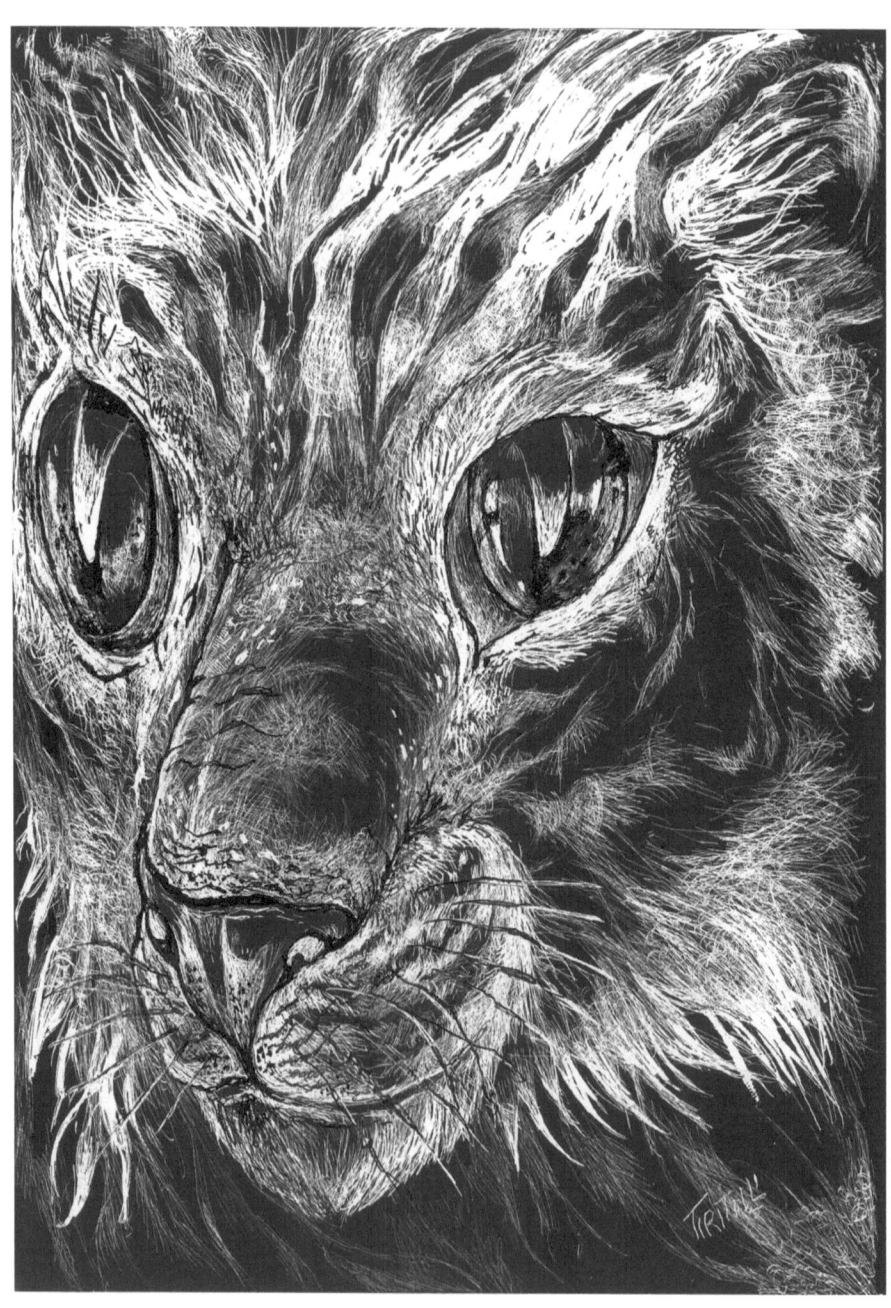

The White One

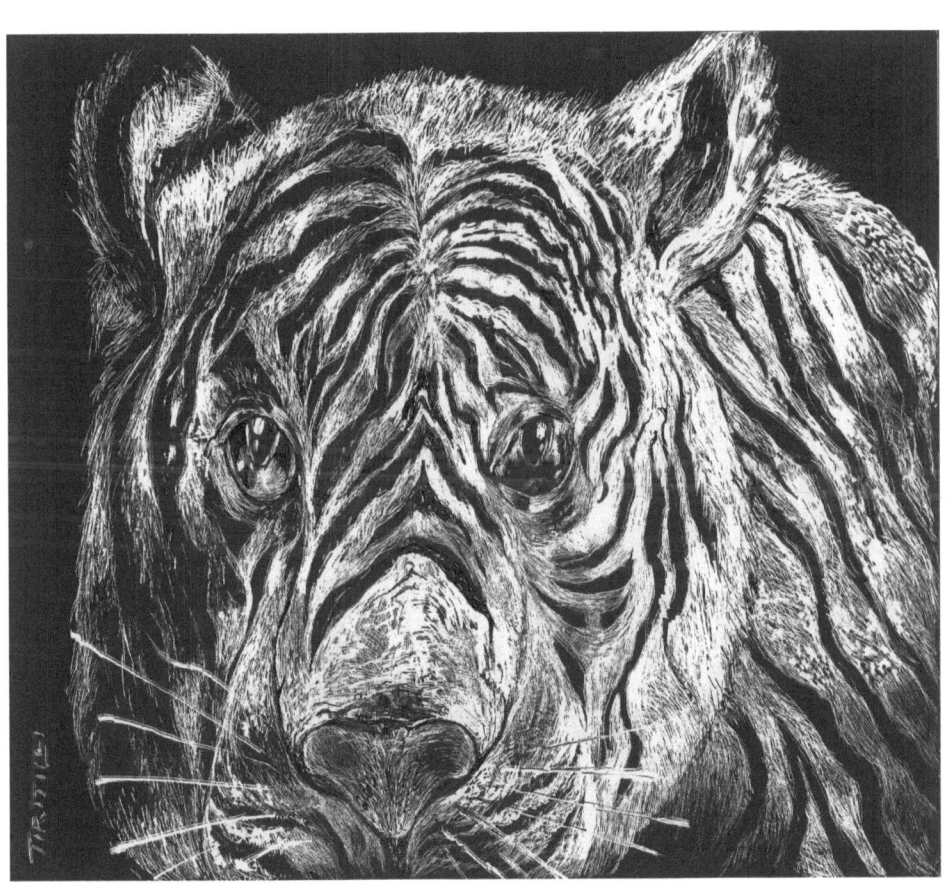

Big Cat

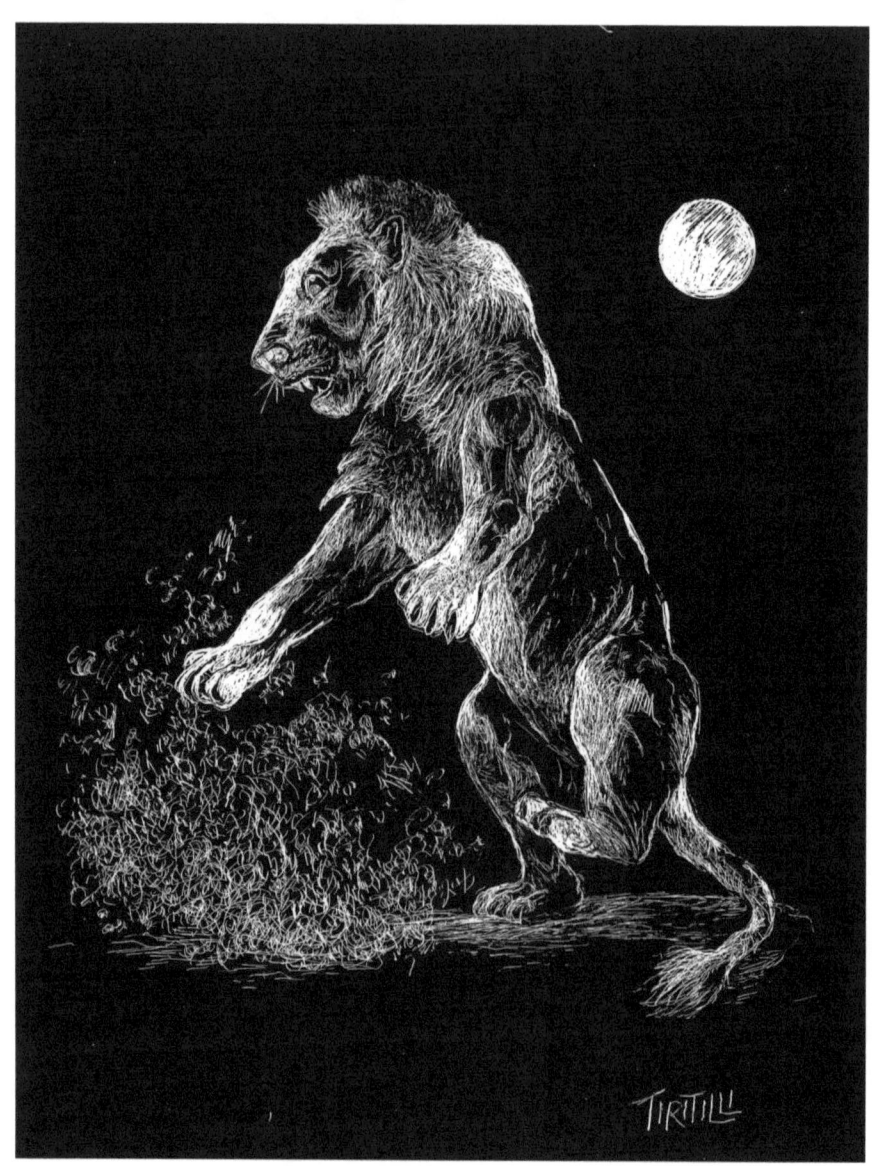

Misc Scratchboard

Round-up

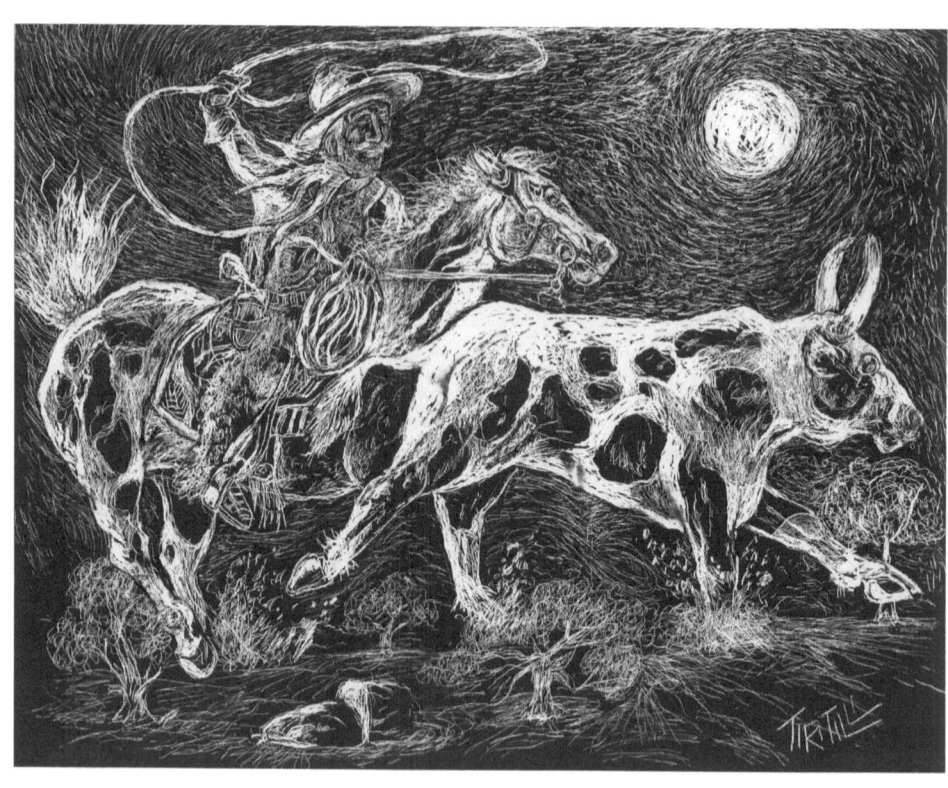

Philosopher

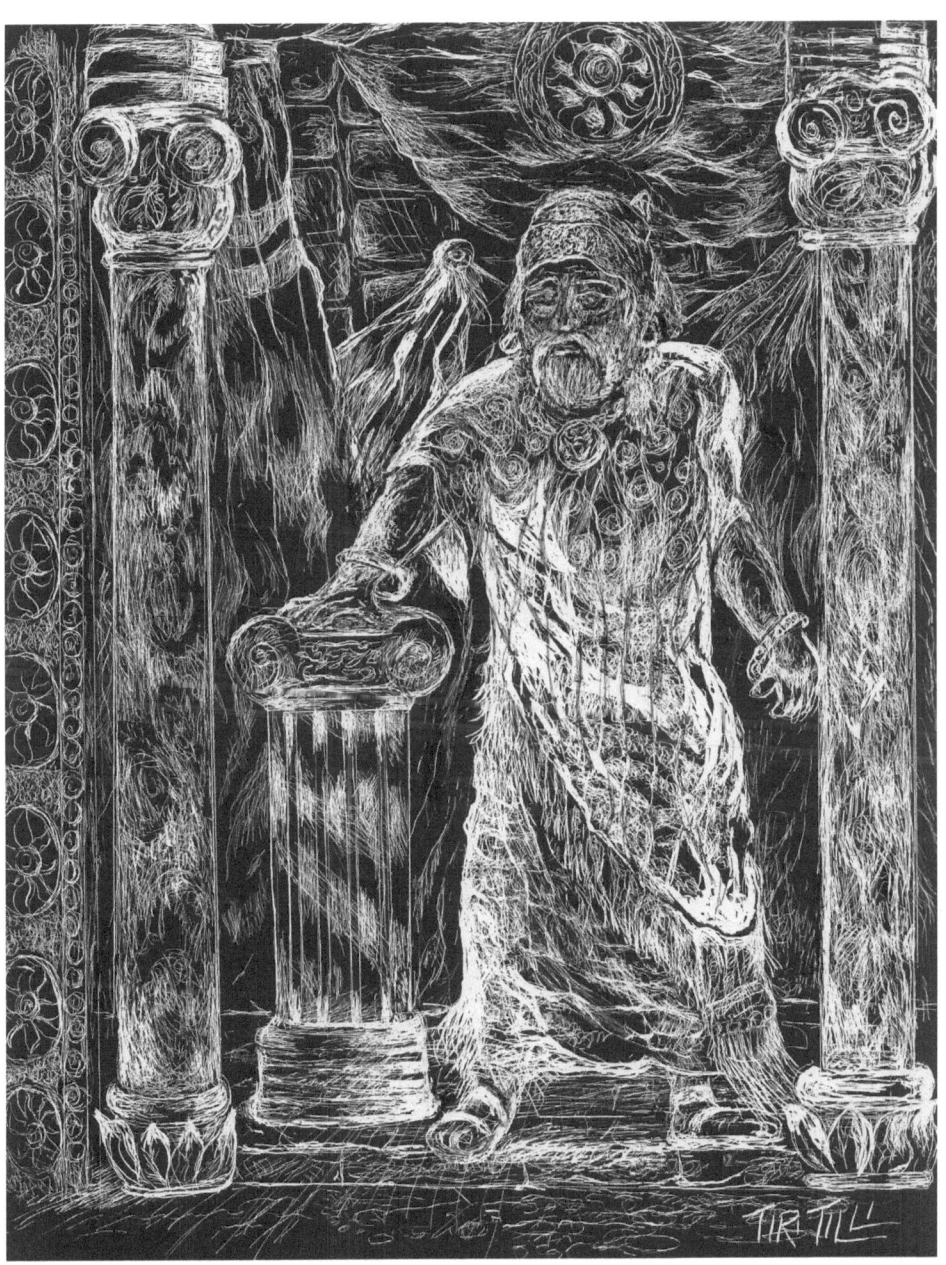

Thrown

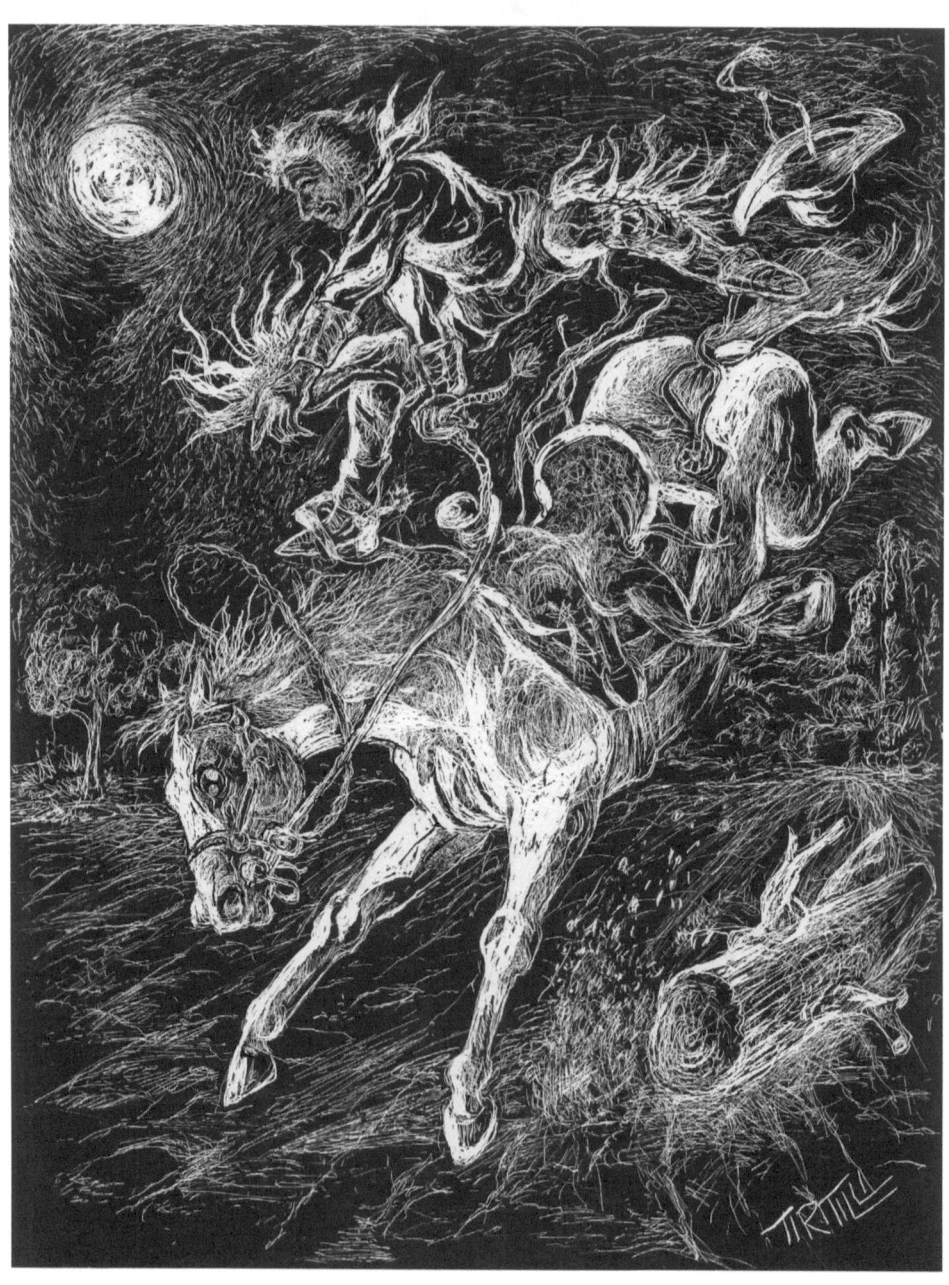

Shoot Out

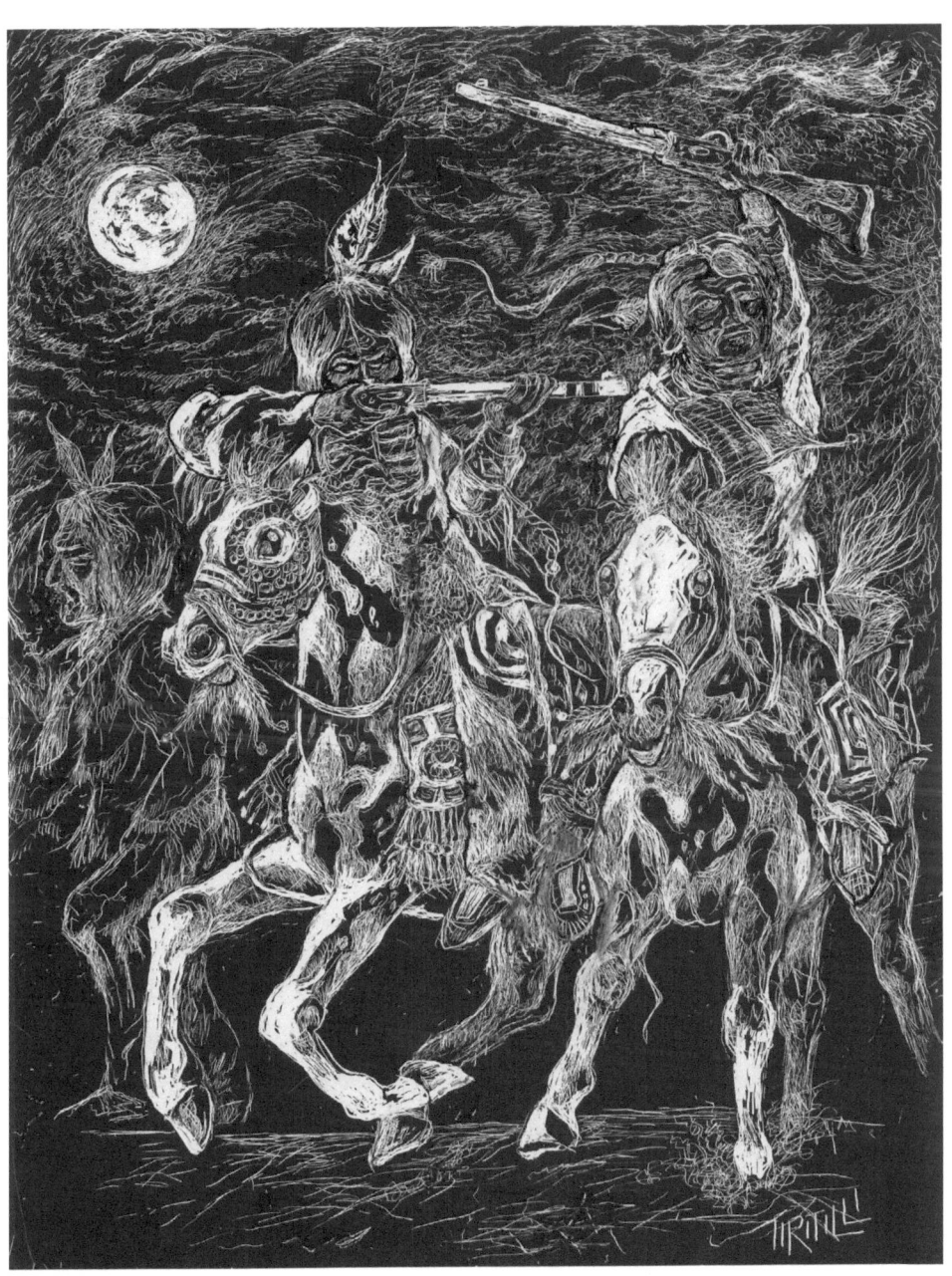

Slave

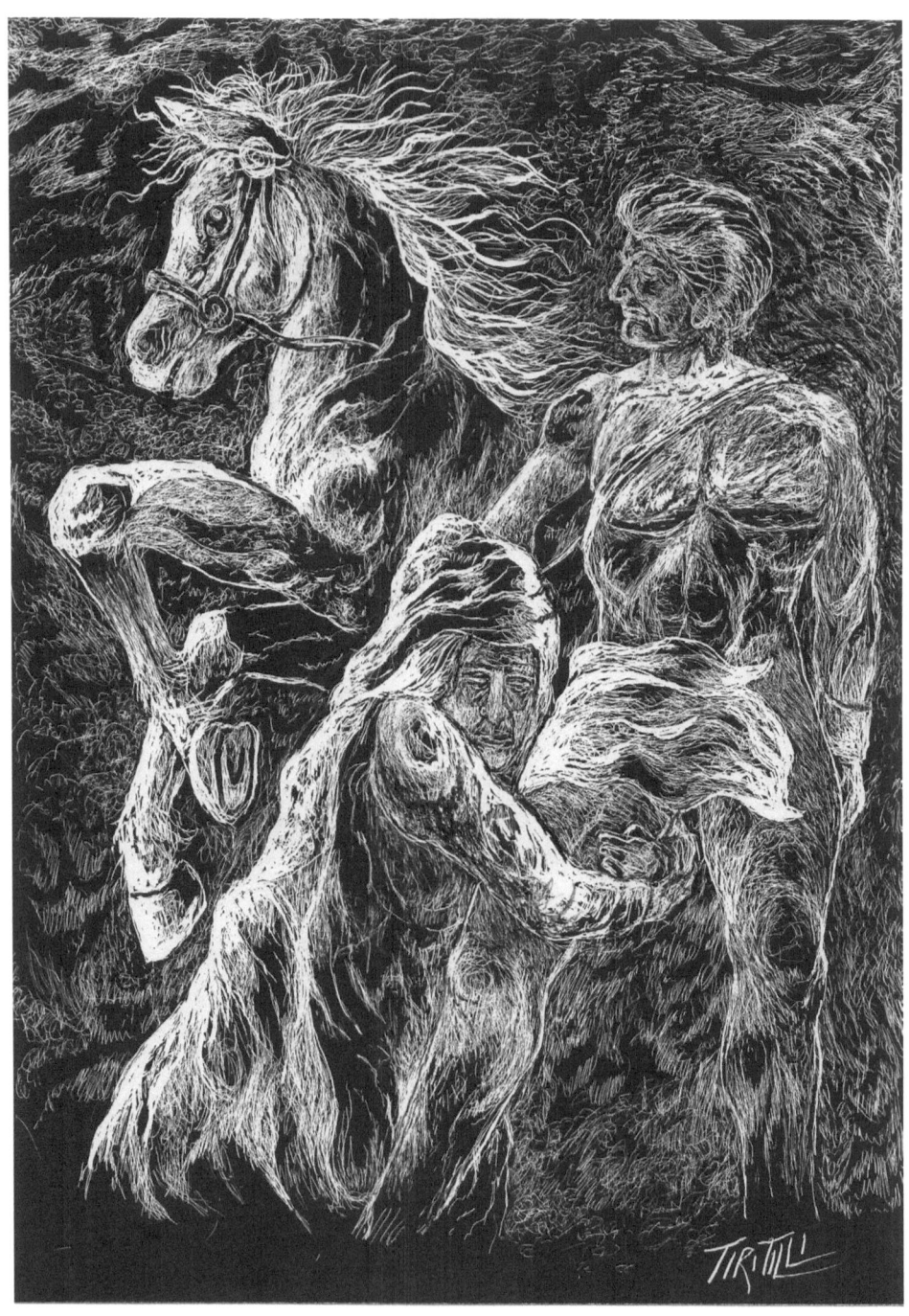

River Crossing

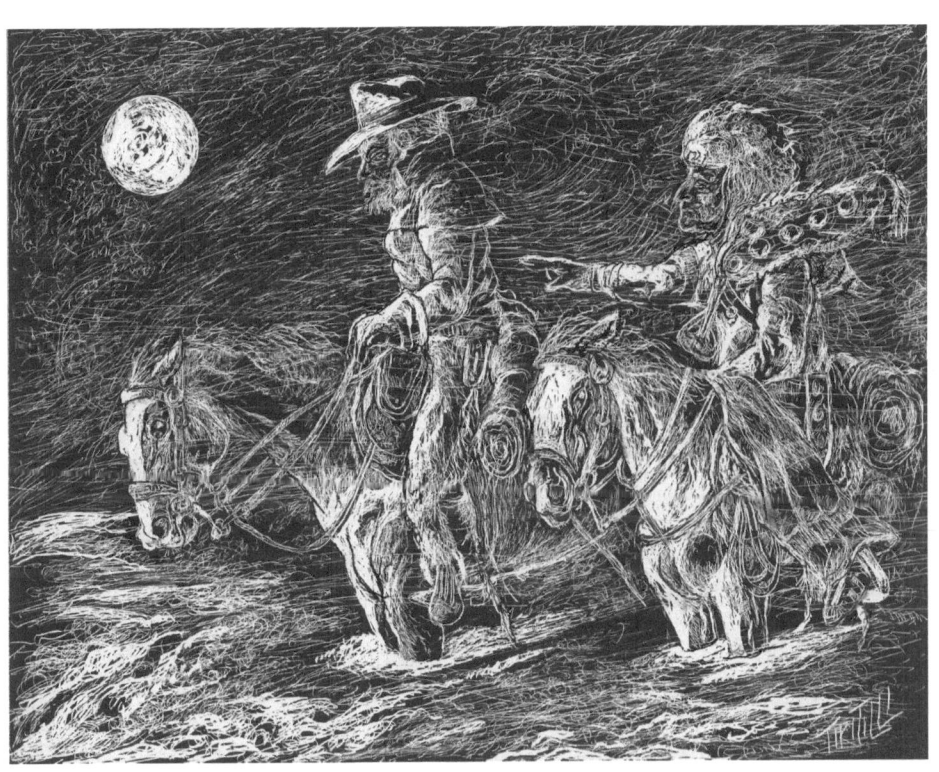

Warrior

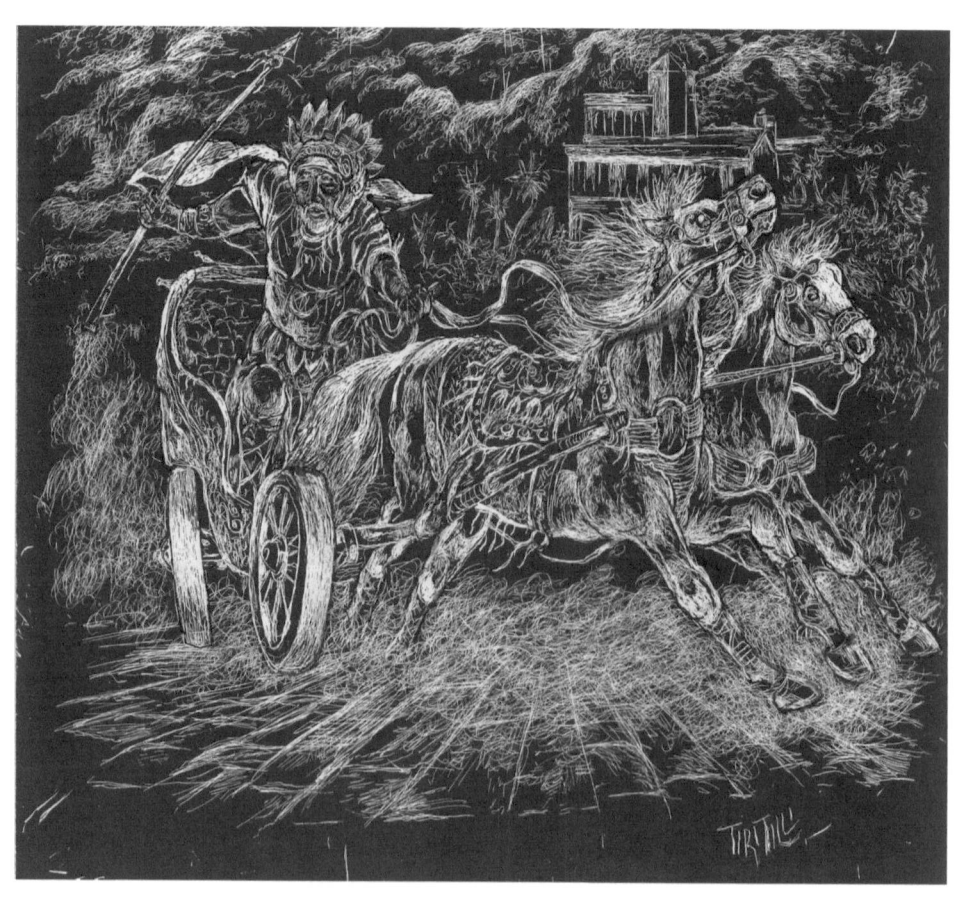

Soldier

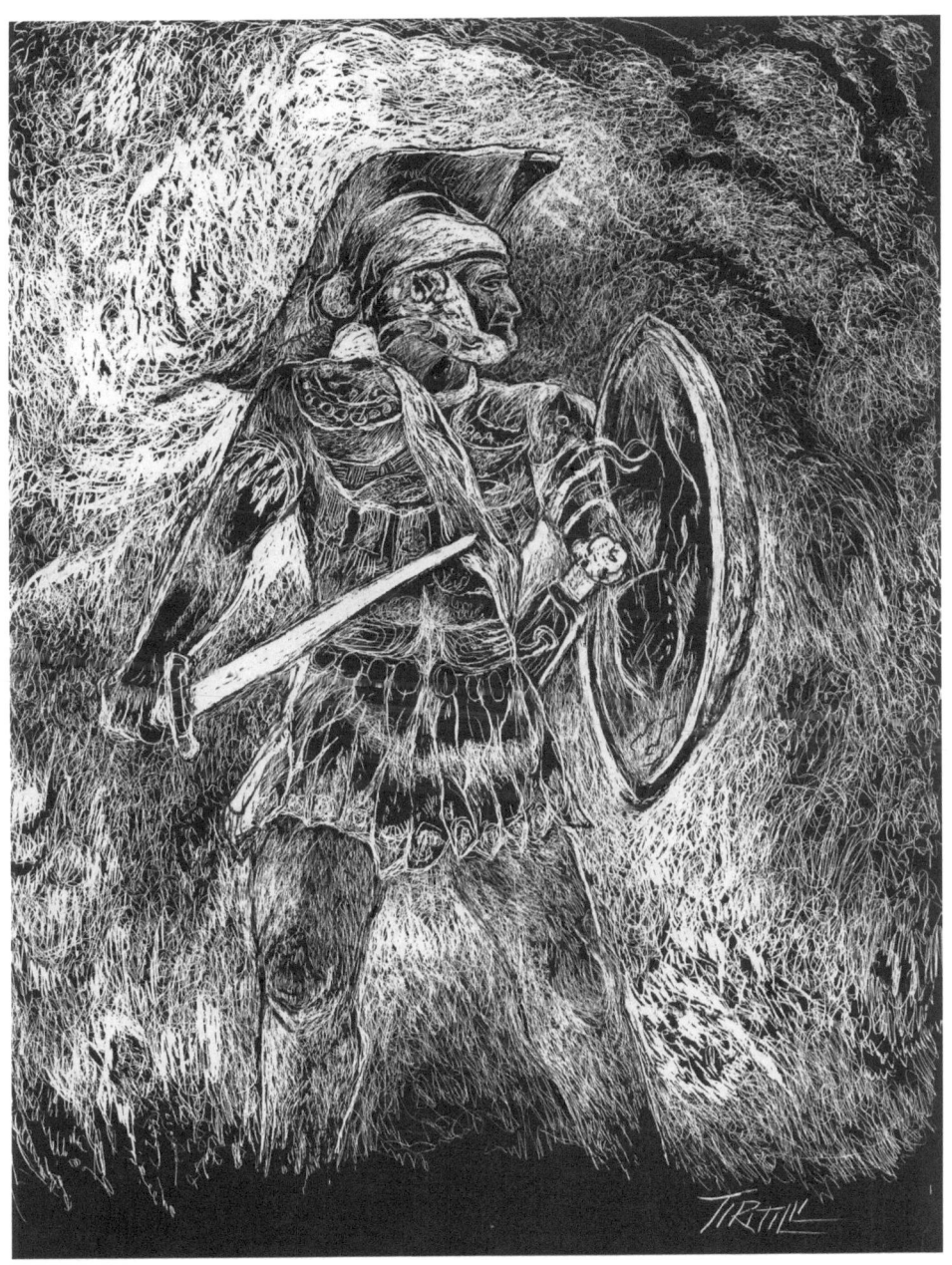

The Chase

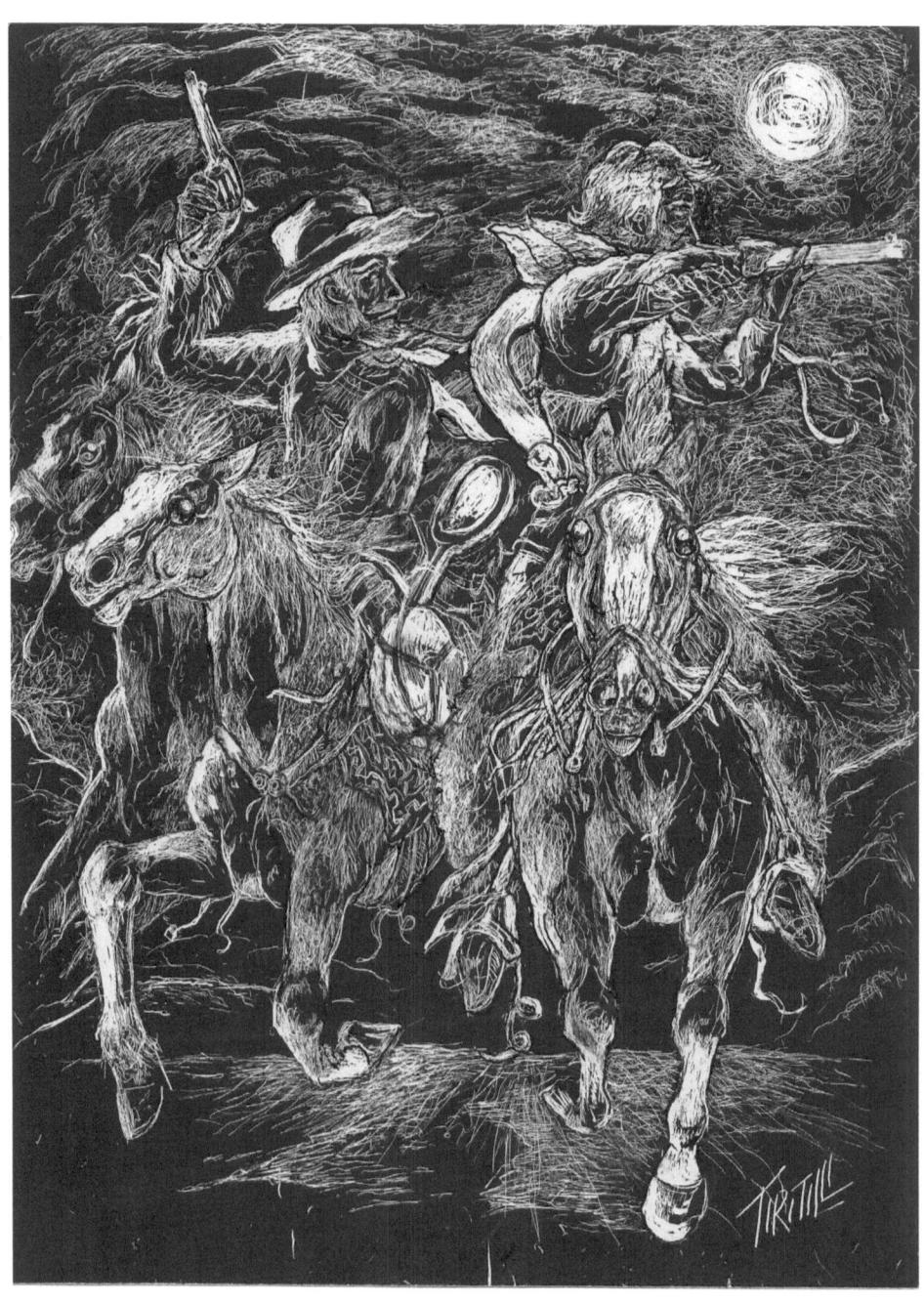

Forgivness

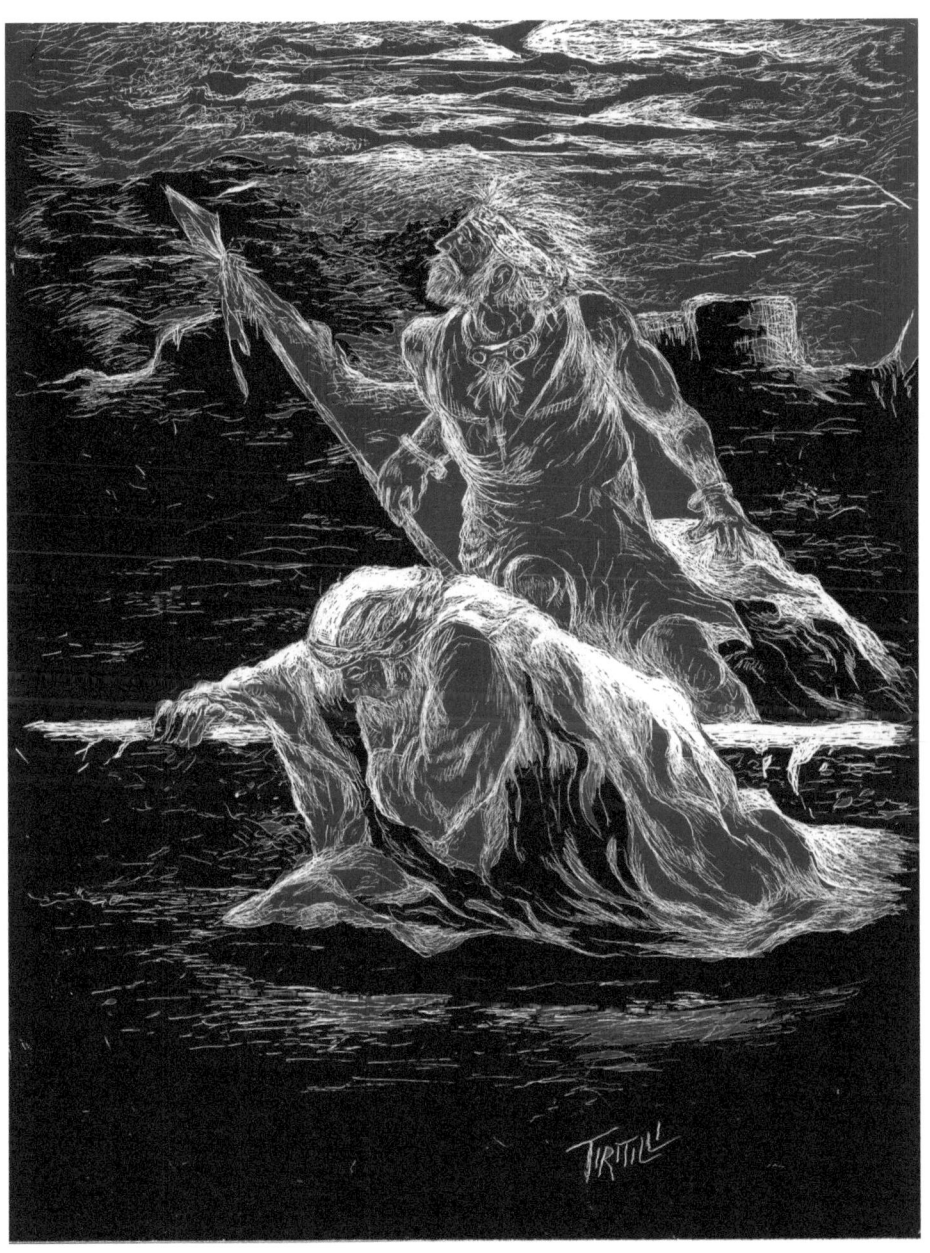

Victor

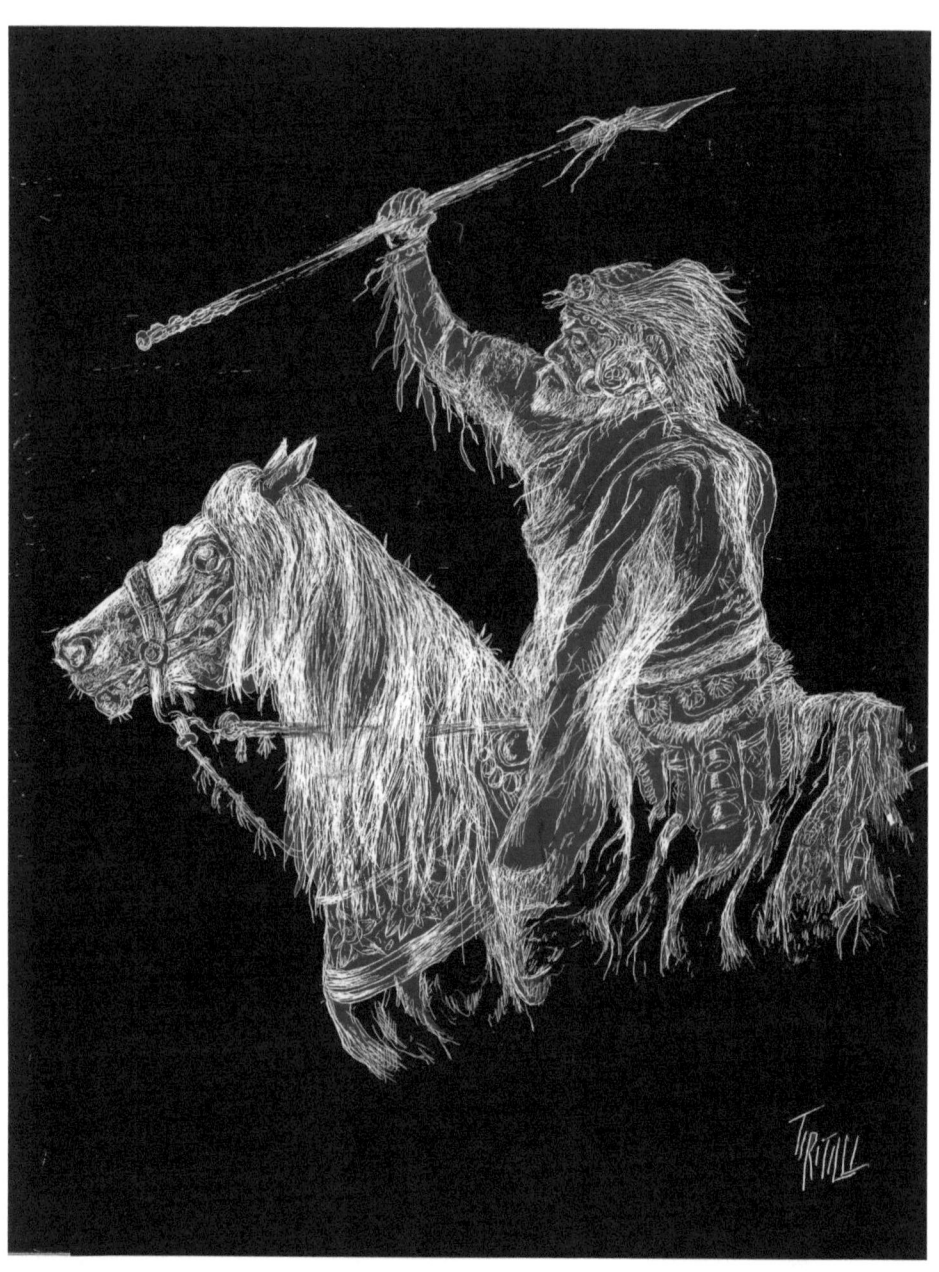

Relaxing

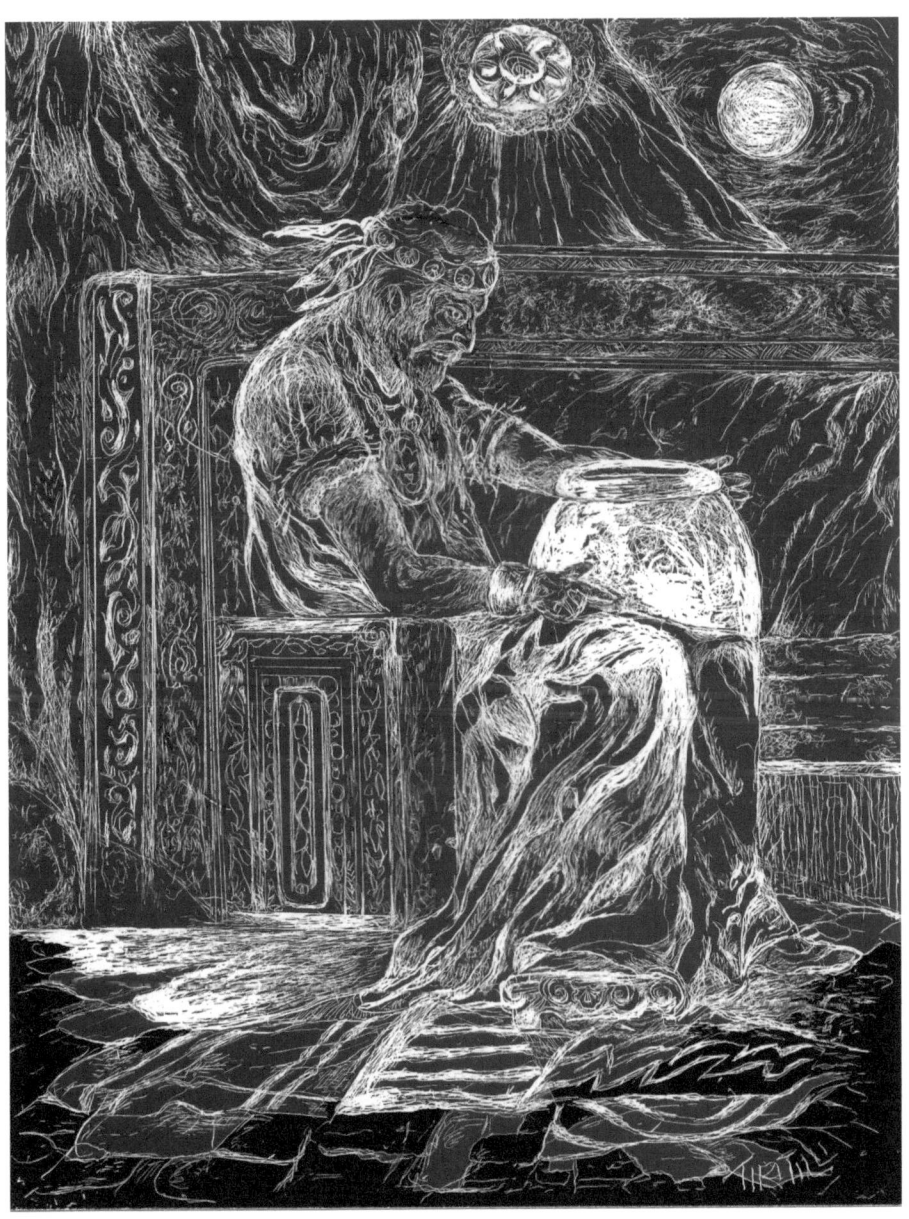

Thinker

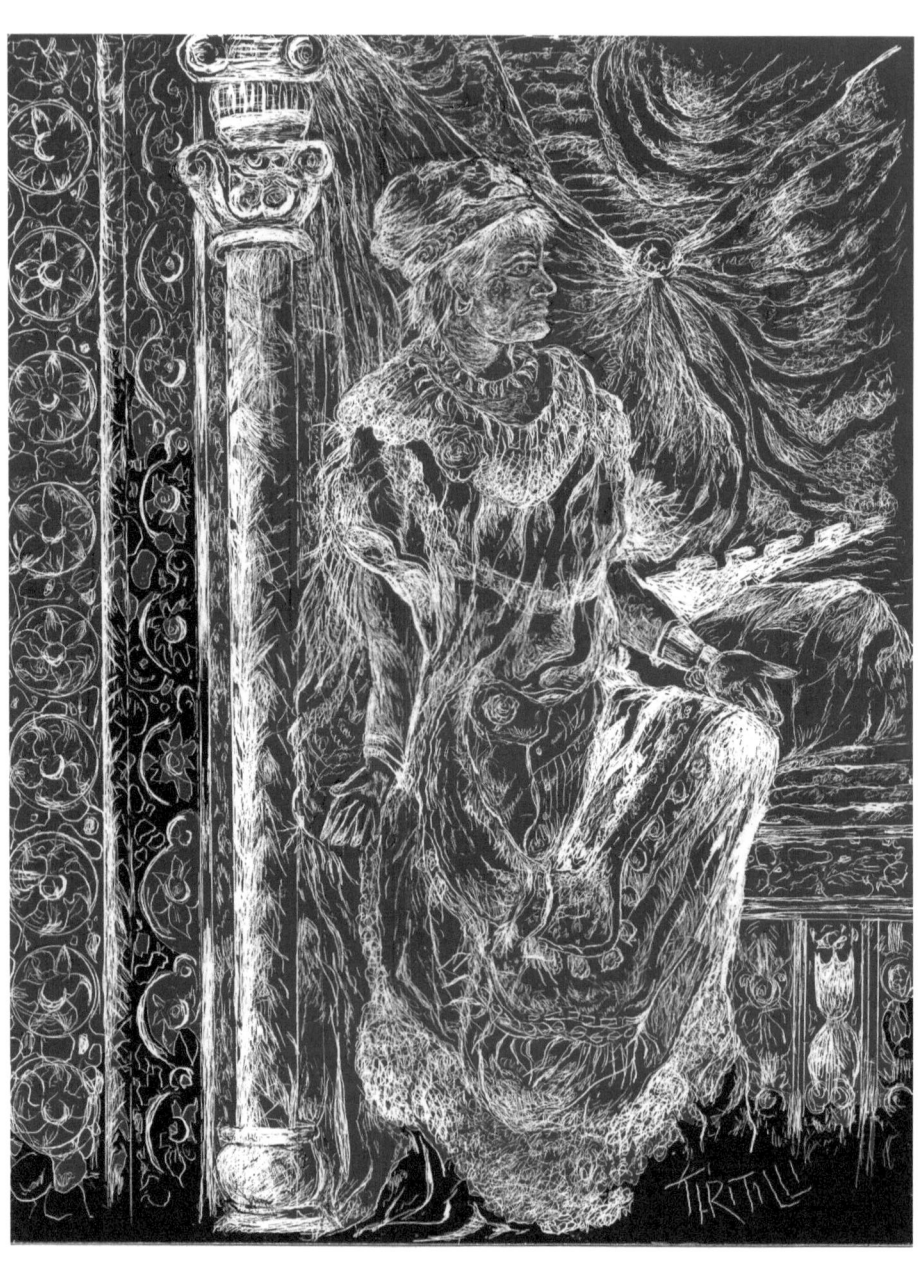

Resting

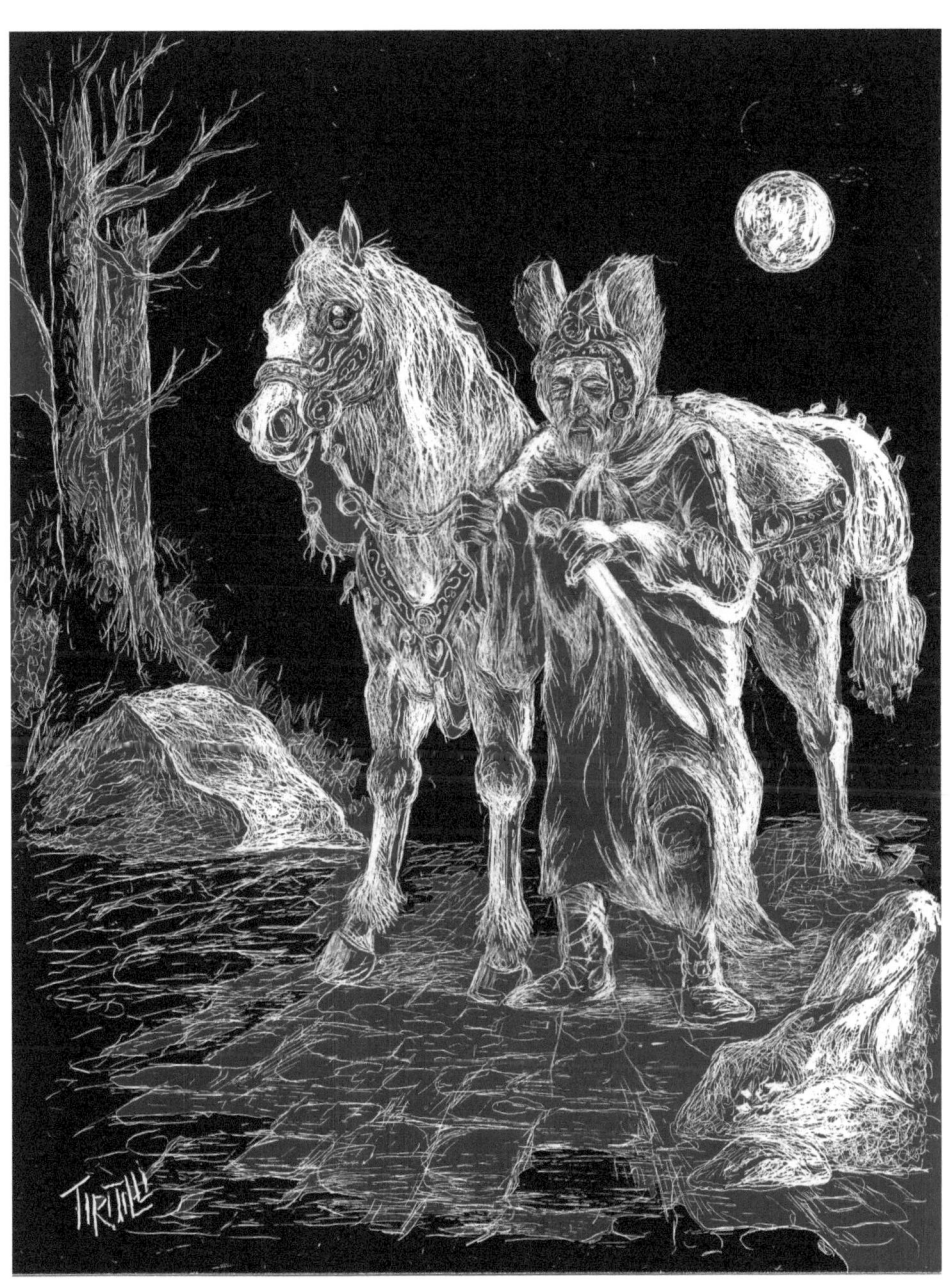

Searching

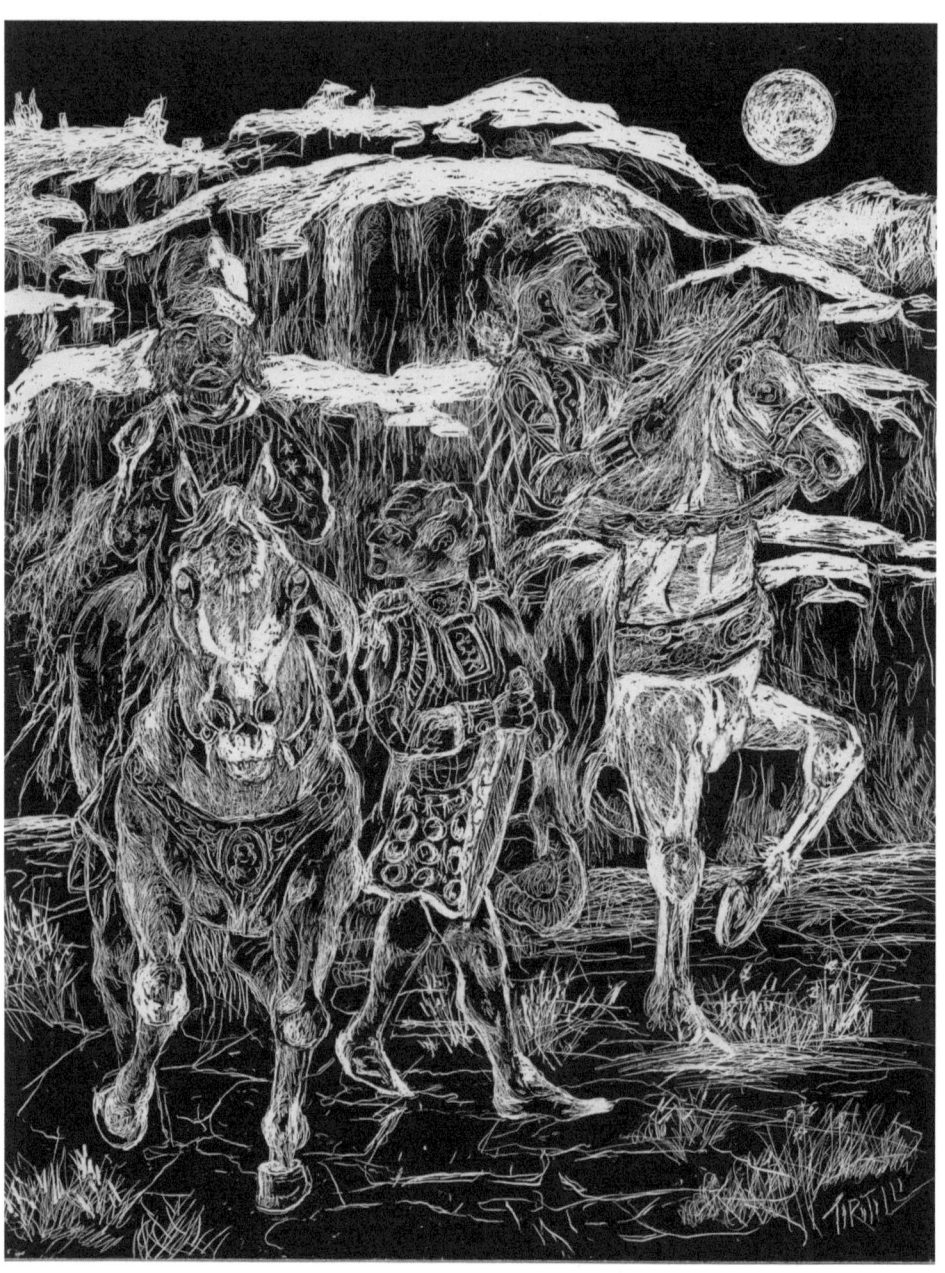

Dinner

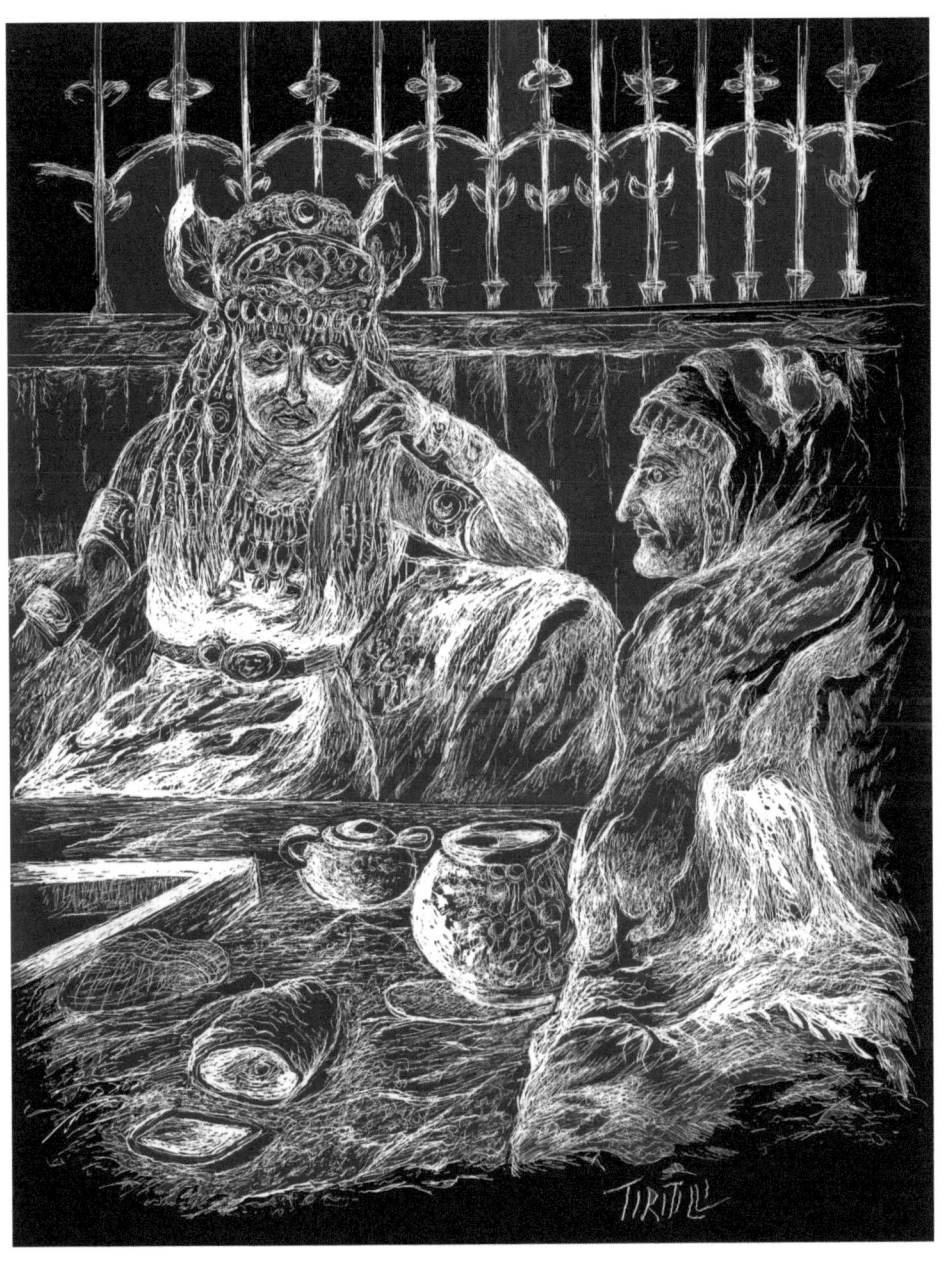

Joyous

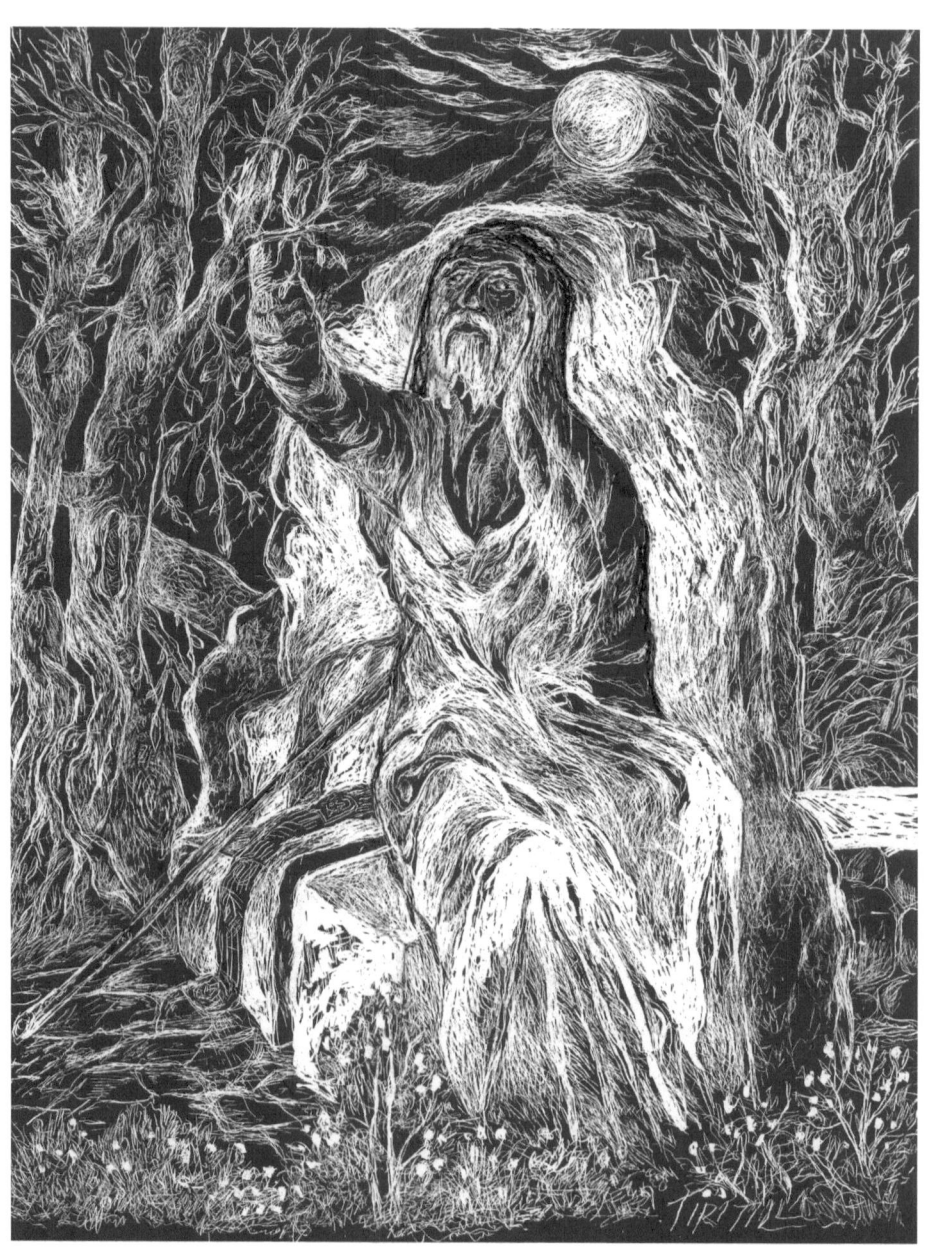

African Moonlight

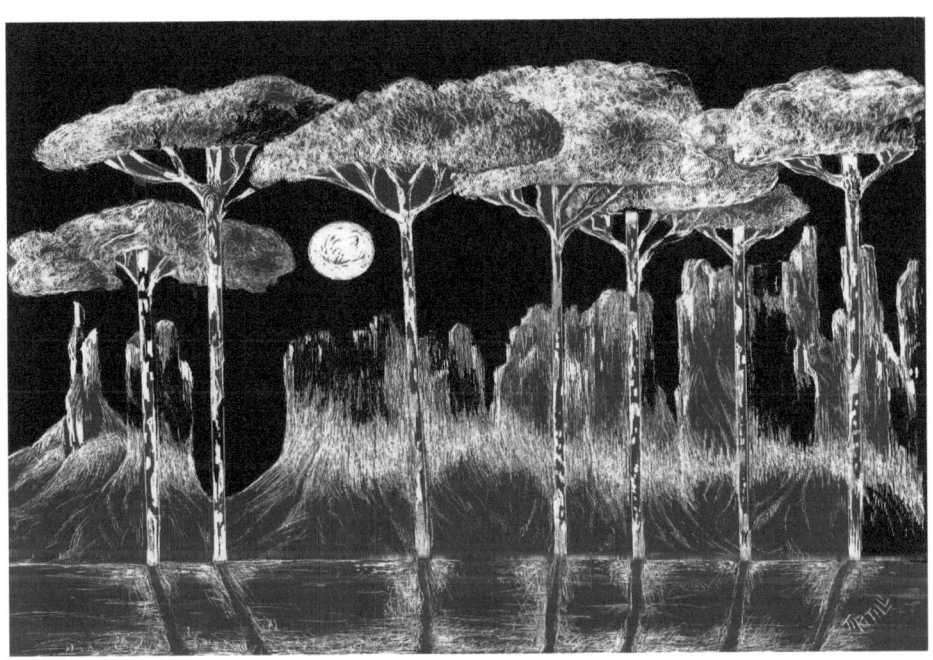

Palm before Storm

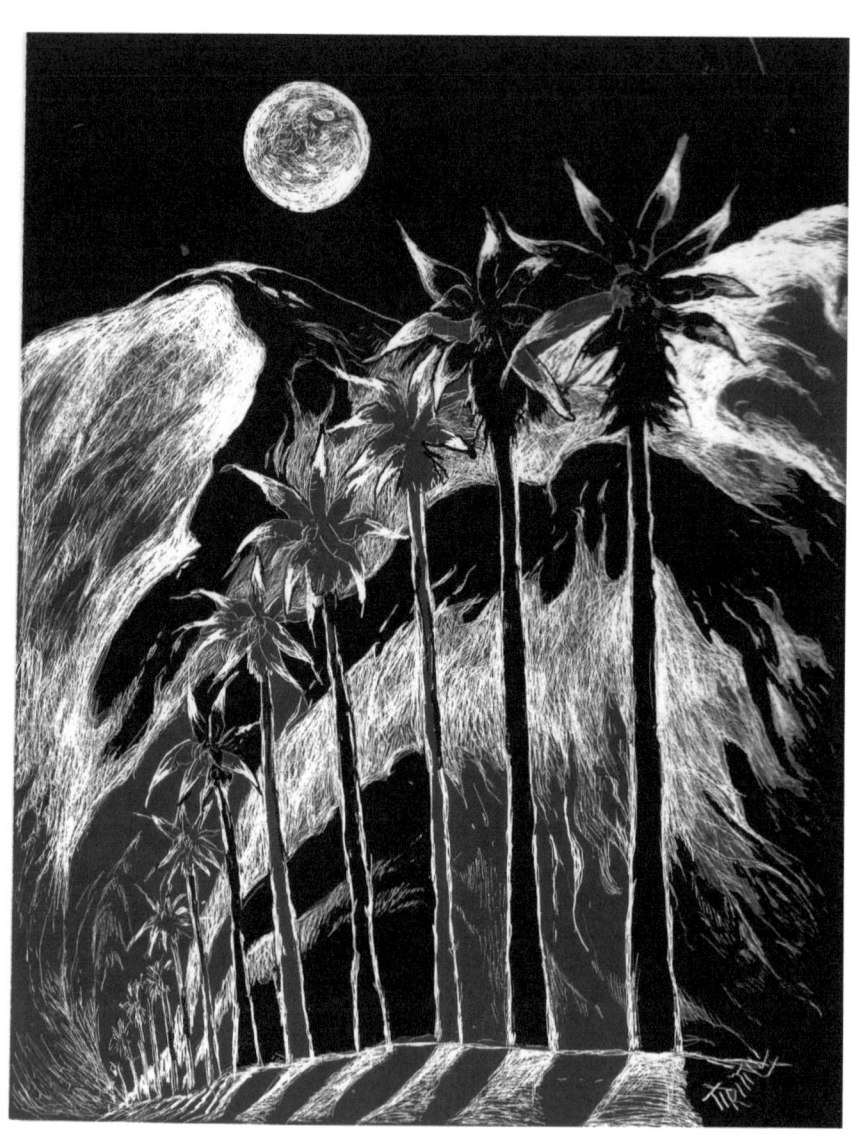

Moonlight Serenade

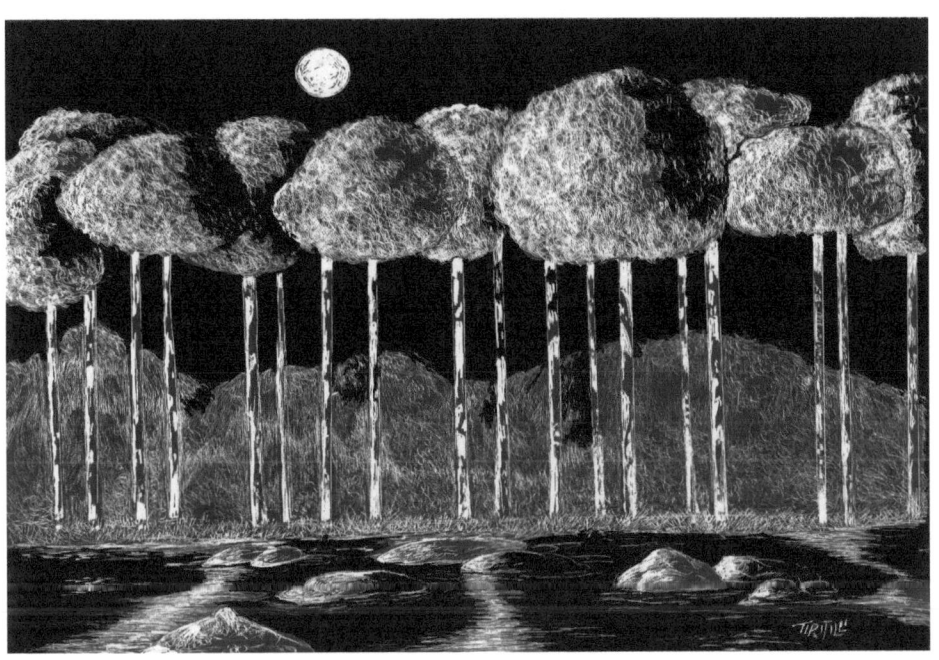

Monterey

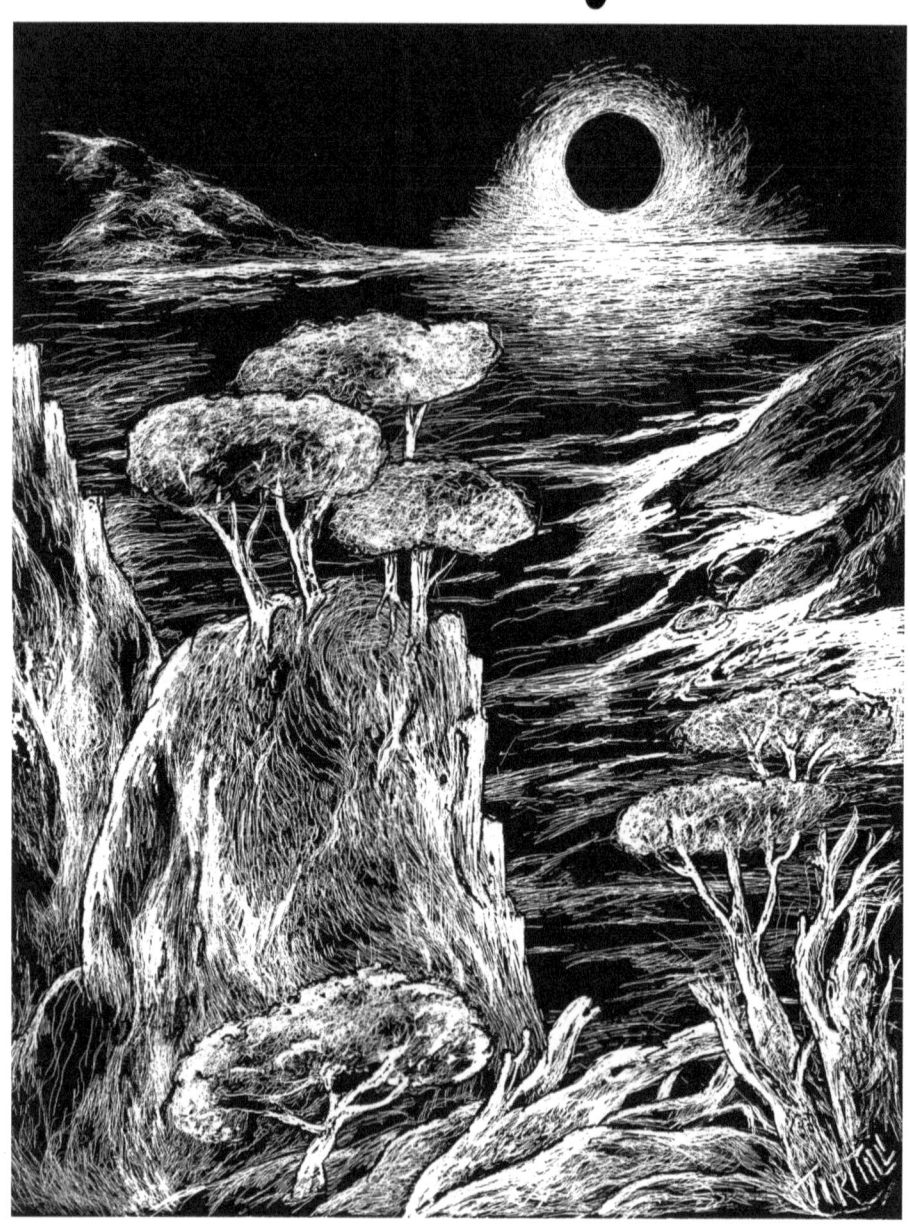

Never Forget

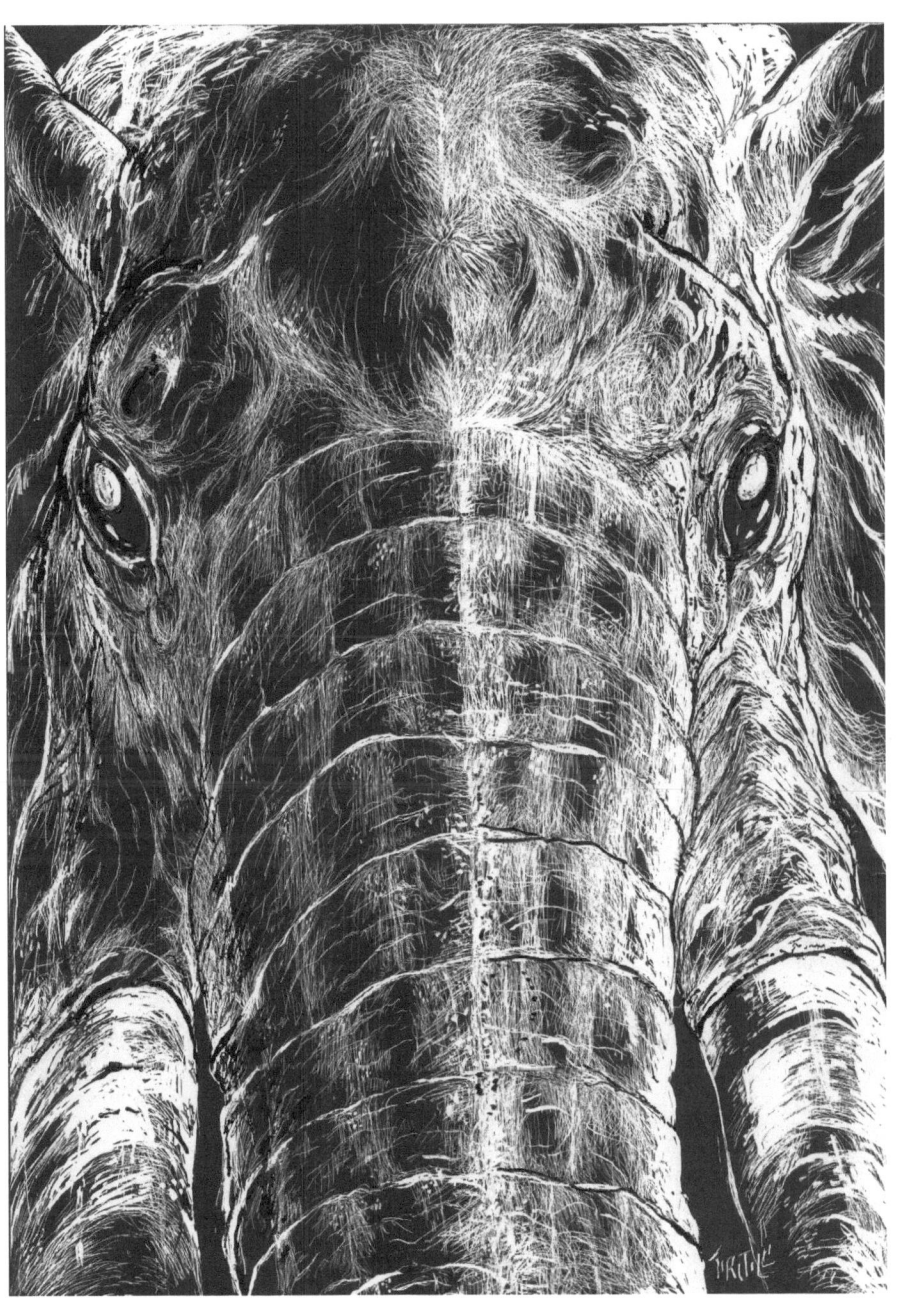

Their Country

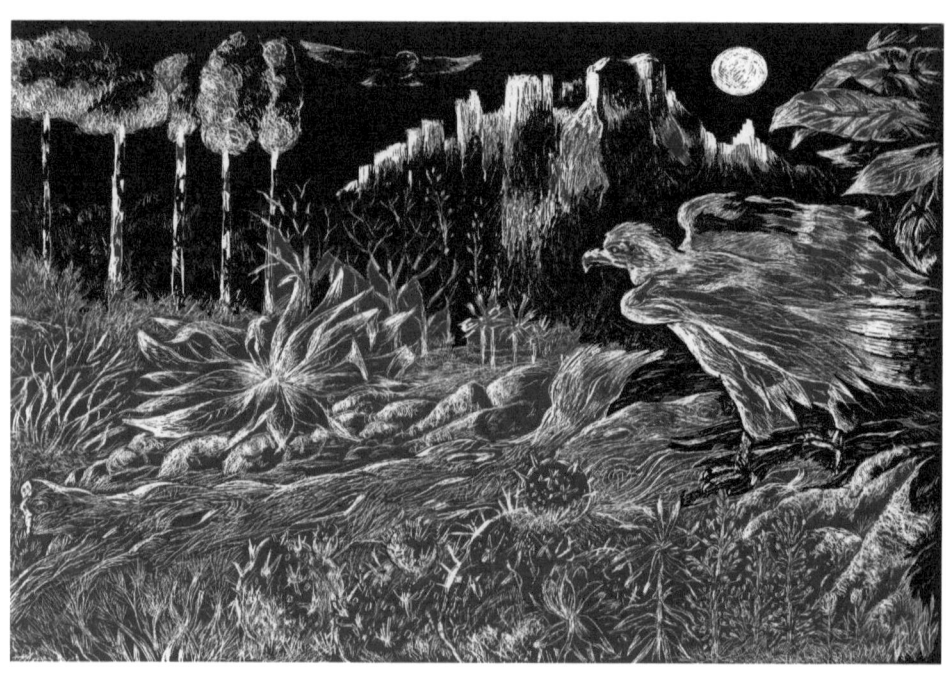

Tsar Bomba

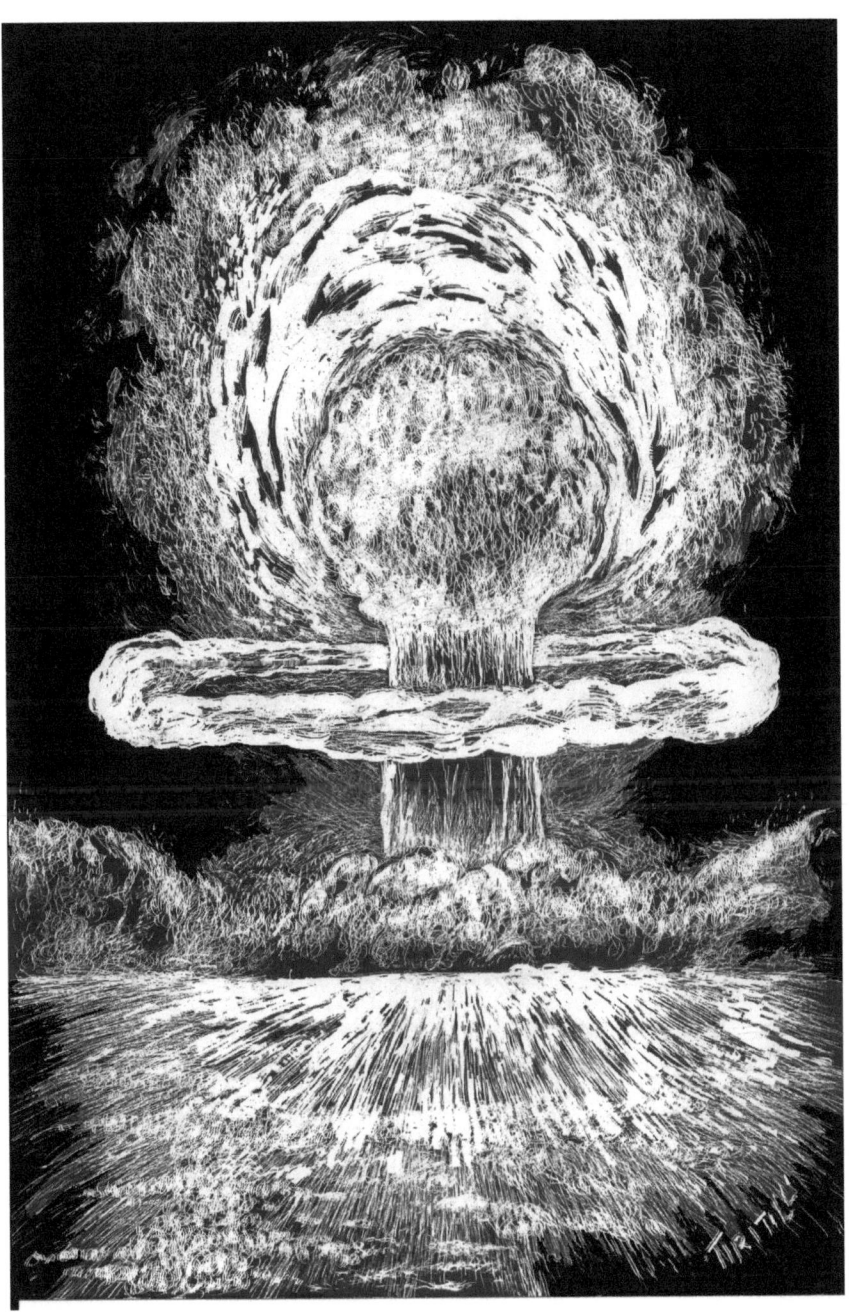

Mission

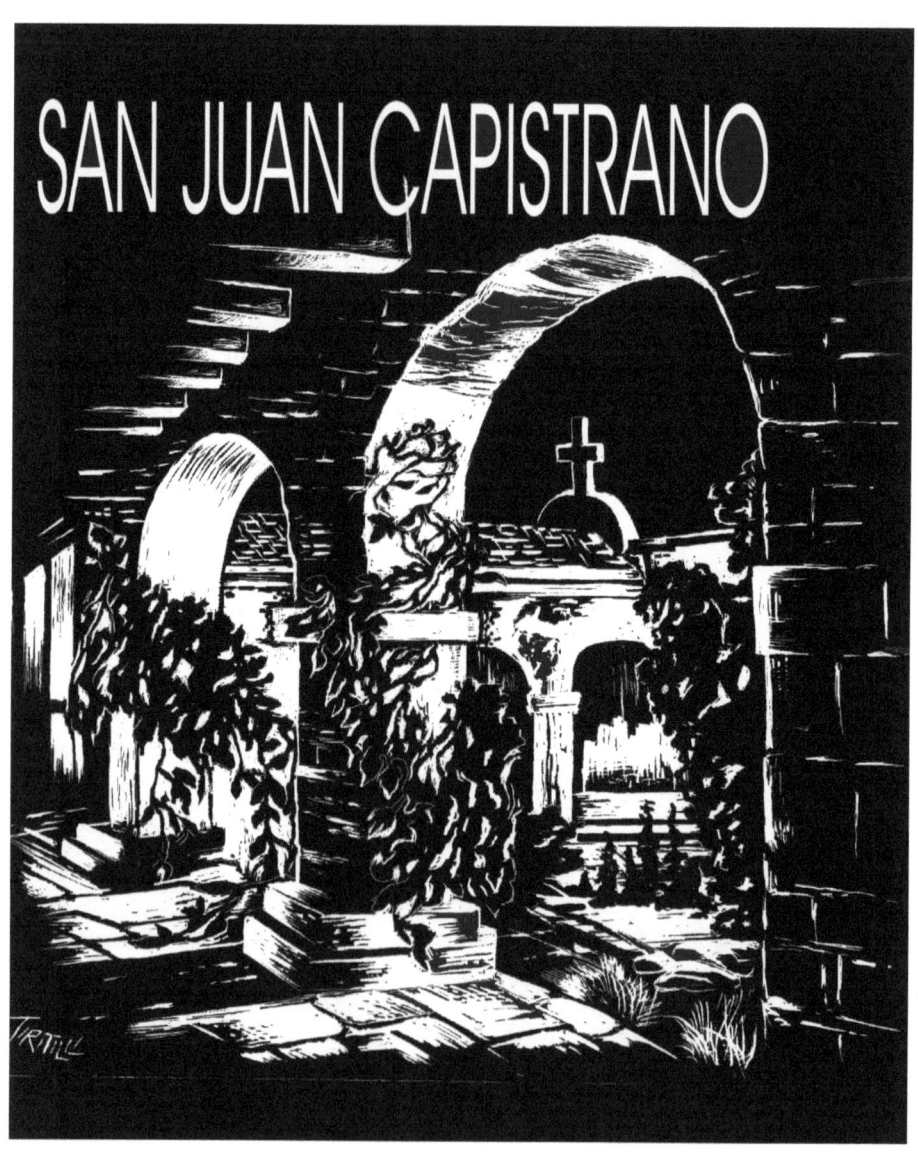

The Bells Toll

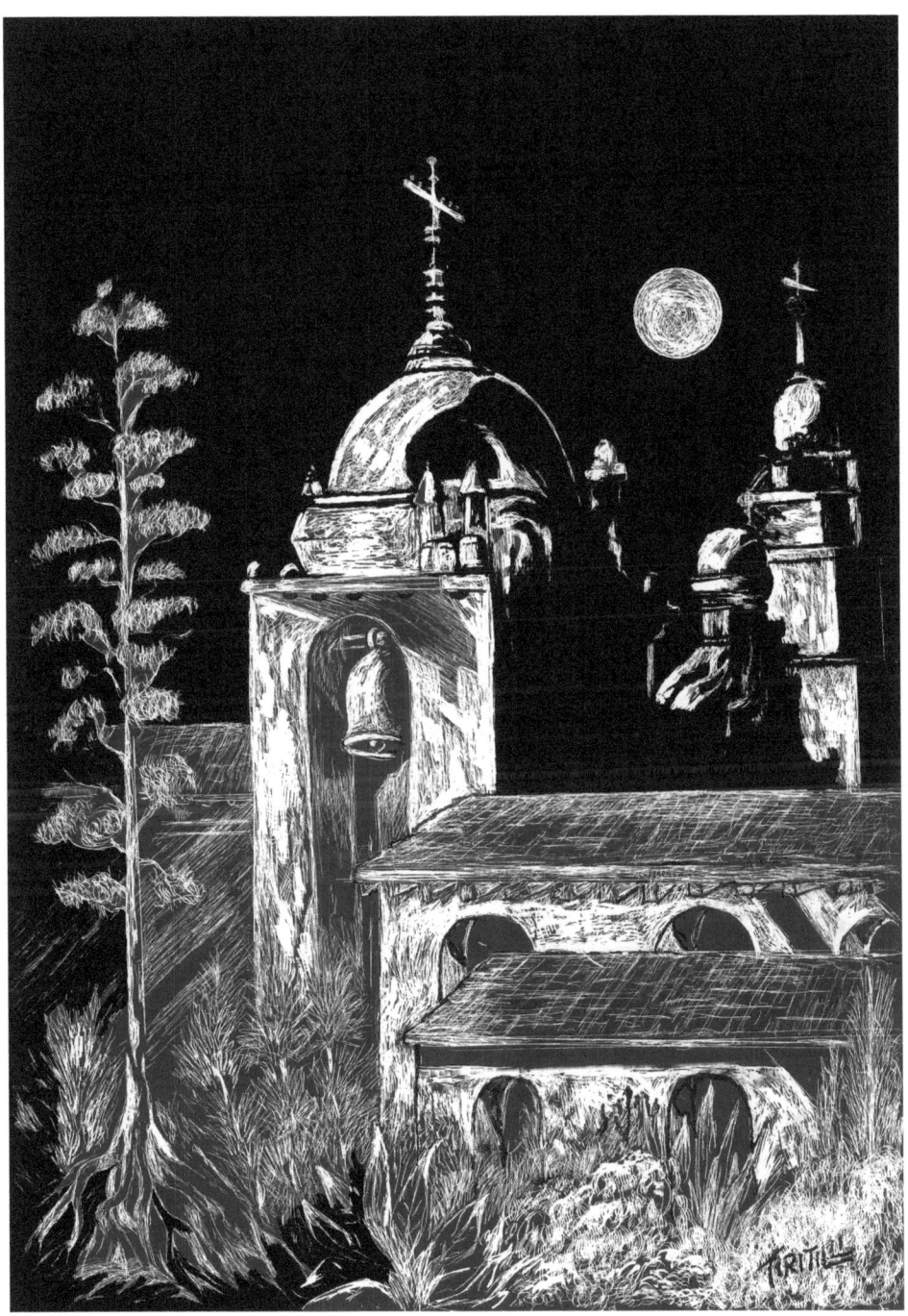

Heaven's Home

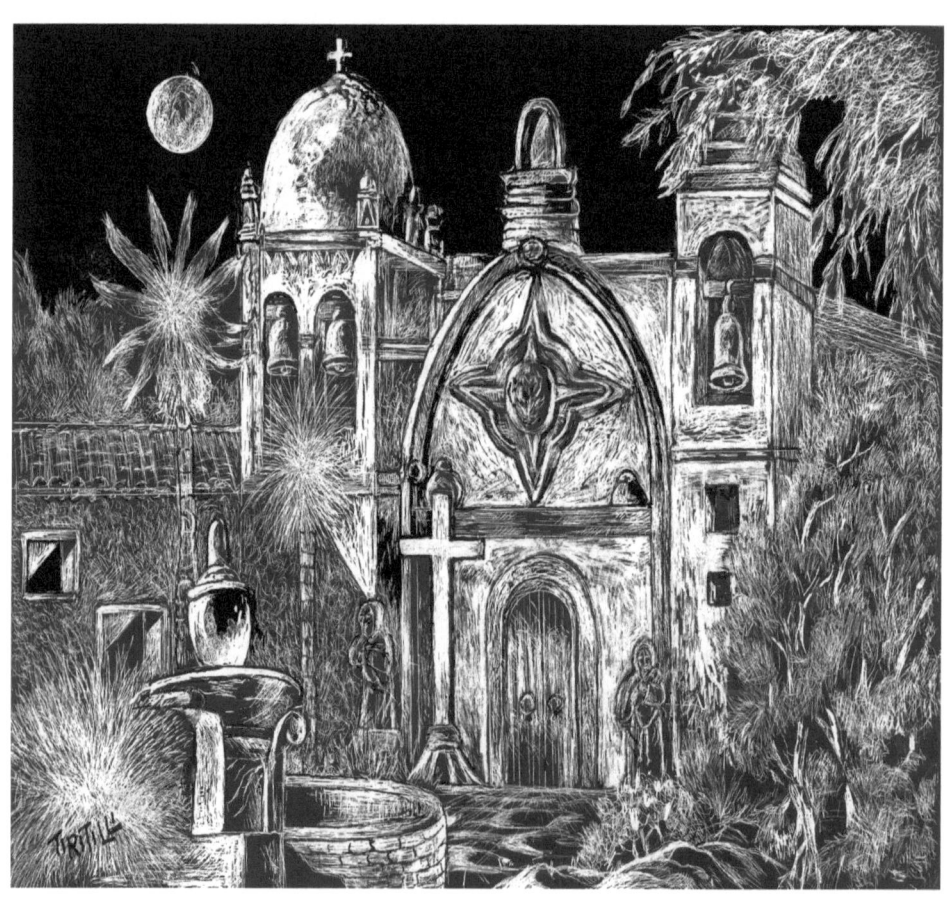

Military

The Enforcer

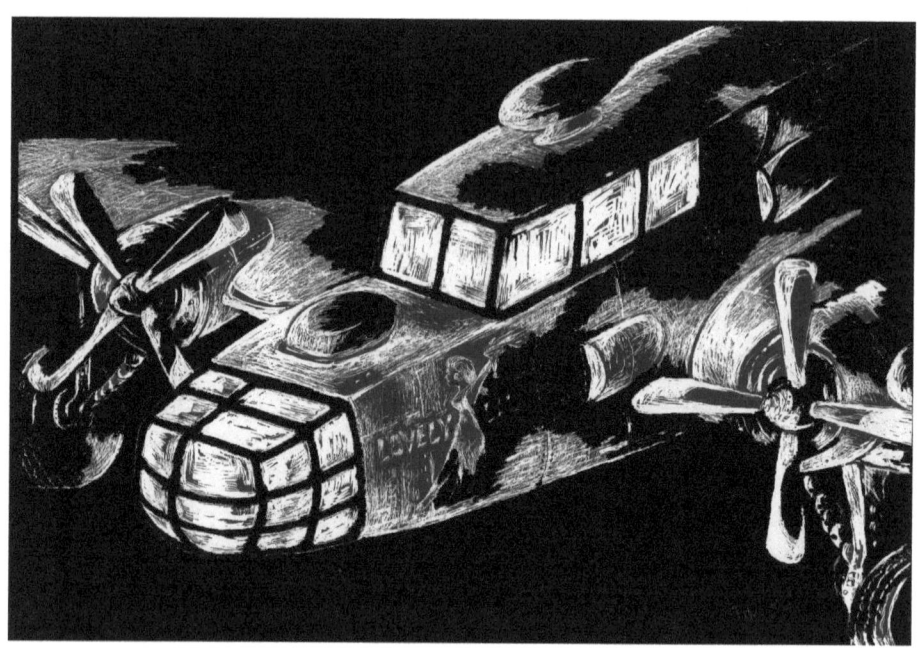

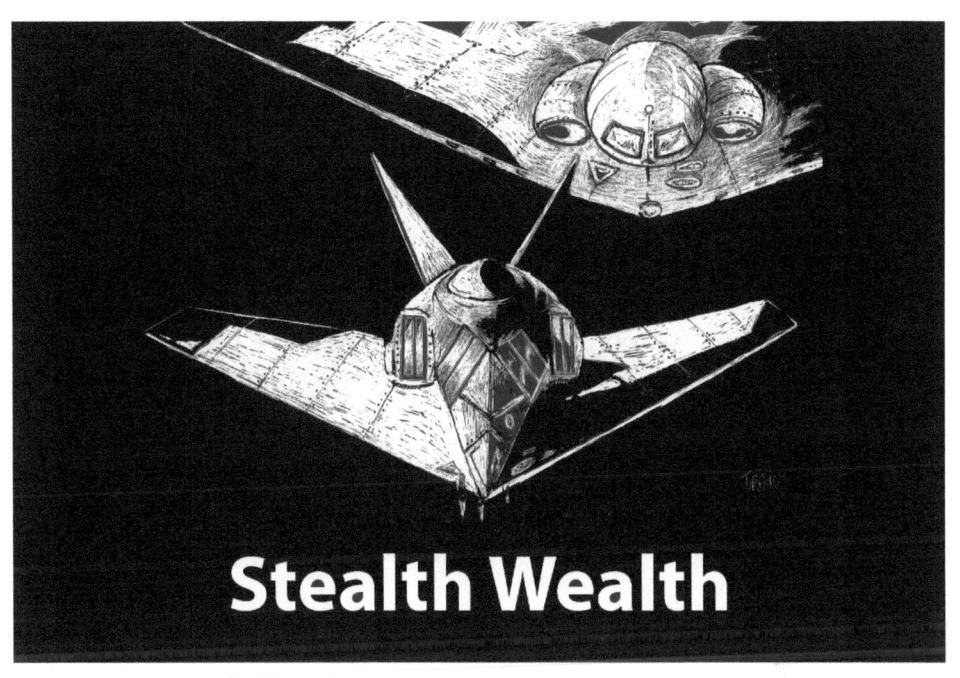

Stealth Wealth

Burning Bright

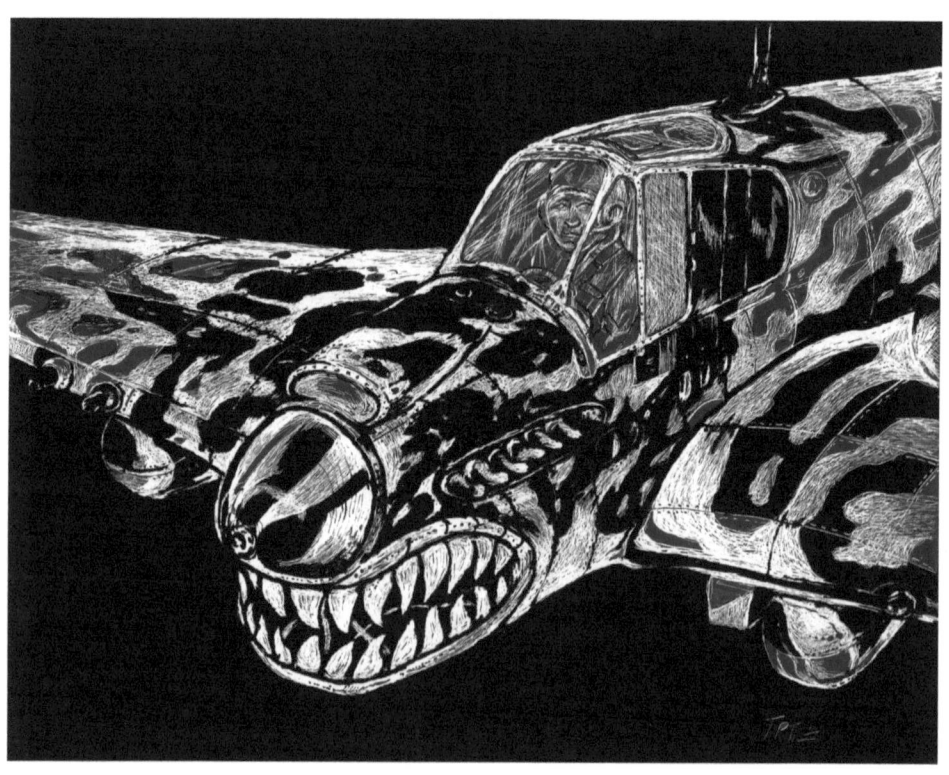

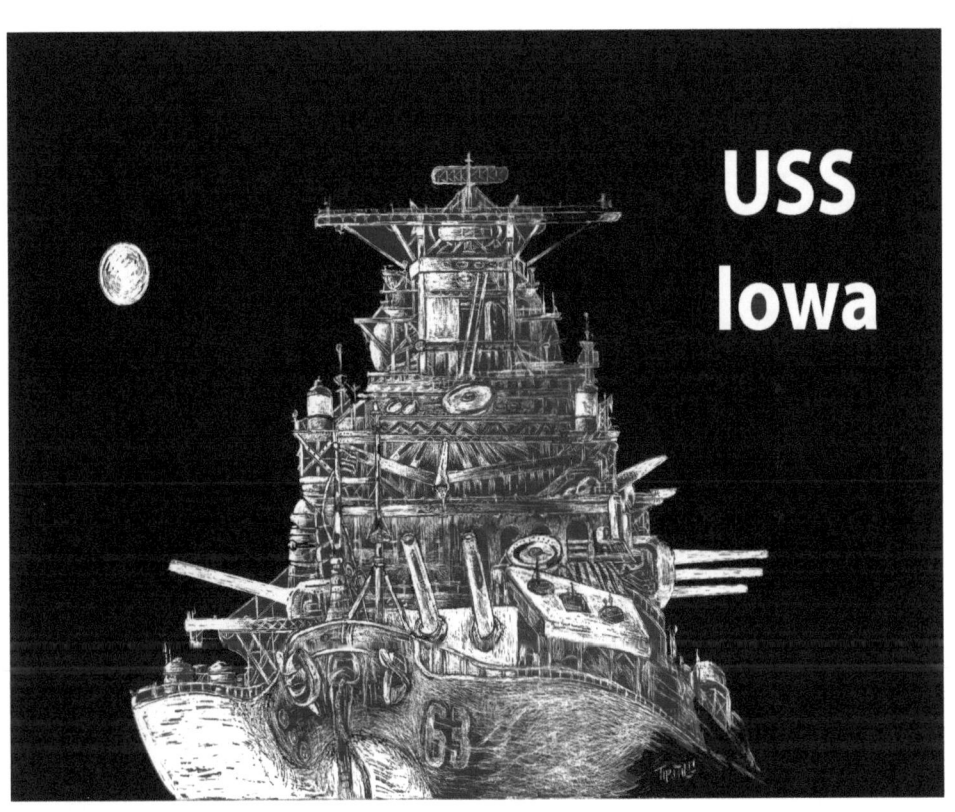

USS
Iowa

Hot Shot

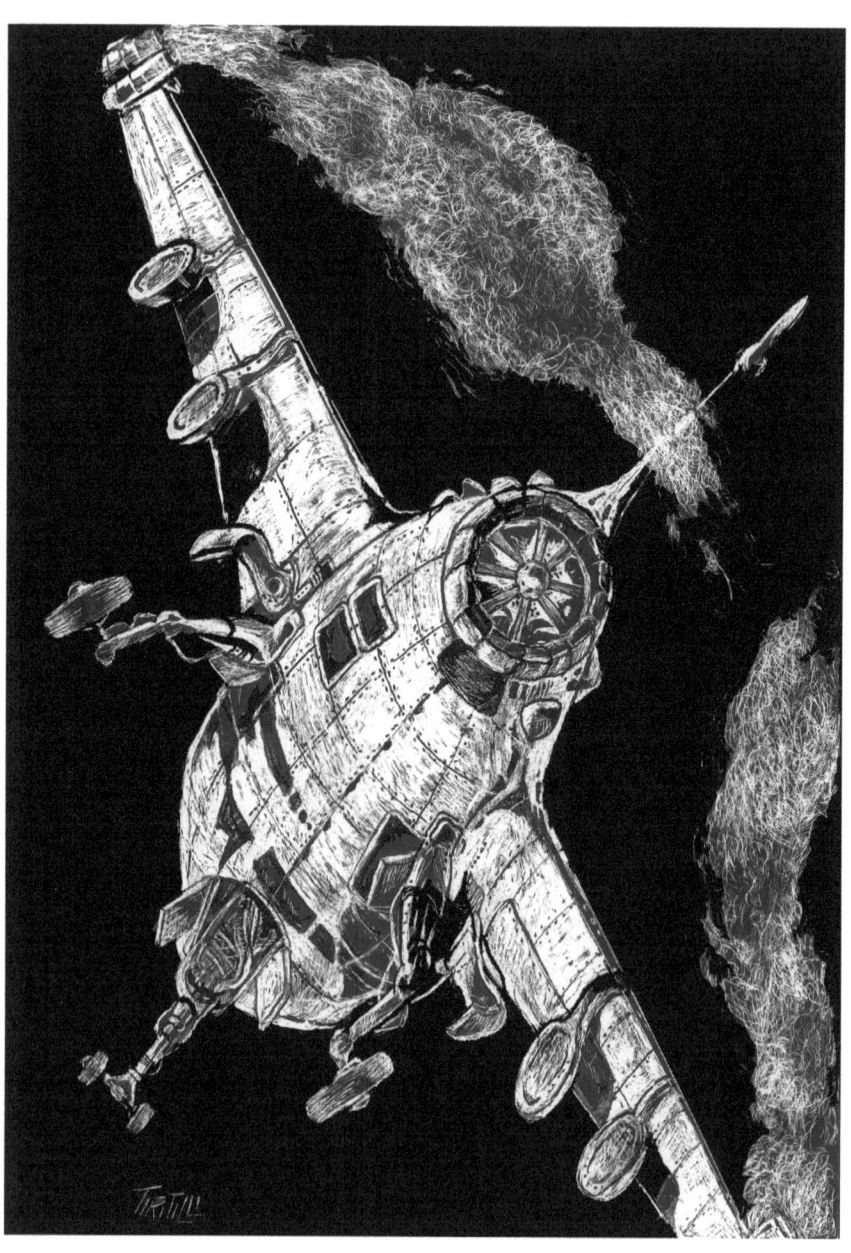

Coastal

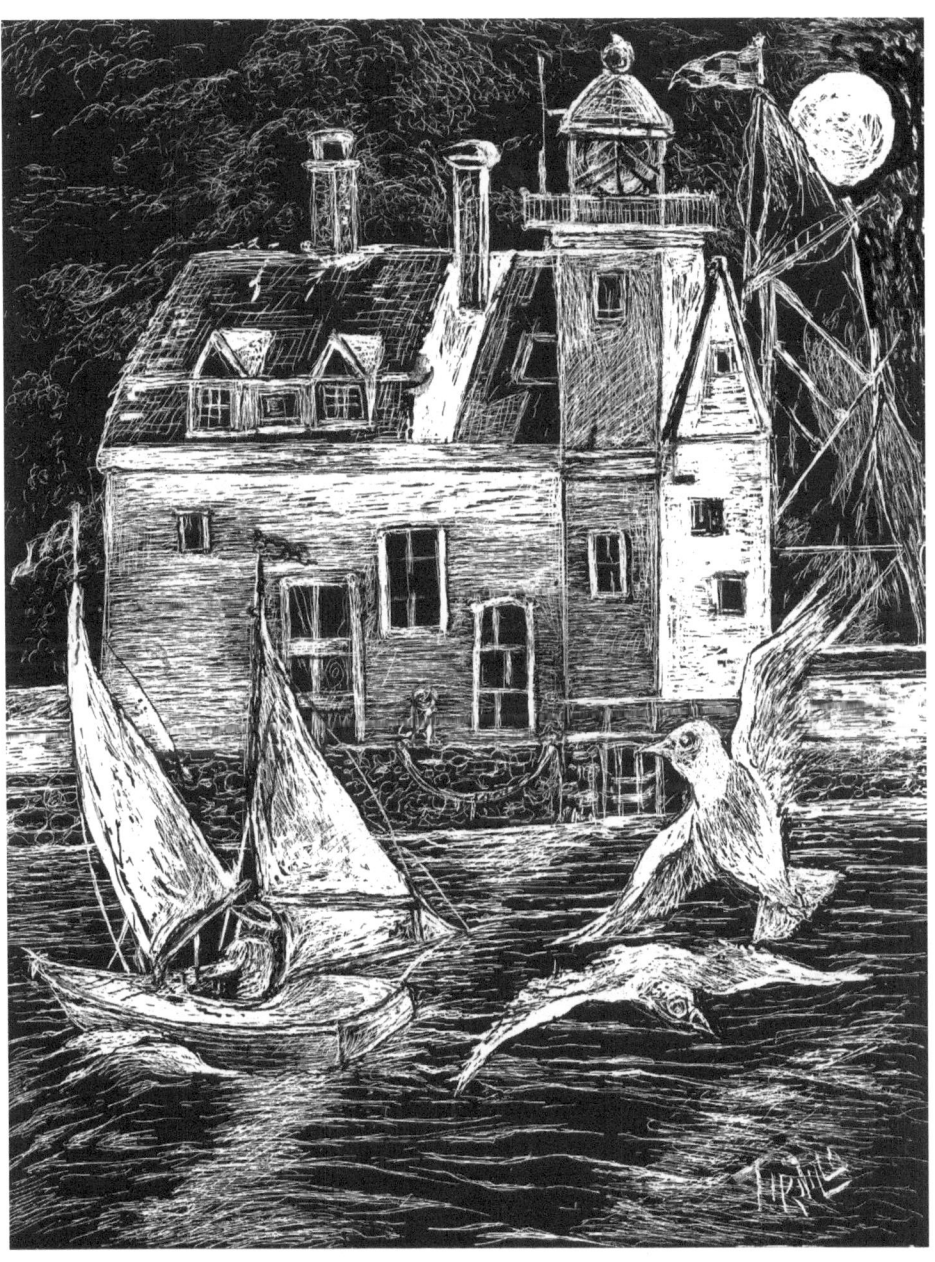

Old Church

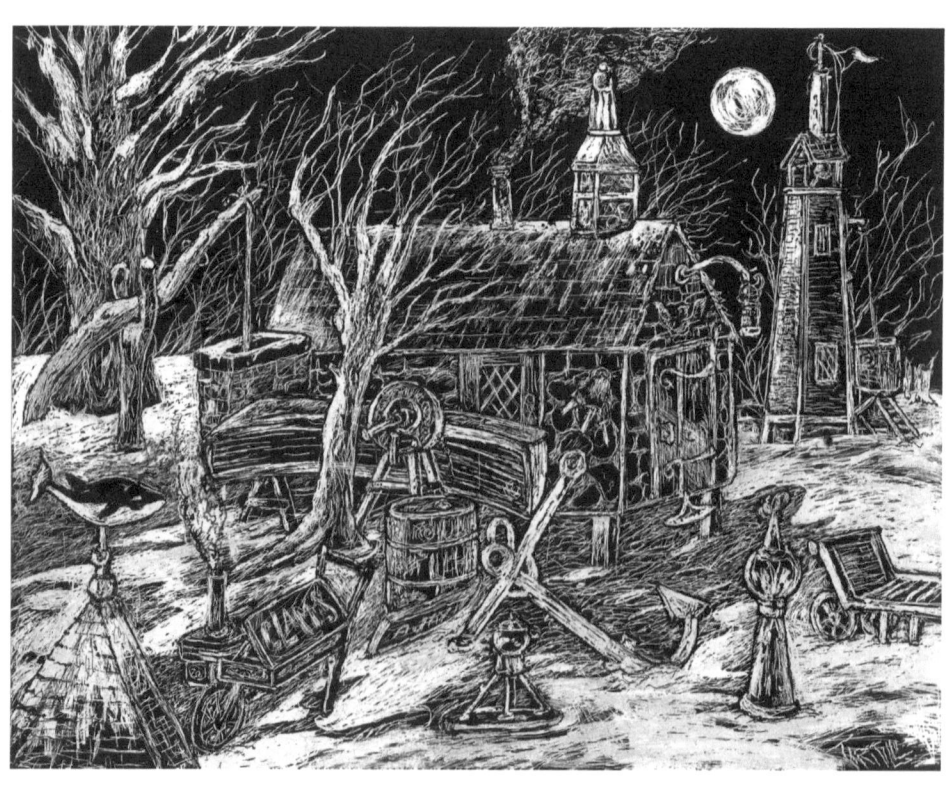

Electrical Power

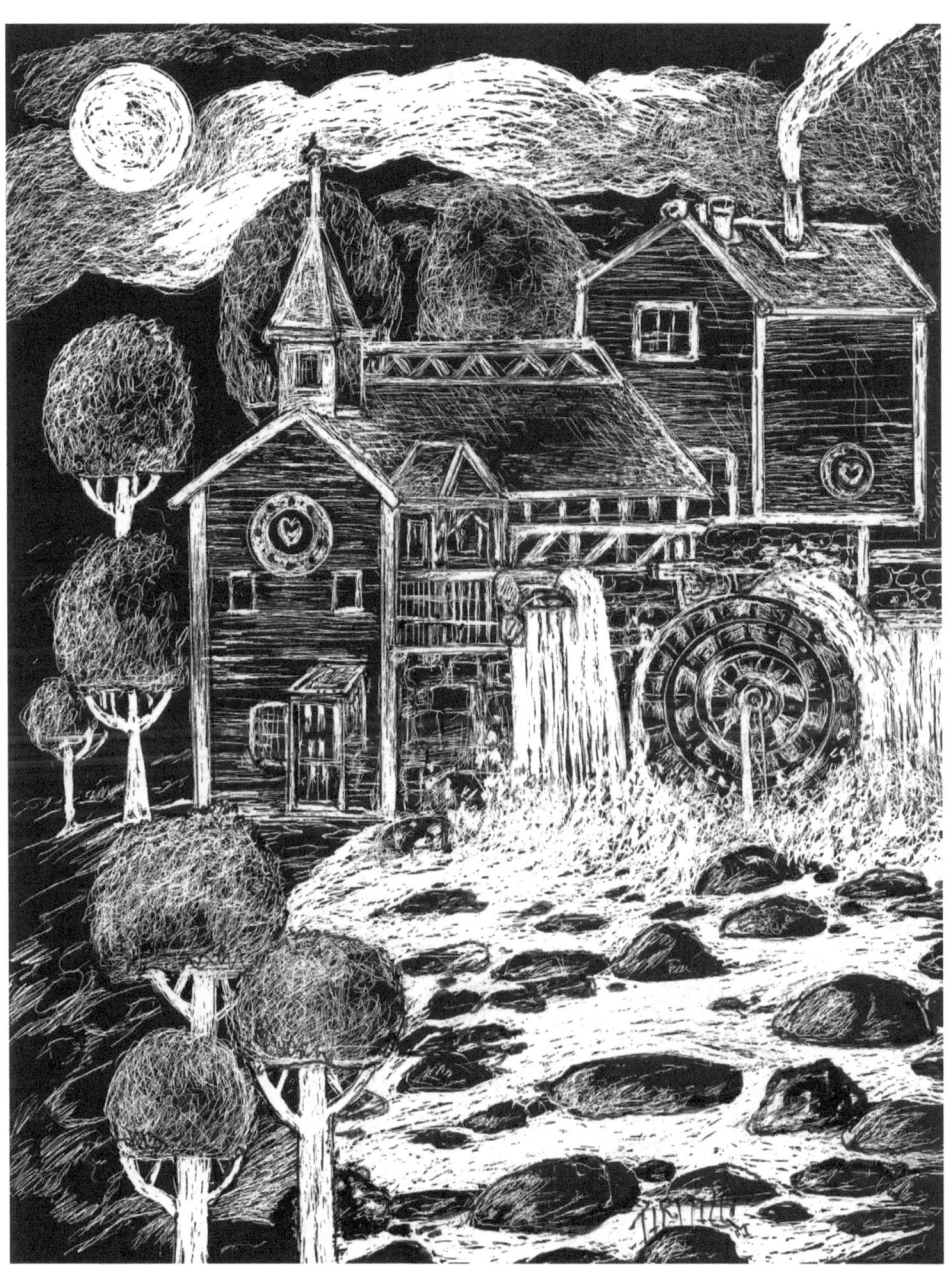

Pump

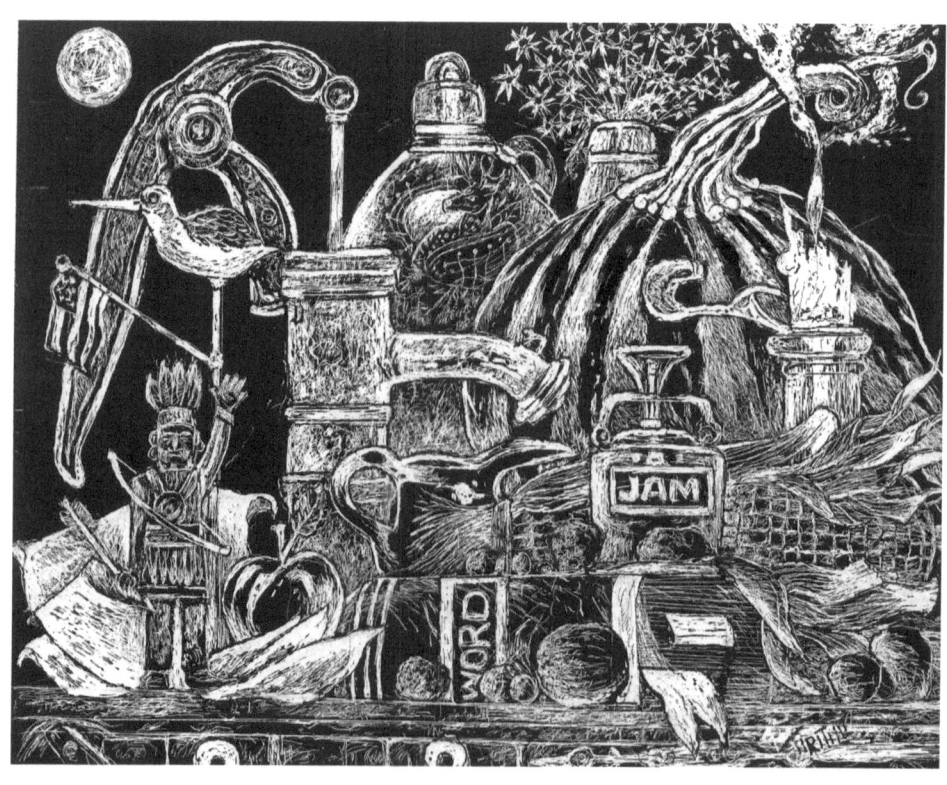

Kitchen Table

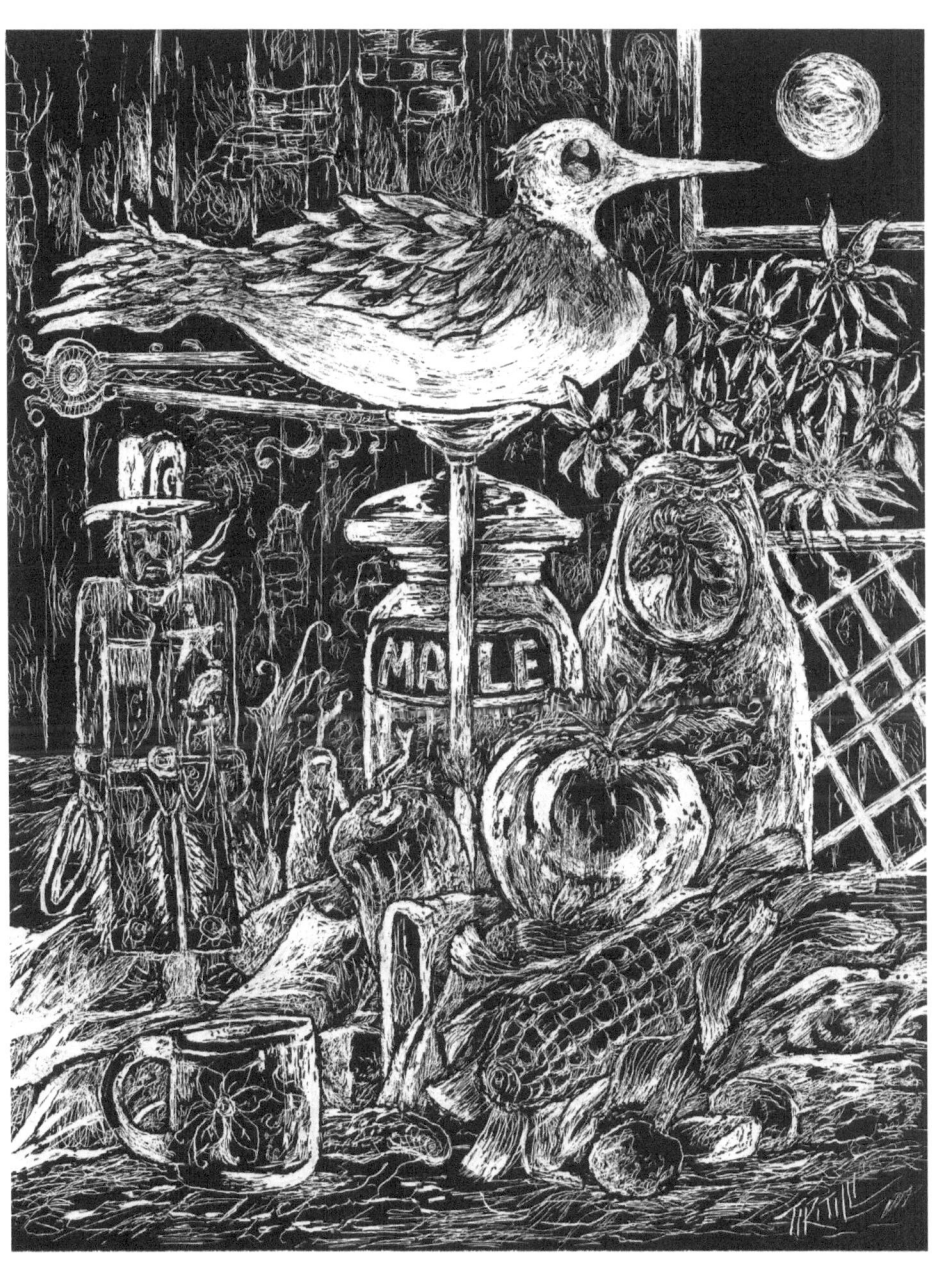

Two Ships

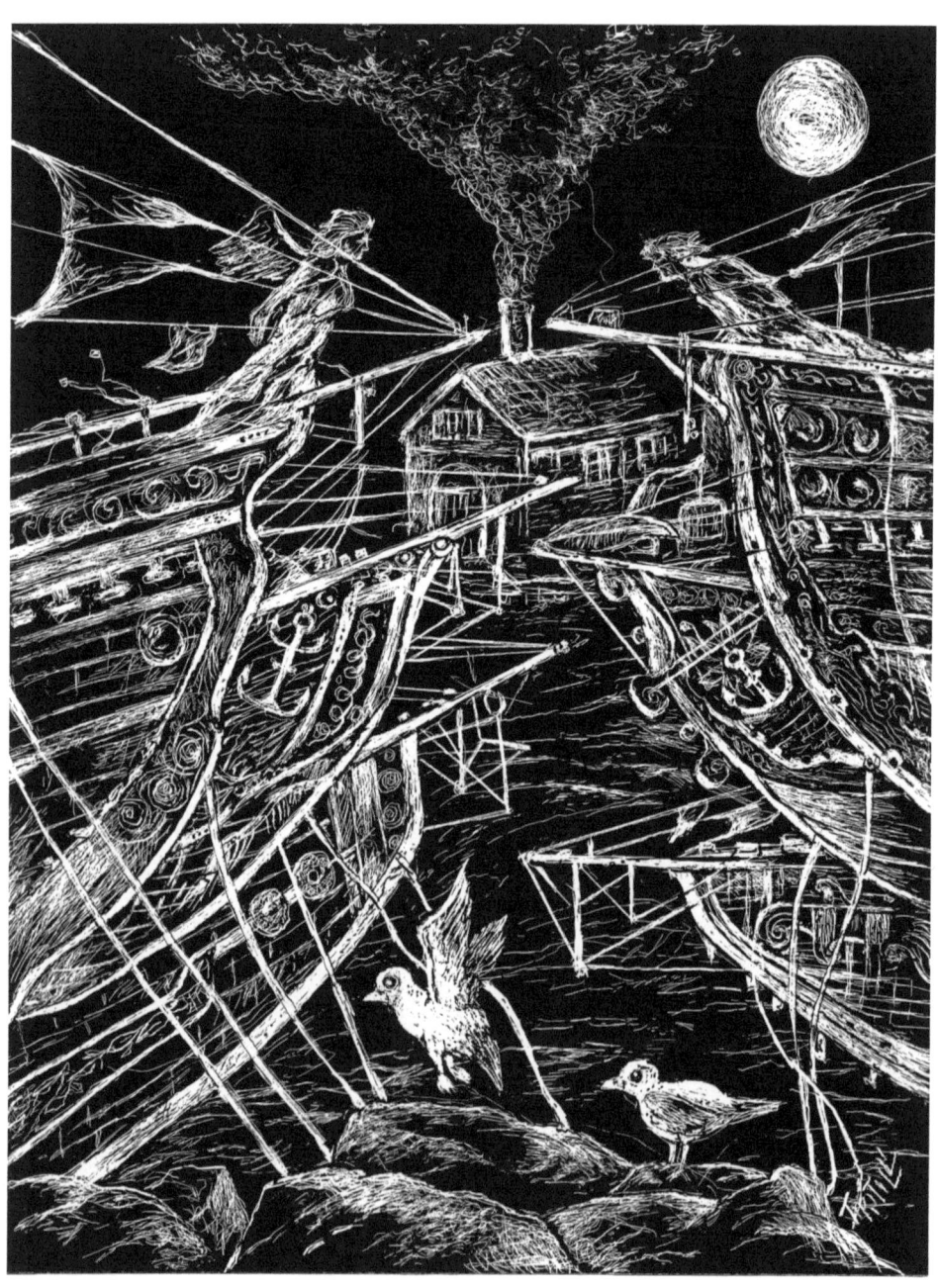

Wharf

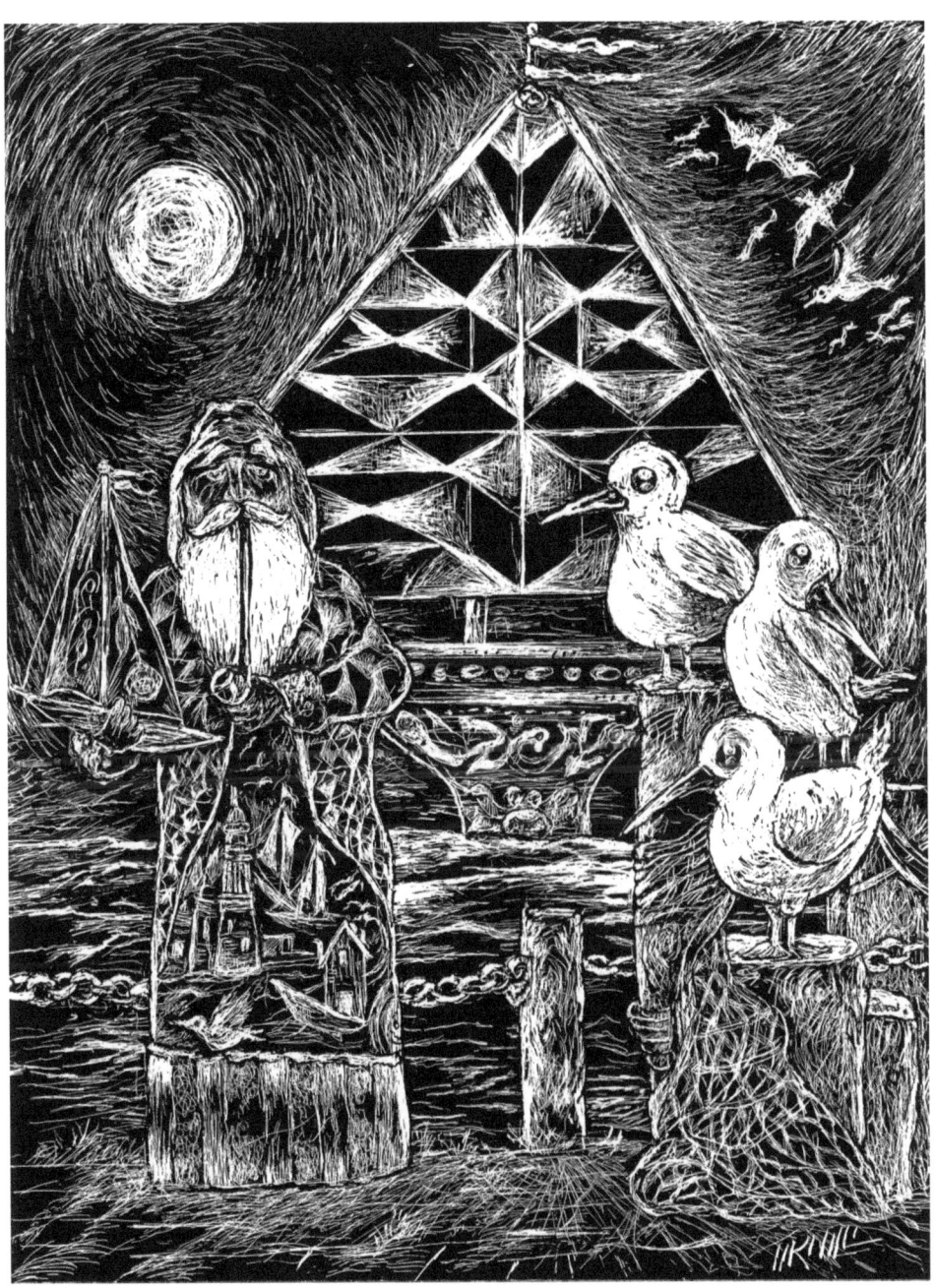

Potpourri

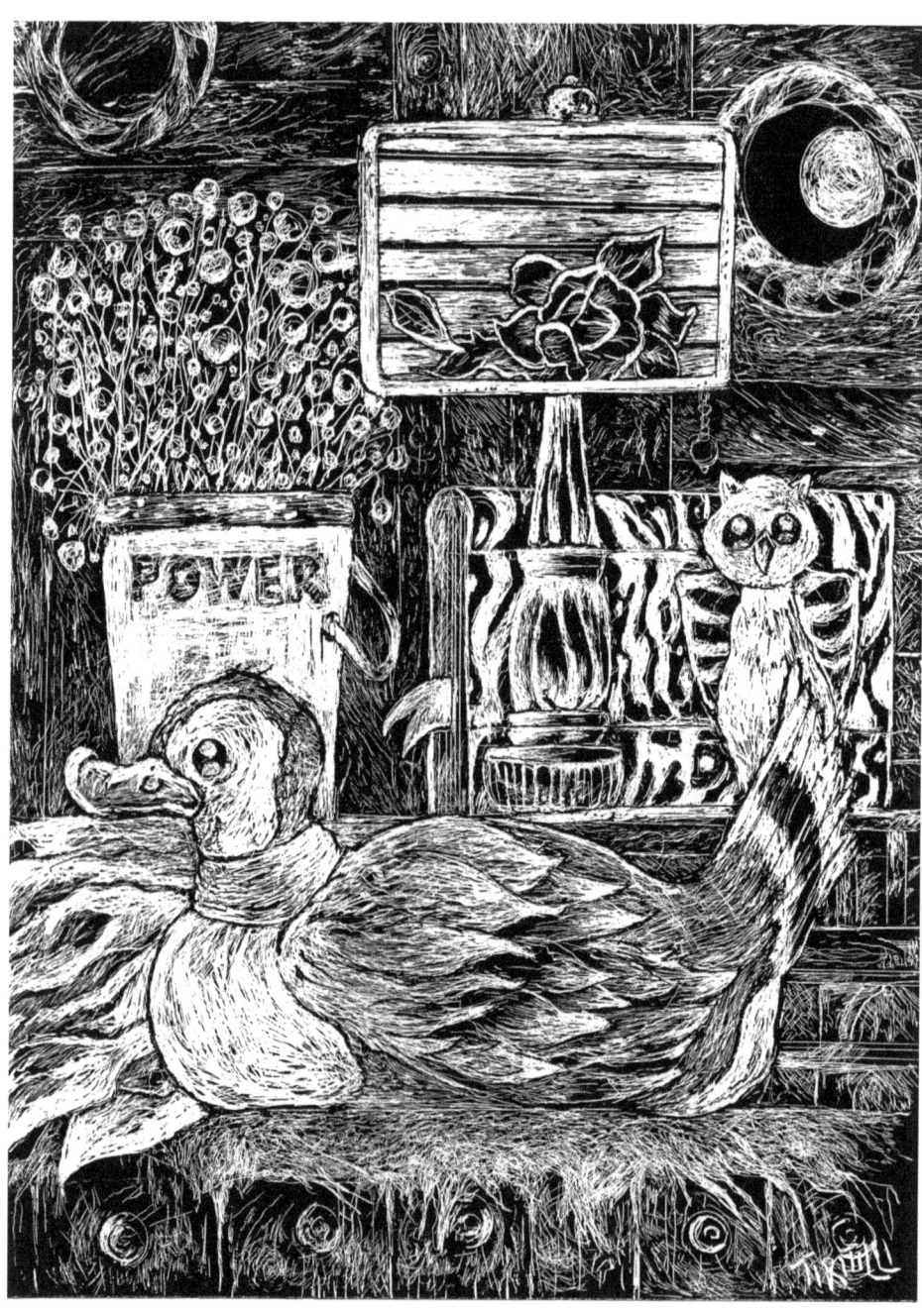

Birds

Baby Hawk

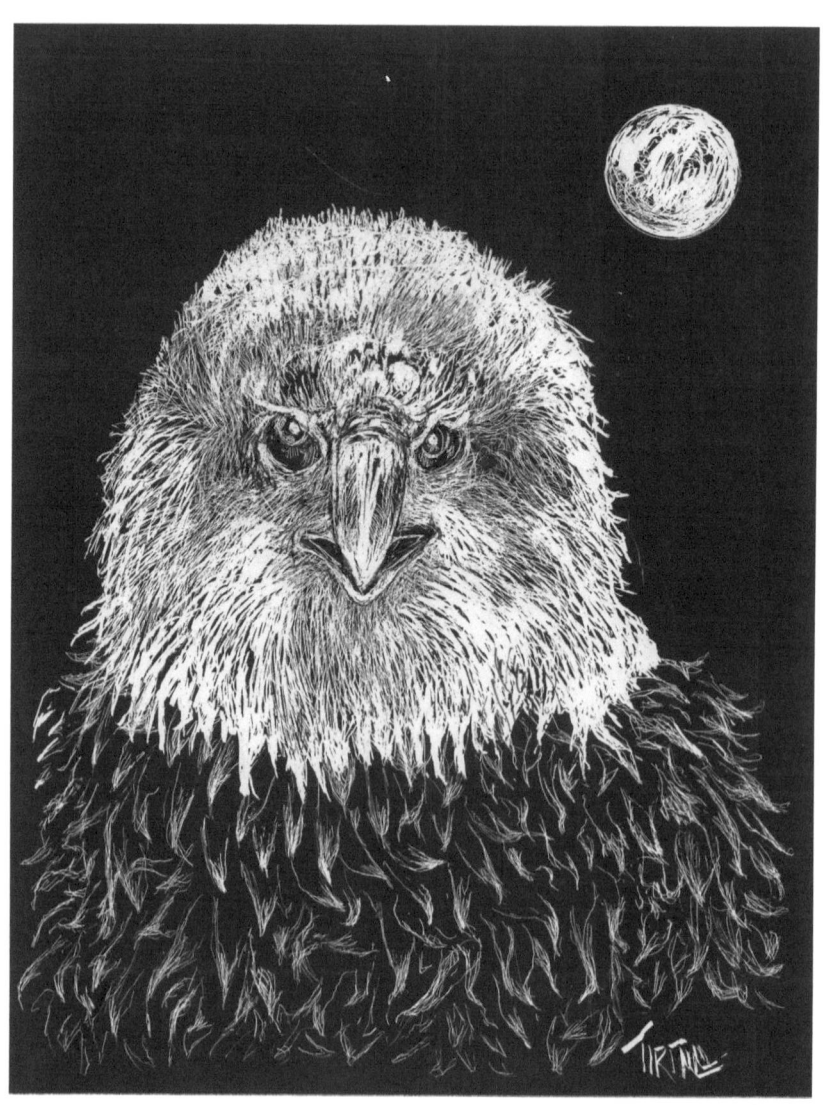

Duck

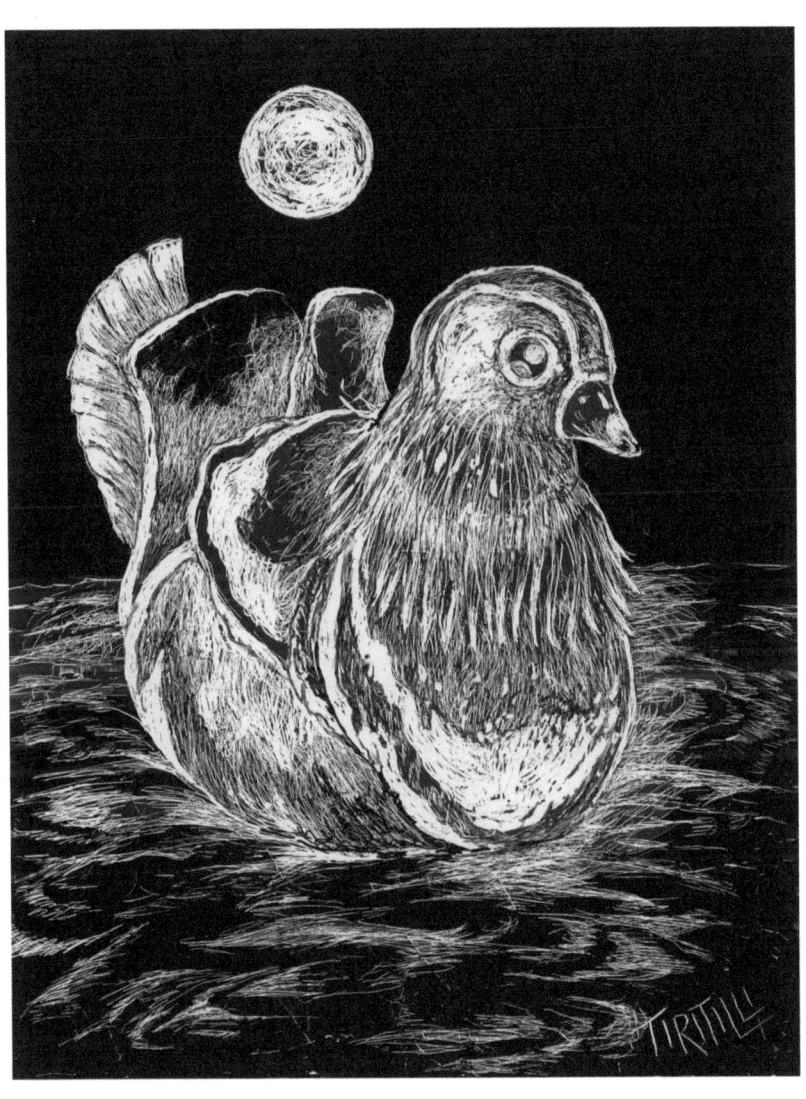

Flying Goose

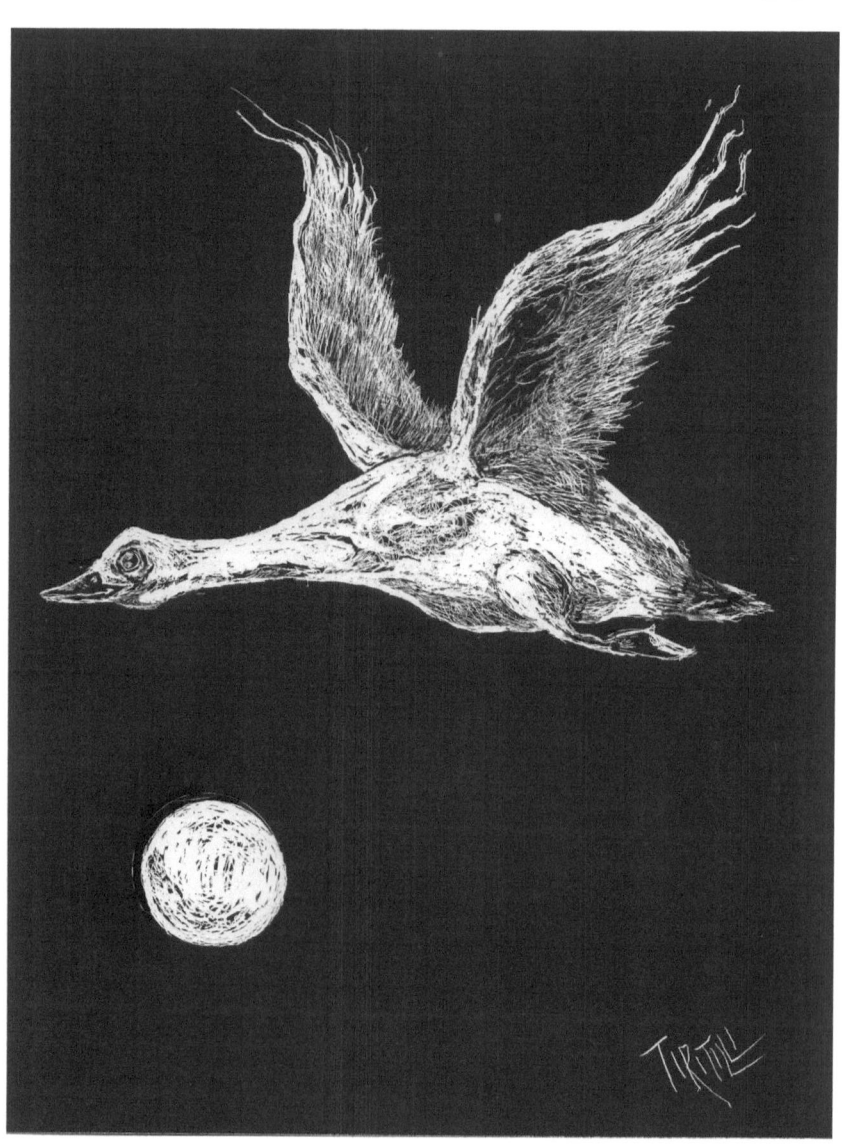

Flying Geese

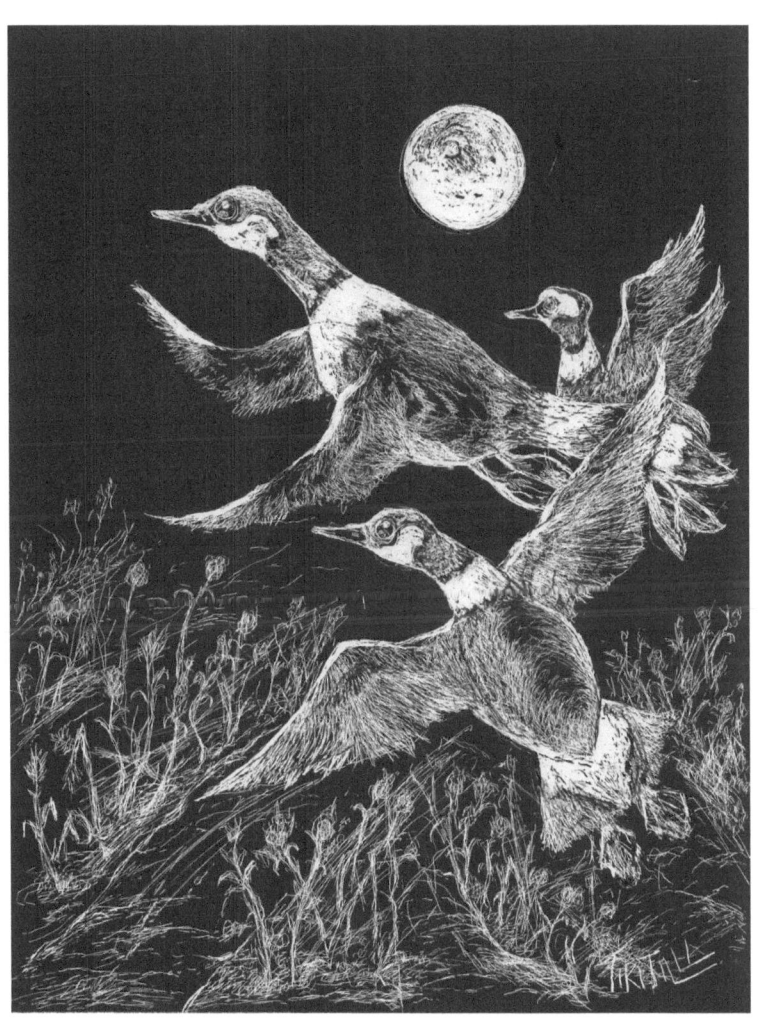

Geese Dynasty

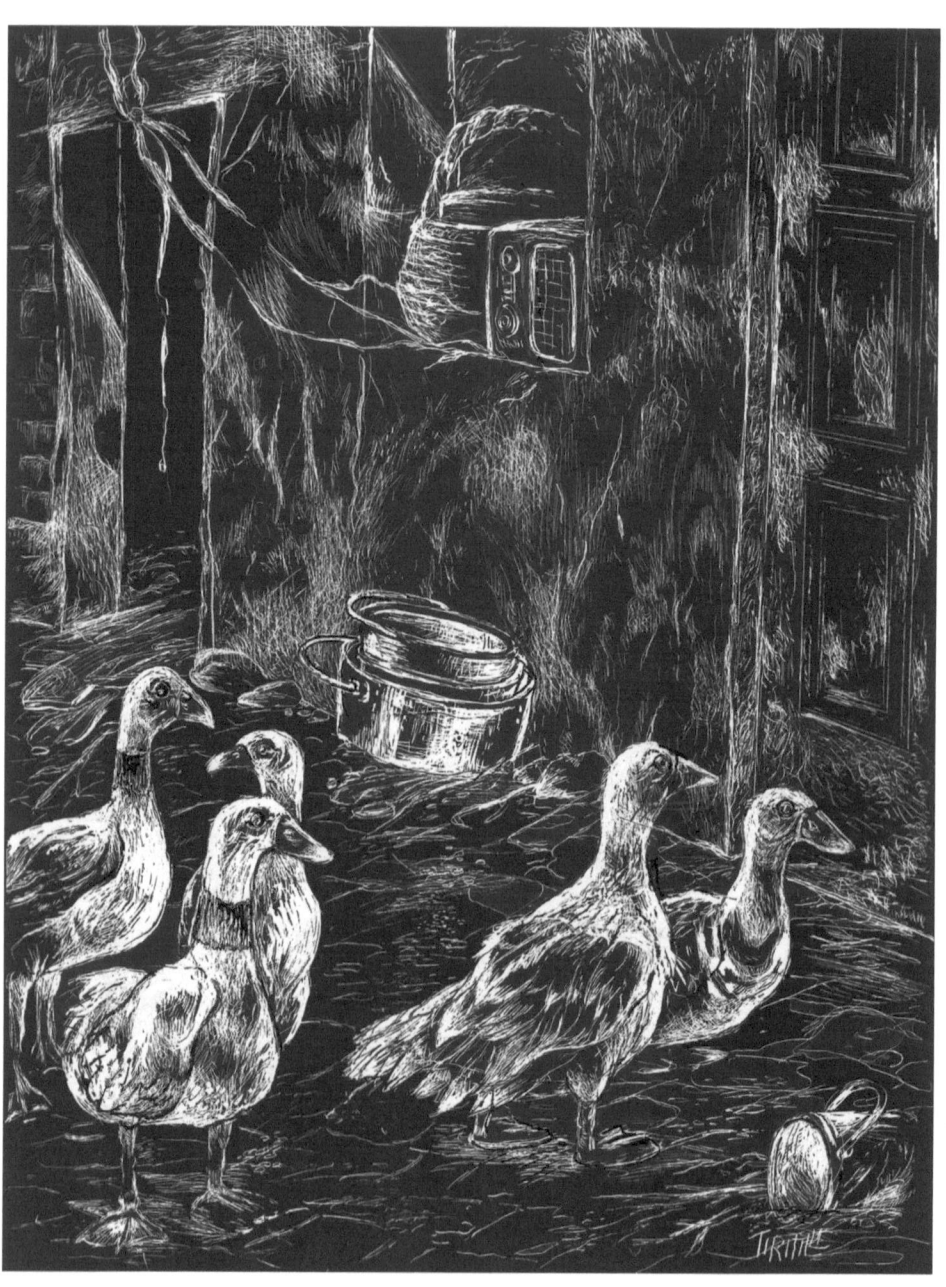

Eagle

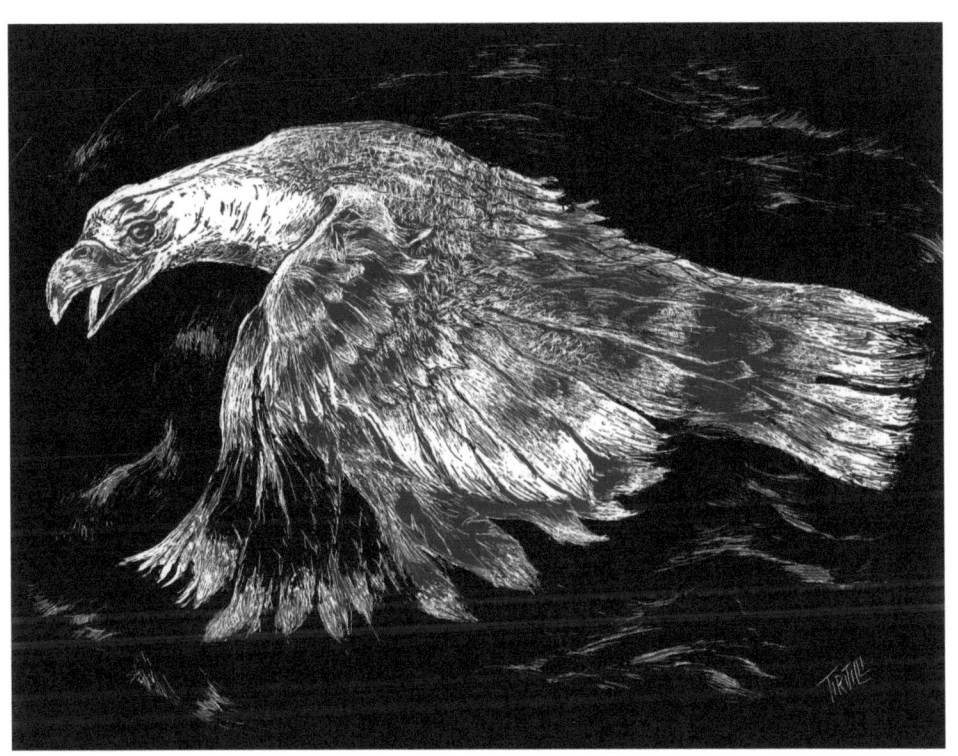

Flying Hawk

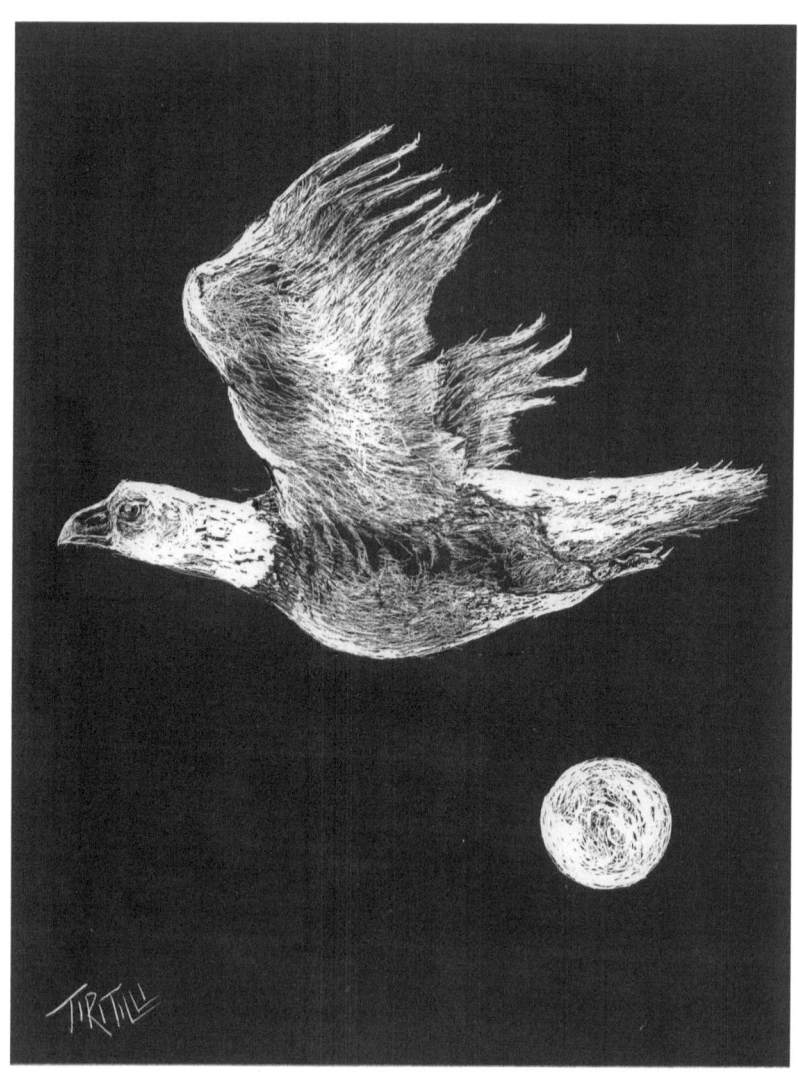

One-eyed Owl

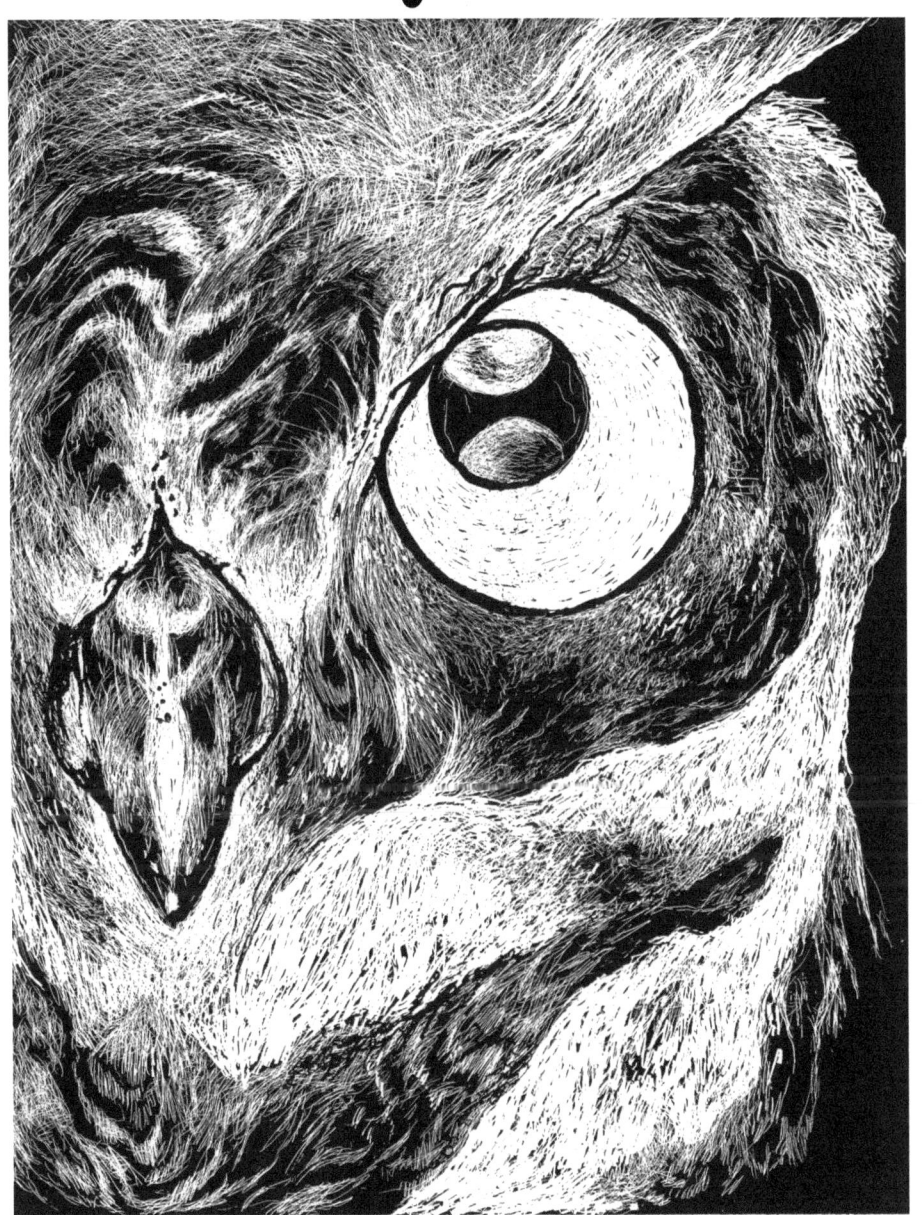

Two Owls

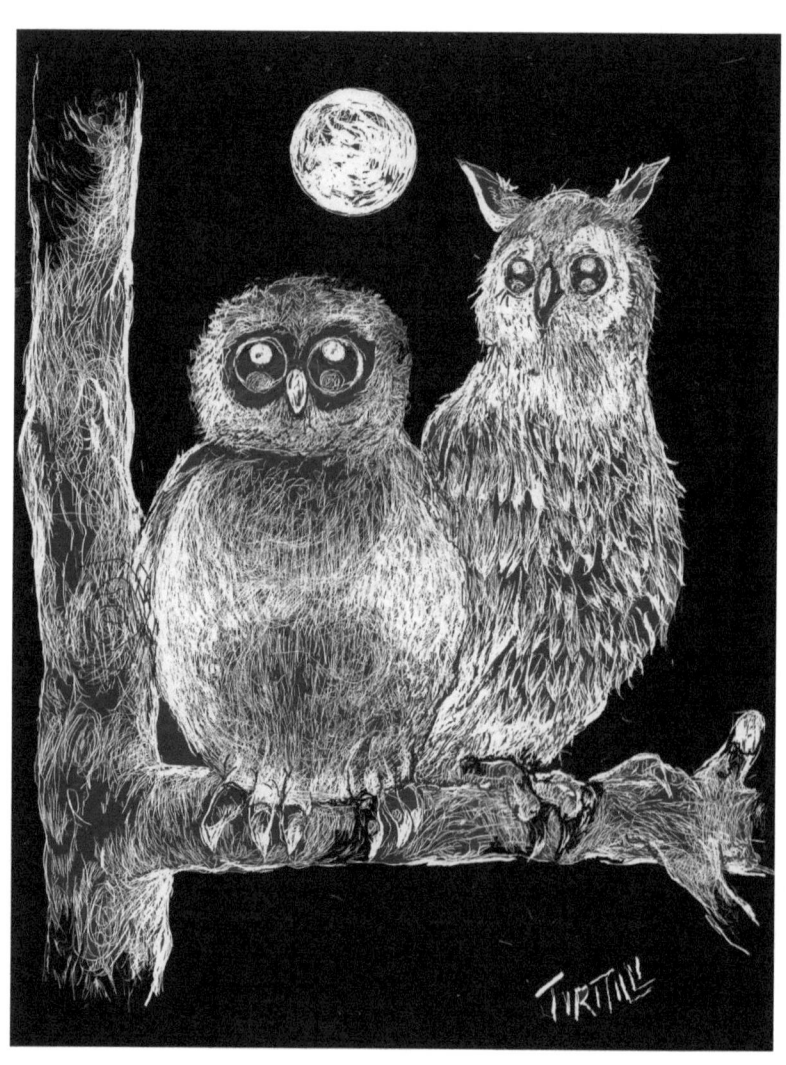

Torero

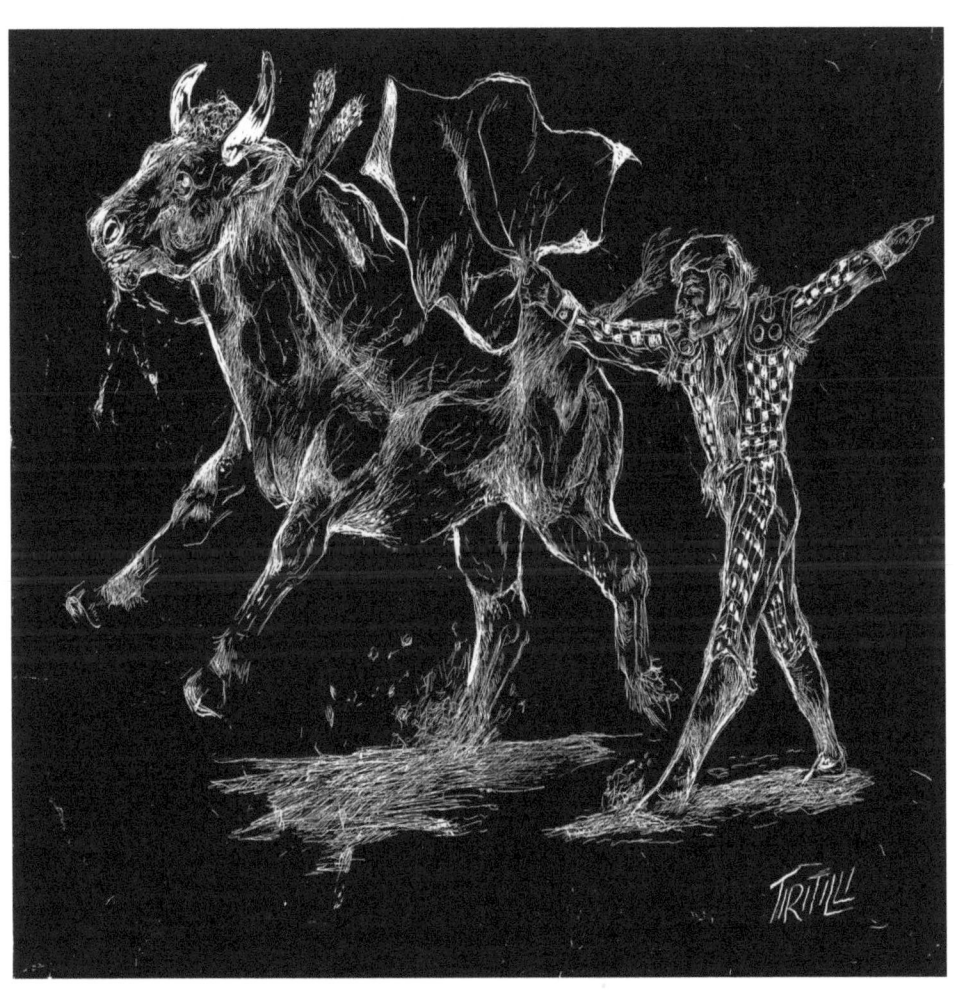

Fish

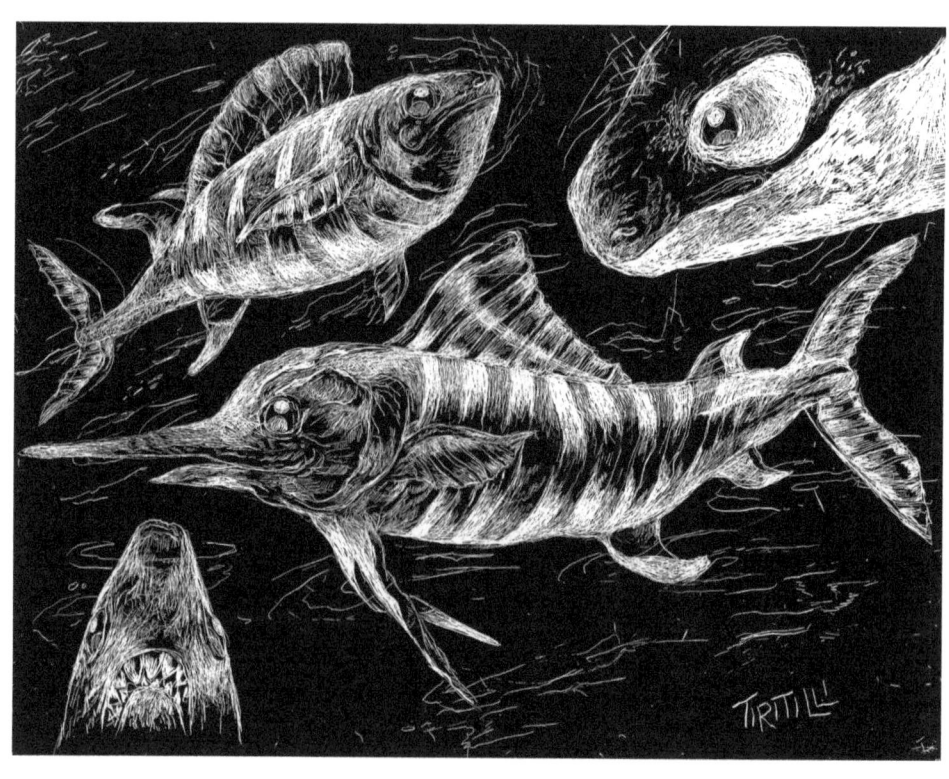

Whale

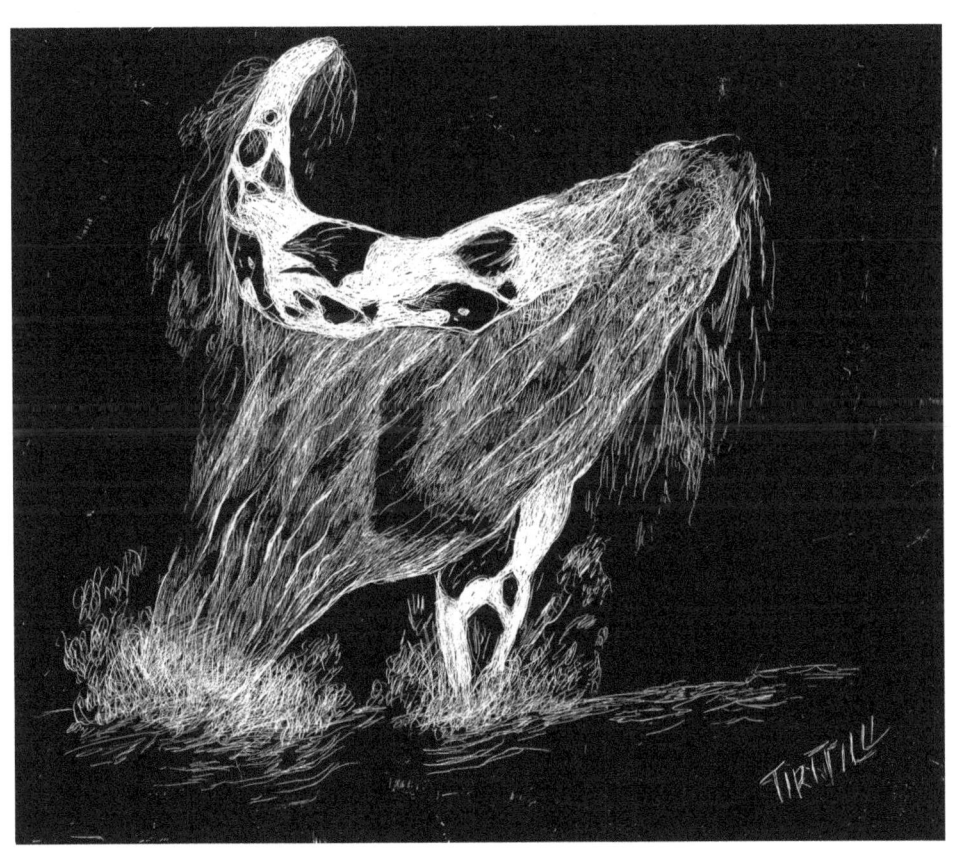

Baseball

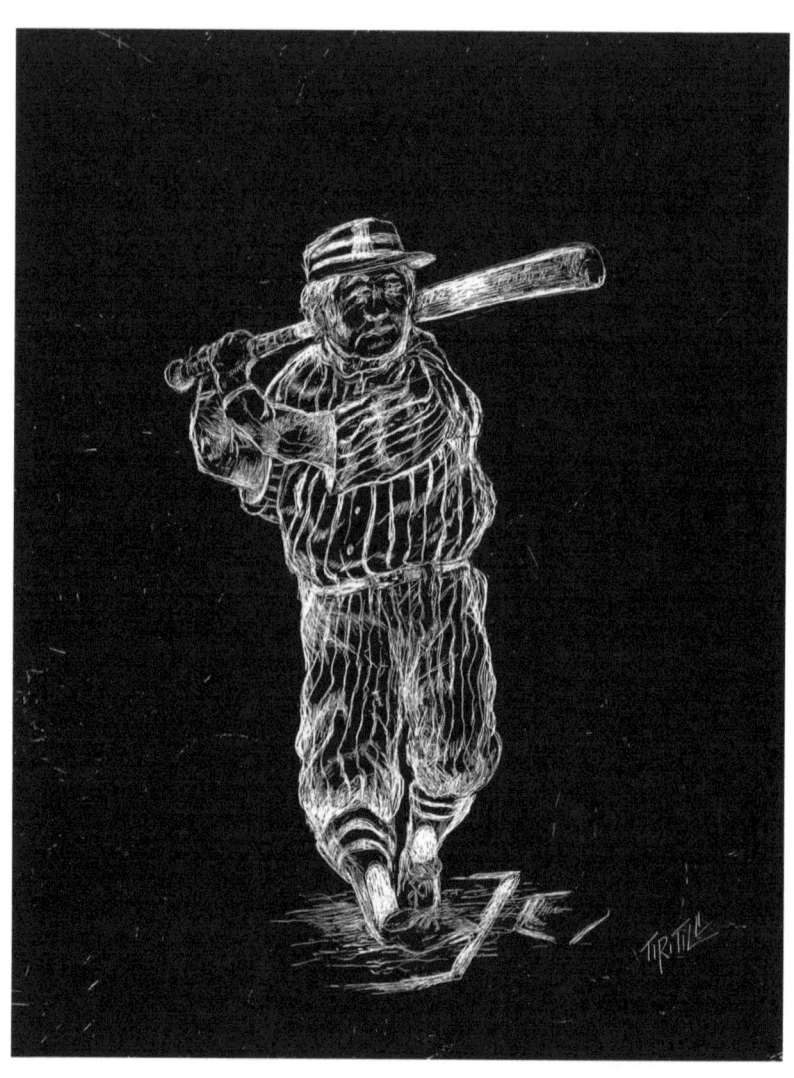

Football

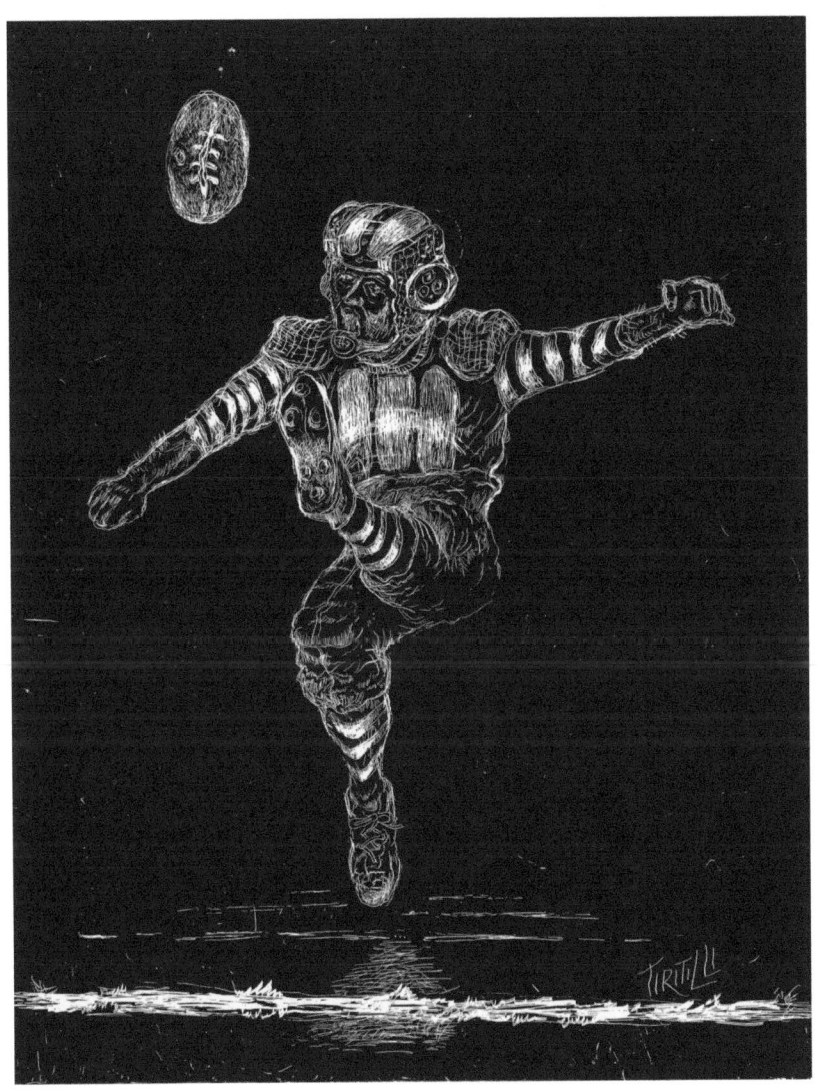

Other Sports

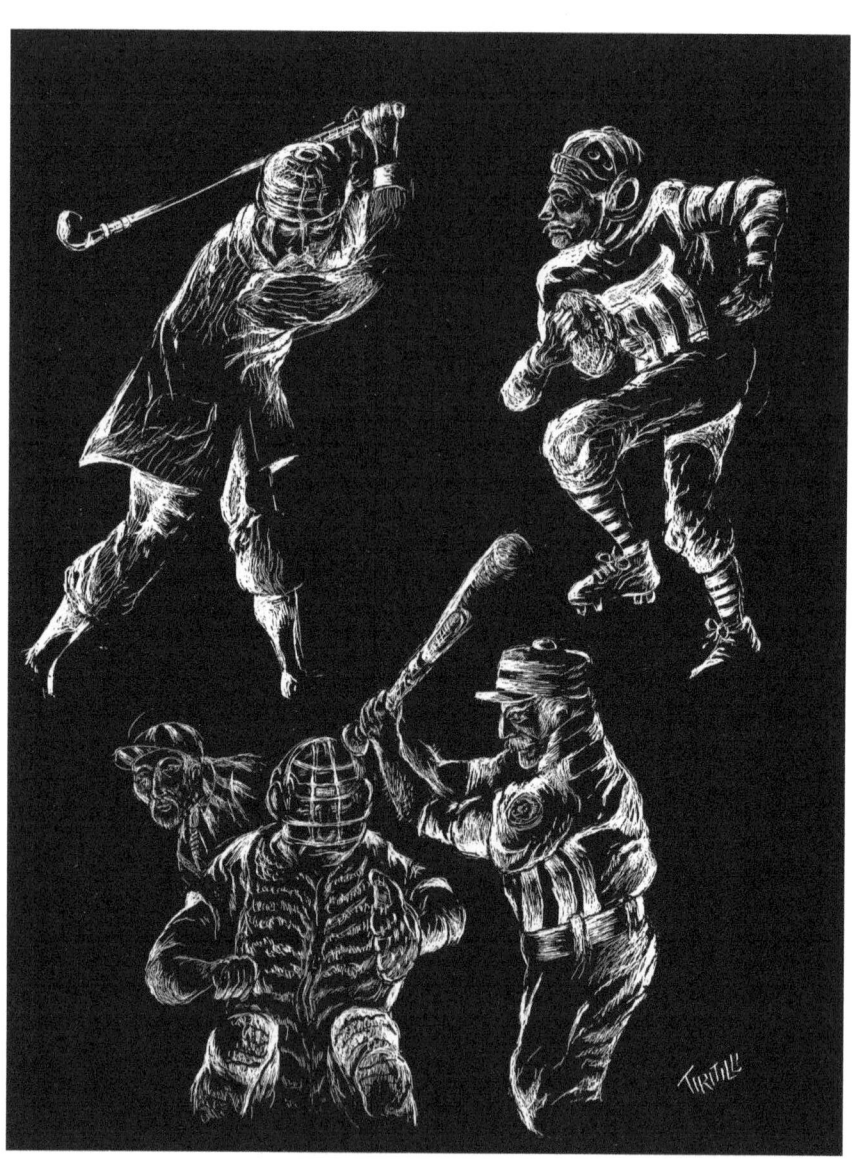

Cars/Planes

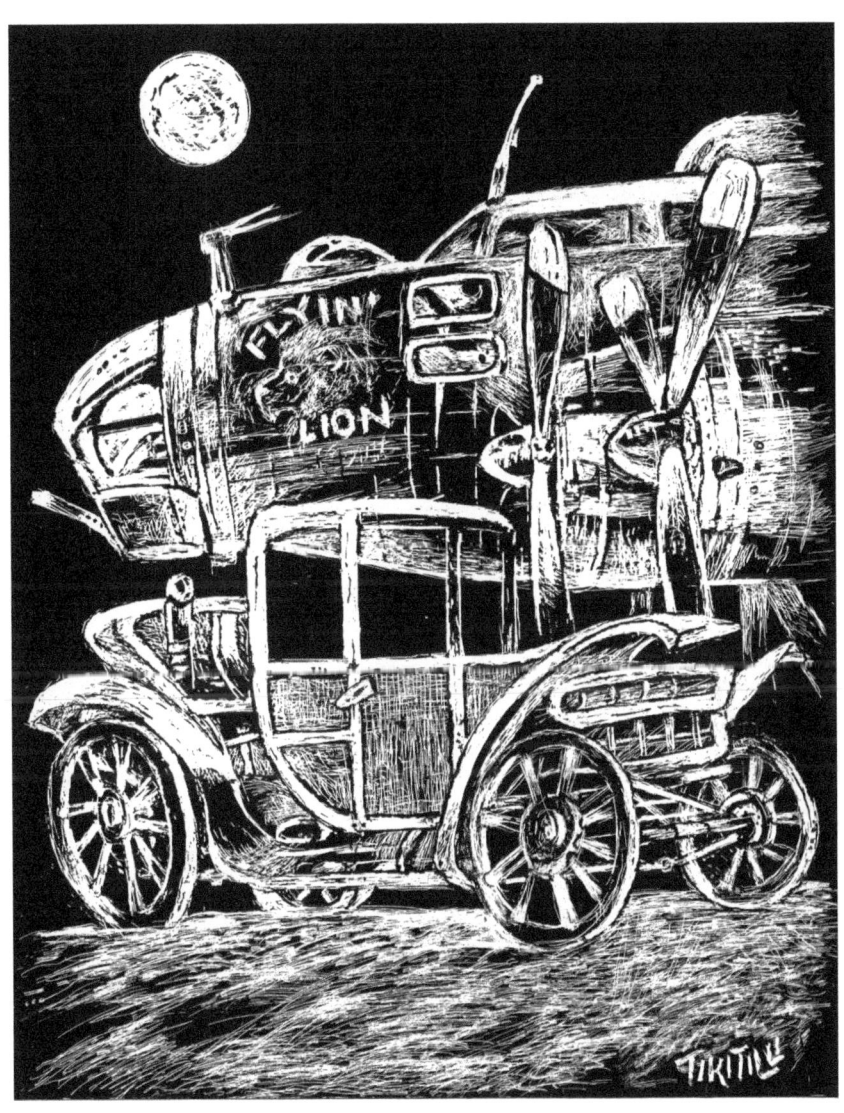

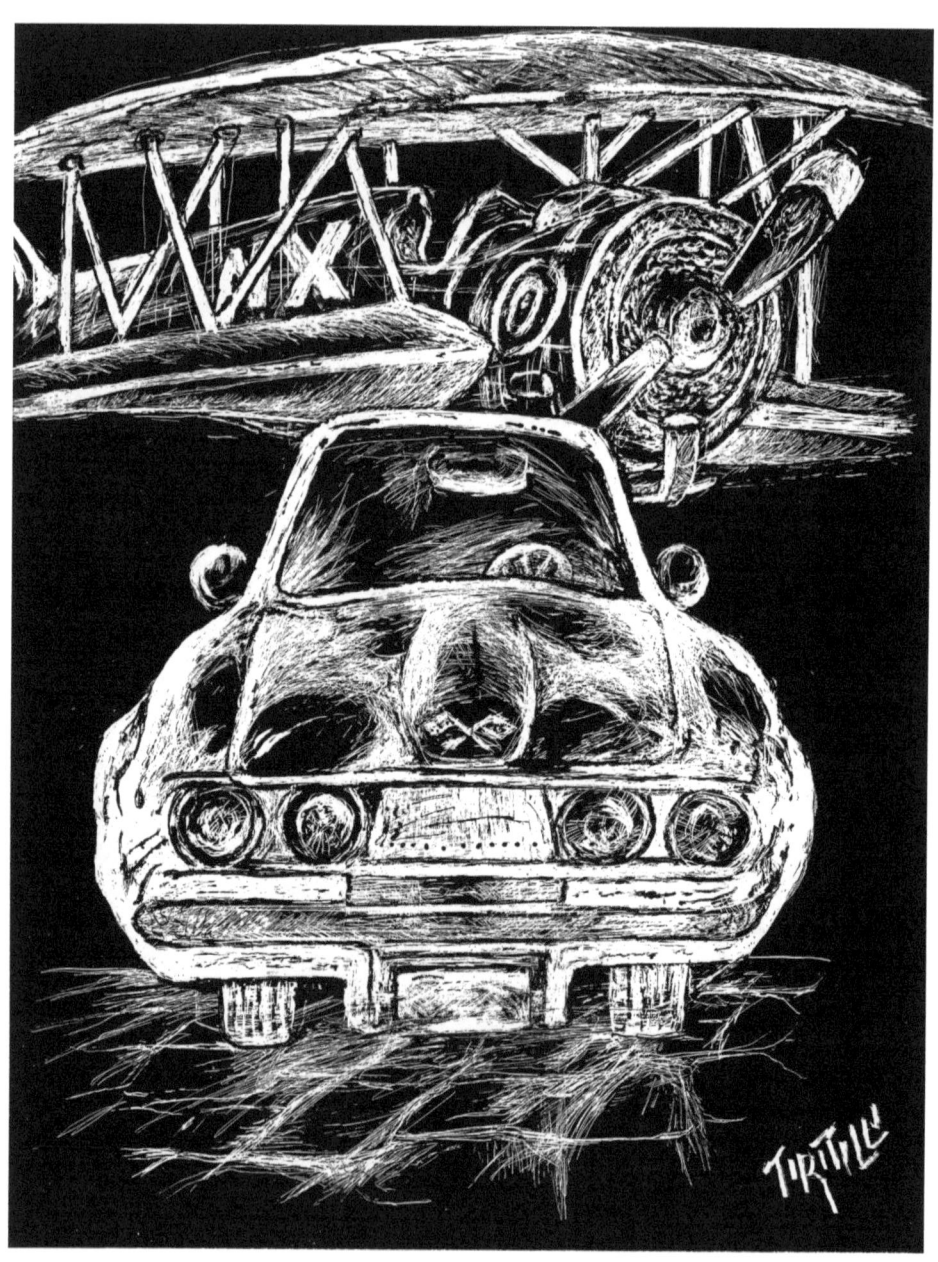

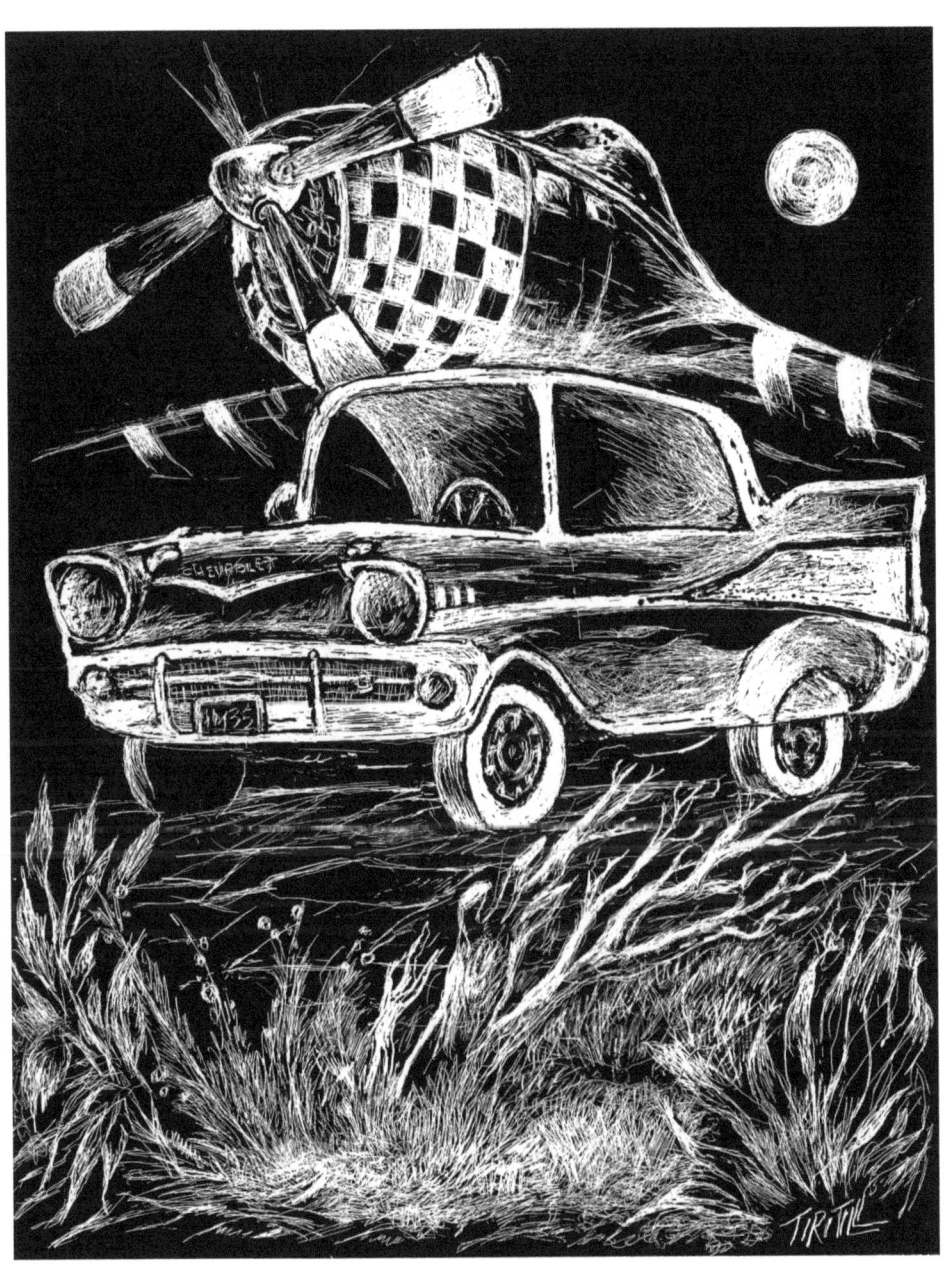

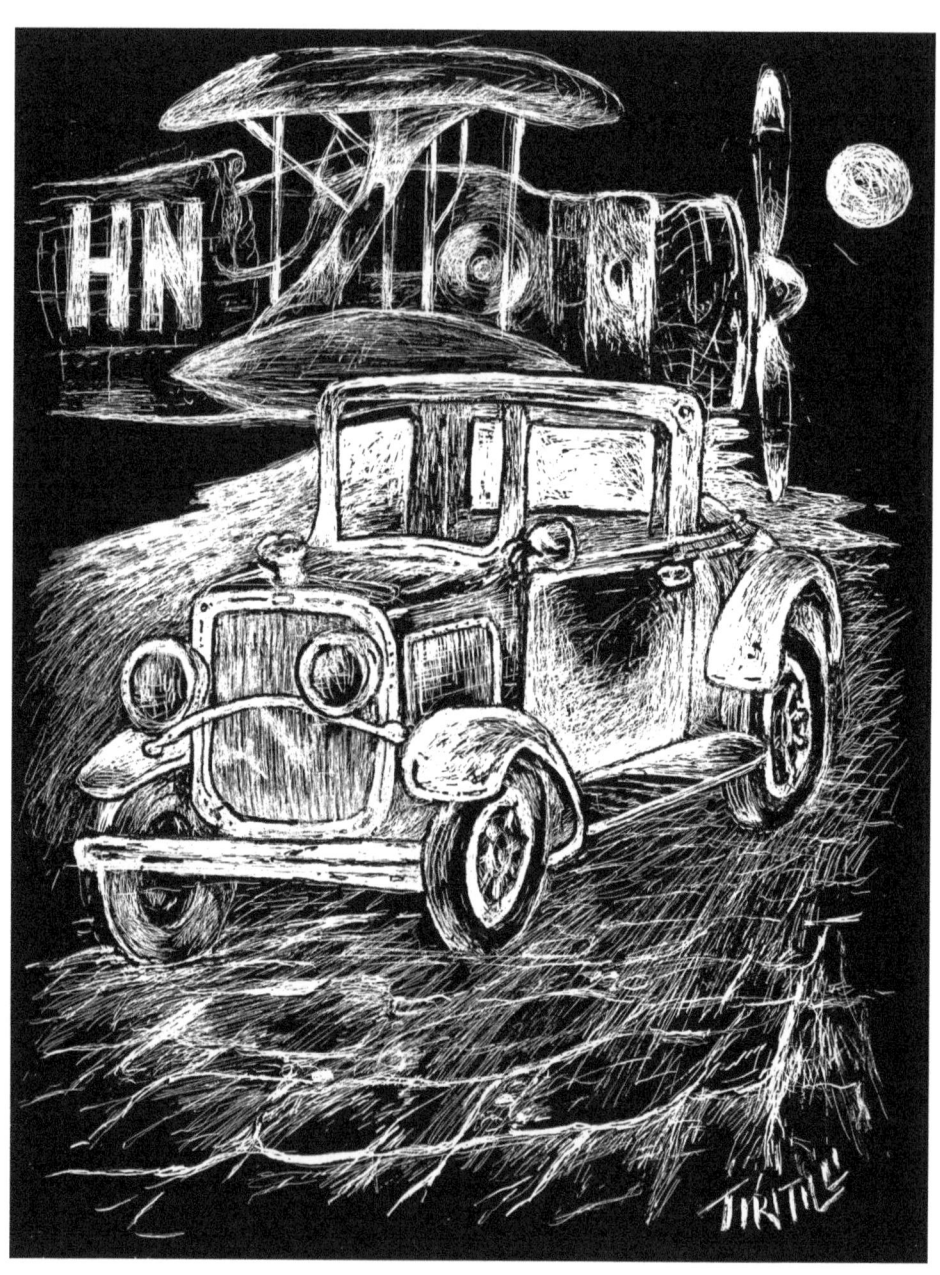

Butterfly

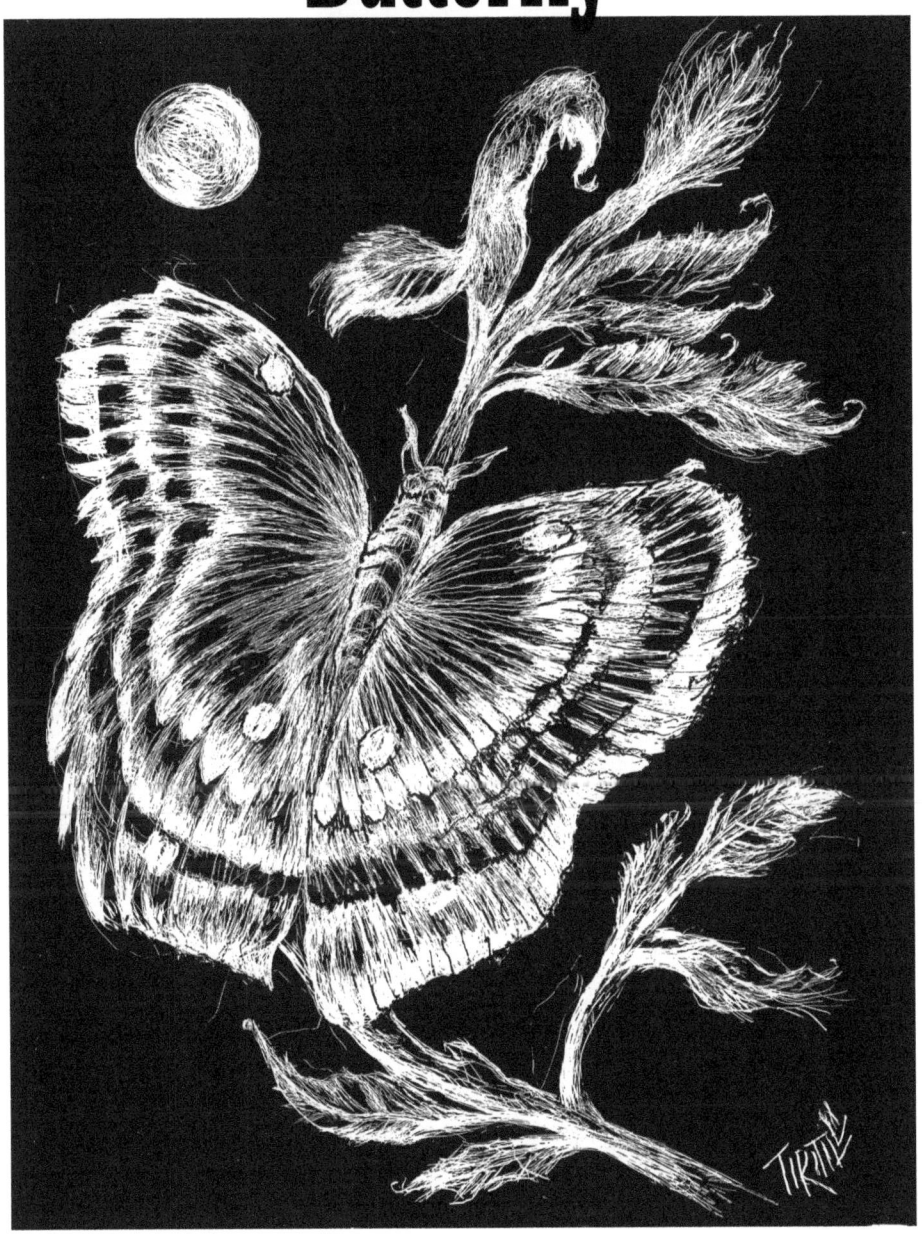

Trains

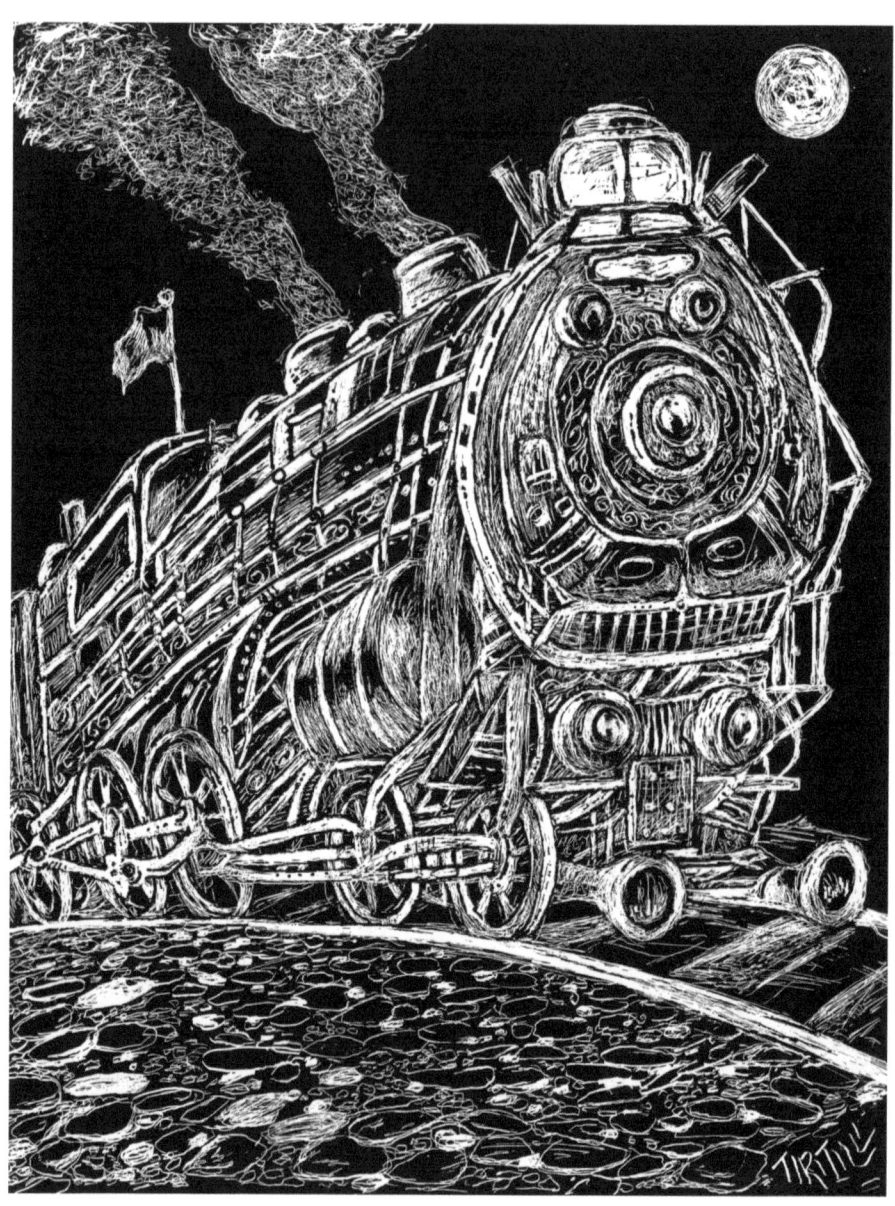

Steam Engine

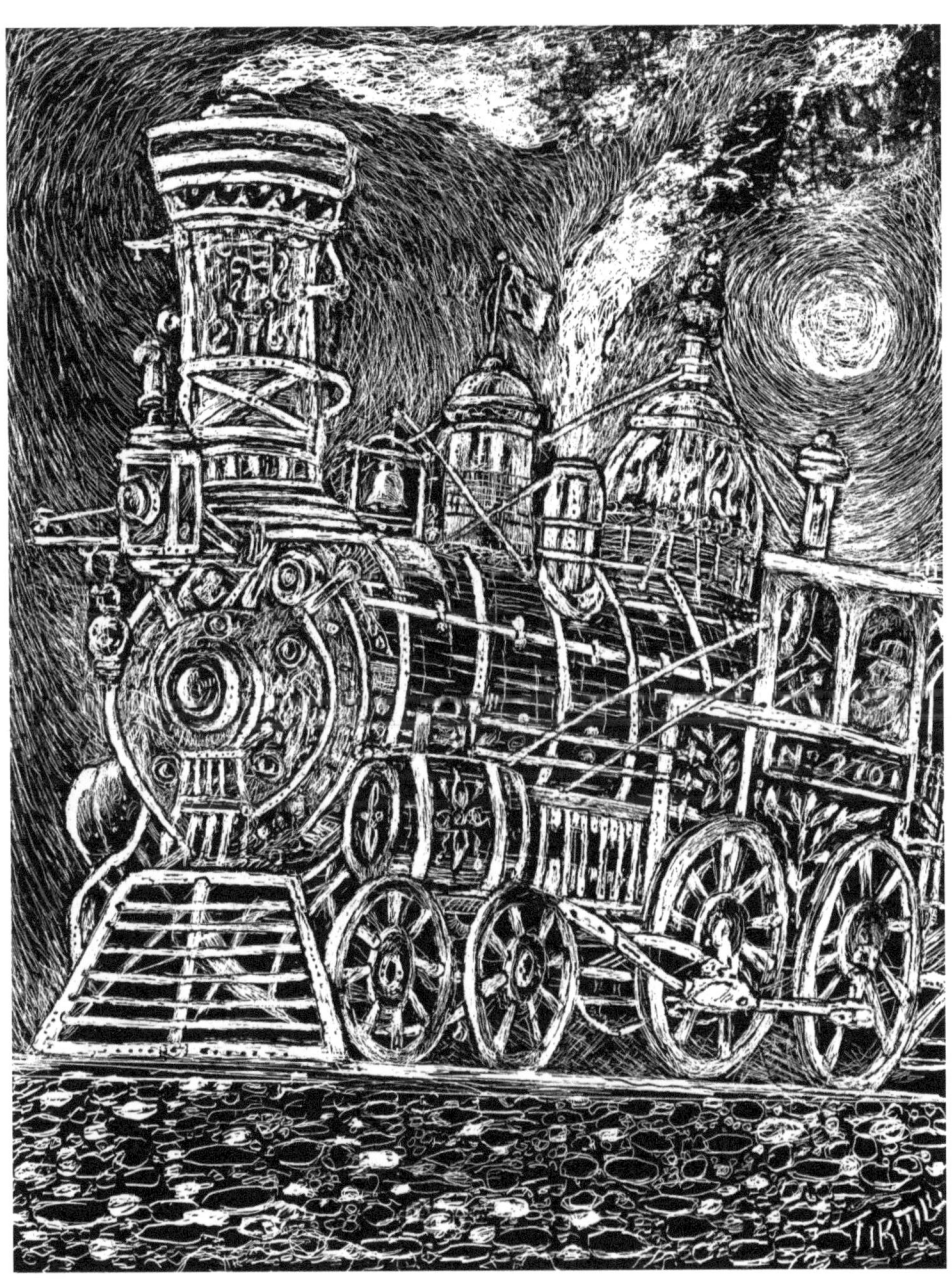

Country Side

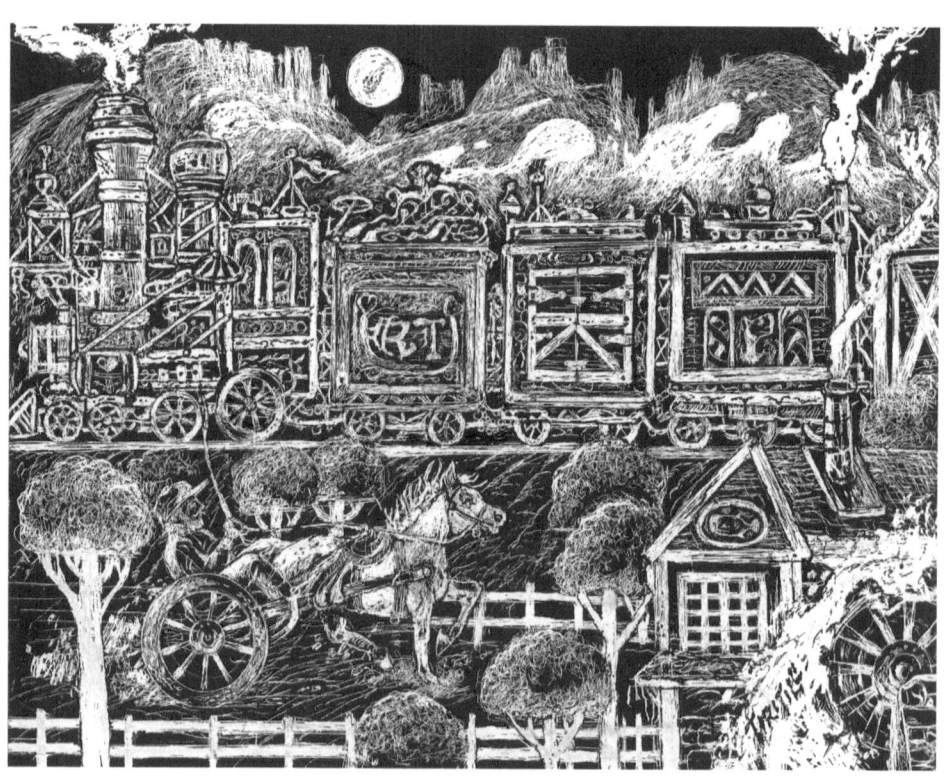

Robert A. Tiritilli

Robert A. Tiritilli is an artist who works in several mediums.
His favorite is the traditional pen & ink technique, which he
has produced thousands of detailed artworks. Recently,
he has created several works of graphic fine art in the
labor-intensive and time-consuming medium of scratchboarding.
Scratchboarding is a drawing technique whereby you scratch
or carve a design on the surface of a black board, revealing white
underneath. It has the opposite effect of drawing with black ink
on white paper. Since it is a reverse drawing method,
it requires learning special techniques to master it,
which Tiritilli did.

www.ingramcontent.com/pod-product-compliance
Lightning Source LLC
Chambersburg PA
CBHW041241200526
45159CB00028B/19